WHY ALTHUSSER KILLED HIS WIFE

ESSAYS ON DISCOURSE AND VIOLENCE

GERALDINE FINN

HUMANITIES PRESS
NEW JERSEY

First published in 1996 by Humanities Press International, Inc.
165 First Avenue, Atlantic Highlands, New Jersey 07716

Library of Congress Cataloging-in-Publication Data

Finn, Geraldine.
Why Althusser killed his wife : essays on discourse and violence / Geraldine Finn.
p. cm. — (Society/religion/ /religion/society)
Includes bibliographical references and index.
ISBN 0-391-03907-5. — ISBN 0-391-03908-3 (pbk.)
1. Postmodernism—Controversial literature. 2. Feminist theory.
I. Title. II. Series.
B831.2.F56 1995
190'.9'04—dc20 95-8841
CIP

A catalog record for this book is available from the British Library.

CONTENTS

INTRODUCTION

THIS BOOK CONSISTS OF three parts corresponding to both the chronology of the writing, which constitutes its chapters and developments within and among the discourses and practices of the modernism, postmodernism, and feminism with which it is engaged. It begins as a project of critique—inaugurated by Althusser's killing of his wife and focused on the totalizing categories of modern and postmodern thought and the unacknowledged violence(s) of their effects. It ends as a project of affirmation of the possibility of a philosophy and a future that can be different: which do not rely on the totalizing categories of the past nor, therefore, reproduce the violences of their effects by liquidating particularity, contingency, and chance.

The uncompromising oppositional critical voice of the early essays, addressed to the equally uncompromising uncritical prescriptions—the categorical imperatives—of modern and postmodern thought (specified precisely and in detail in the relevant chapters), clears the way for and eventually gives way to a different voice, that is, the voice of différance,[1] which informs the articulation of alternatives in Parts II and III. It is a tentative, conditional voice of the saying and the not-yet-said; of particularity, contingency, and chance; of undecidability, response-ability, vigilance, and change. This affirmative project of articulating alternatives—an alternative politics, spirituality, ethics, and future, for example—takes the (lived) experience of contingency/the contingency of (lived) experience rather than the (abstract) categories of necessity/the necessity of (abstract) categories as both its point of departure and its intentional end, in the elaboration of a praxis of politics and philosophy which moves us beyond the familiar aporia of (post)modern thought (the aporia of all or nothing and more of the same demonstrated in Parts I and II) toward the space of the *ethical* encounter with others, beyond and between the categories of institutionalized thought. An encounter that disarms me (of my name and my place in the polis), in which the contingency of the categories and the violence of their effects are visible (experienced) and available for intervention and change.

The first essay, "Why Althusser Killed His Wife," was written in 1980 and sets the political and intellectual agenda of the collection, though not its direction and tone, which shift in the course of Part II from an uncompromising *political* critique of the totalizing tendencies of (post)modern thought to the affirmation of alternatives to it grounded in the standpoint of contingency and the *ethical* possibilities of the space-between. "Why Althusser

Killed His Wife" is a short, angry, polemical piece that proposes links between science and violence, theory and practice, and the personal and the political (between Althusser's commitment to scientific marxism and his dead wife in this case), which were routinely and dogmatically obfuscated or denied in the response of the media and cognoscenti to the murder and which are explicated in detail and at length—together with the effects of violence of their obfuscation—in the chapters that follow.

The last essay on "The Future of Postmodernism" was written in 1992 for the Annual Learned Societies' Conference of The Royal Society of Canada. It uses the question of the conference—the question of "The Future of Postmodernism"—as an opportunity to explore the temporal imagination(s) informing postmodernism and the future(s) at stake in its various contestations and debates. And it repeats the argument of earlier chapters (chapter 6 in particular) that postmodernism (the postmodernism that has succeeded in capturing the category and the institutions that authorize the terms and relevancies of its praxis) tends toward the same political ends and the same effects of violence as the modernism it purports to displace or distance itself from—the totalizing ends/effects of "final solutions."

The intervening essays, written between those two dates, link the two sets of concerns—the effects of violence of modernism's commitment to Reason and Science on the one hand and postmodernism's tendency to "final solutions" on the other—within an alternative discourse of politics and philosophy which take its point of departure from the particularities and contingencies of the flesh and the ethical experience of the space-between the categories (rather than the pre-scribed and pre-scriptive categories of established thought) which becomes increasingly explicit as the collection proceeds.

Part I, *On Modernism*, presents a feminist critique of the practical and political implications of modernism's unquestioned and unquestionable assumption of Reason and Science as the privileged instruments and ends of human being, that is, of human dignity, community, freedom, fulfillment, and control. The first three chapters show how Reason and Science function as both mechanisms and mystifications of patriarchal power and how they are inseparable from a praxis of institutionalized violence and a politics of division, denial, and domination, which both constitutes and defines them and supplies them with their social, material, and ideological conditions of possibility. Chapters 4 and 5 extend this critique to the culture of modernism in general and to its organization of identities, differences, privilege, and power through *sexual spectatorship* in particular. They demonstrate the links between the objectivity, rationality, and abstraction of Science and the constitution of masculinity through (and as) sex and power and throw into question the effectiveness of feminist and would-be *post* modernist critiques that challenge modernism on its own terms by calling for more-albeit new and improved—forms of reason, science, spectatorship, sexuality, freedom, control, self, identity, difference, and desire. These chapters argue for a postmodern feminism—a feminist postmodernism—that eschews the categories and values of modernism and the violences of their praxis, as well as the political ends of domination, division, and denial those categories institute and provoke.

Part II, *On Postmodernism*, extends this analysis to the ideologies and practices of postmodernism, the would-be *after* or *other* of the modernism discussed in Part I. The essays in this section identify tendencies in postmodernism that replay and reproduce the suppositions and strategies of modernism and thereby the political realities which postmodernism purports to repudiate and resist. This is perhaps best exemplified by the epistemological standpoint assumed by the most authoritative discourses of the postmodern, which remains the standpoint of the masculine spectator, the detached observer outside the frame of his own discourse. (What I call the standpoint of the Prince in chapter 10—the standpoint of privilege and power.) It is identified as the standpoint of Man/men in Part I, both conditioned by and reproductive of domination, division, and denial and the effects of violence these strategies of privilege entail. The four essays in Part II explore the political tendencies and effects of postmodernism as well as its material and ideological conditions of possibility, applying to postmodernism the analyses developed earlier in the critique of modernism's attachment to Objectivity, Rationality, and Science. The dominant and dominating discourses of postmodernism emerge here as but another set of moves on patriarchy's chessboard: one aspect of the continuing negotiation of white Eurocentric male privilege in face of the threats to its hegemonic self-righteousness from feminism, from what is now being called the post-colonial critique, and from the massive shifts in the organization and dynamics of national and international economies and powers that are currently underway.

Part III, *On the Future*, explicates the affirmative constructive implications of this critical engagement with modern and postmodern discourse. It takes up the challenge of earlier chapters to articulate a philosophy and a politics that neither reproduces nor relies on the politics and taken-for-granted categories, strategies, and values of the modernism and postmodernism it aims to criticize and surpass. The essays in this section attempt to rethink politics, ethics, spirituality, and the future from the standpoint and for the sake of the other(s) of modernist and postmodernist thought: a standpoint *inside* discourse, language, politics, and texts; *inside* the concrete, contingent specificities and determinations of particular persons, places, and times, particular bodies, contexts, projects, and relations. The immediate political and theoretical context motivating these reflections on politics, ethics, spirituality, and the future are the various divisions and debates in contemporary society and scholarship over questions of identity, difference, representation, privilege, and voice: over the interconnections of race, sex, and class for example in the determination of complex subjectivities, subordinations, resistances, and powers. These essays argue that the political realities which have provoked these divisions are the political realities of modernity—realities articulated to, by, and for the politics of the Prince: a politics of division, denial, and domination for which issues of identity, difference, representation, privilege, and voice are absolutely central. The theoretical and political aporia dividing contemporary scholars will not therefore be resolved by the application of more of the same, more politics of identity—of division and difference and freedom and representation. On the contrary they call for a completely new kind of reflection and praxis, one on that does not rely on nor therefore reproduce the familiar political ends—the "final solutions"—of the (post)modern past. The essays in this concluding section of the book take up this challenge. Although they appear at the end of this study, they are presented not so much as ends of an accomplished thought but as points of departure in a praxis of reflection/a reflection of praxis, which is always already underway, which is always beginning, which cannot and must not be concluded, which does not repeat the patterns of the past, and which opens up the possibility of a future that can be different.

It is at once both fitting and ironic that Althusser's memoir, *L'Avenir dure longtemps*,[2] written in 1985 and subtitled "Brève histoire d'un meurtrier," should be published just as I was putting the finishing touches to this manuscript which bears his name and takes the discourse and violence of that particular man as its point of departure for a study of the effects of violence of the discourse(s) of Man/men in general. Fitting because Althusser actually makes an attempt to answer the question posed by the title essay of this book in his memoir. And ironic because his answer responds almost word-for-word to the criticisms articulated there of the systematic obfuscation of such questions among colleagues and cognoscenti, in the rhetorics of Reason and Science, and in the politics and philosophy of Althusser himself. In *L'Avenir*, by contrast, Althusser establishes the links between the privileging of abstraction, totality, and control in his (conscious) 'objective' theoretical and political work, and the (unconscious) 'subjective' fantasies of mastery and power—the desire for "la domination et la maîtrise de toute situation"[3]—which was the motor of his existence. He explicates the links between these and the politics of the family, the psychodynamics of his own early childhood, and the organization of his sexuality and gender in relation to power in particular, as well as the links between all of these and the murder of his wife.

The tragedy is, of course, that Althusser did not (would not or could not) acknowledge these links between science and violence, theory and practice, and the personal and the political, until it was too late—too late for Hélène, anyway: until her murder and the subsequent living death of his own confinement in a kind of madness in a psychiatric hospital forced them upon him. Until, that is, the agonie/anomie of his existence in the *space-between* the categories of institutionalized thought deprived him of (the authority of) his name and place in the polis and precipitated him into the space of the *ethical* encounter (with self and other) within which both the contingency and the violence of the polis and its categories became visible and available for change. It is the argument of this book that such violences will continue to occur as long as the links between the personal and the political, and theory and practice, are obfuscated or ignored; and that violence is both the condition of possibility and the effect of the severing of those links and of their systematic denial in the politics and praxis of authorized knowledge.

* * *

The difference between poetry and rhetoric
is being
ready to kill
yourself
instead of your children[4]

Audre Lorde makes this distinction in a poem called "Power" (cited in full at the beginning of chapter 13). It is about a black woman who was a member of a jury the rest of whom were white men, which acquitted a white policeman who had killed a ten-year-old black boy.

Today that 37-year-old white man with 13 years of police forcing
has been set free
by 11 white men who said they were satisfied
justice had been done
and one black woman who said
"They convinced me" meaning
they had dragged her 4'10" black woman's frame
over the hot coals of four centuries of white male approval
until she let go the first real power she ever had
and lined her own womb with cement
to make a graveyard for our children.

Althusser never went to trial for killing his wife. Like the white policeman in Lorde's poem (and more recently in the case of the beating of Rodney King), the rhetoric of institutionalized thought was on his side, and he too went free. Lorde's poem, like the essays in this book, is about the power of language in the determination of who lives and who dies, who kills and who is killed, who speaks and who is silent—and who will survive. It is a political poem that advocates poetry rather than rhetoric as the more powerful instrument in the struggle against the politics of the Same—the dominant politics /the politics of dominance of final solutions.

> *But unless I learn to use*
> *the difference between poetry and rhetoric*
> *my power too will run corrupt as poisonous mold*
> *or lie limp and useless as an unconnected wire*
> *and one day I will take my teenaged plug*
> *and connect it to the nearest socket*
> *raping an 85-year-old white woman*
> *who is somebody's mother*
> *and as I beat her senseless and set a torch to her bed*
> *a greek chorus will be singing in 3/4 time*
> *"Poor thing. She never hurt a soul. What beasts they are."*

The essays in this collection make a distinction between ethics and politics which parallels the difference between poetry and rhetoric proposed in this poem: identifying politics with the categorical imperatives of established thought, which obfuscate and obscure the possibilities of difference and change, and ethics with the space between the categories, which makes the violences of prescriptive thought visible and available for resistance and change. The relationship between these two sets of distinctions—between poetry and rhetoric as described by Lorde, and ethics and politics as outlined in Part III—calls for further investigation and will be the subject of a future work which takes the problematic of ethics and expression as its explicit and particular focus of inquiry.

NOTES

1. For "différence," see chapter 12 in general and note 14 in particular.
2. Louis Althusser, *L'Avenir dure longtemps*. Suivi de Les Faits, eds. Olivier Corpet and Yann Moulier Boutang (Paris: Stock/IMEC, 1992).
3. Ibid., 163.
4. Audre Lorde, "Power," in *Black Unicorn* (New York: Norton 1978) 108–9. Thanks to Eleanor Godway for introducing me to this poem and this collection.

Part One

1

On Modernism

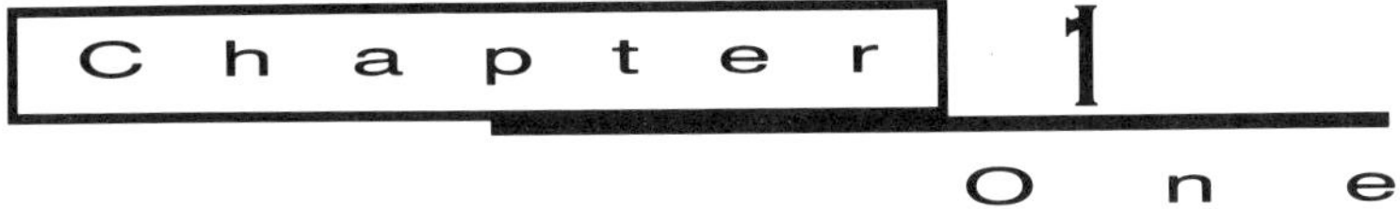

"Why Althusser Killed His Wife."

> One of France's major philosophers walked across the courtyard of the Paris Ecole Normale Superieure mumbling as if in a trance, "My wife is dead."
>
> Wrapped in a dressing gown, Louis Althusser knocked on the door of the college's resident doctor and confessed that he had strangled his wife, Helen, 70, then lapsed into complete incoherence.
>
> It was the end of the career of one of France's most eminent post war intellectuals and stunned the country.
>
> —Graham Tearse, *London Sunday Times*, November 1980

WHEN LOUIS ALTHUSSER KILLED his wife, reports of the killing read like obituaries for *his* death, not hers ("It was the end of the career of one of France's most eminent post war intellectuals"). As if the tragedy was his and not his wife's, who we were routinely informed was ten years older than him, opinionated and argumentative, sometimes sharp of tongue, and not much liked by the couple's friends.[1] Those, like myself, who insisted on making a link between the personal and the political and the public and the private, who insisted that is on examining the relationship between Althusser's ideas and his killing of his wife, were consistently, vociferously, and publically denounced by the primary definers of philosophical and political correctness. As sympathy and compassion, and by implication exoneration, for Althusser were systematically constructed in the academic and popular press.[2]

The tragedy of November 1980 "brought to a head the appalling torture of a man who for eighteen years had been fighting against a grave psychological disorder" wrote K. S. Karol in *New Left Review*.[3] To illuminate what he insisted was their "private drama," he went on to describe what he referred to as "the character and individuality of Hélène's life," that is, her role of "prime importance in everything that concerned her husband's psychological illness":[4]

> She alone during those long years shared her husband's anguish; herself tormented, tormenting him in her turn. It is difficult enough for a psychoanalyst to find words that will help a patient through his nightmare. But for someone so close! For a wife! Often, the hardest of all is not to allow the destructive lucidity of an acute depressive to drag one down as well. And so it was that Louis and Hélène, who could not live without each other, could not find peace through each other.[5]

A few strokes of the pen, *et viola*! Althusser's attack on his wife is transformed into the traditional melodrama of the heterosexual couple. Privatized, individualized, decriminalized, *laid at Hélène's door*, Althusser's killing of his wife and the conditions and consciousness that made it possible are thus insulated from social and political inquiry, sanitized of their social and political determinations, implications, and effects, and (re)written as romance: as the story of one man's private pain and one woman's personal failure to resist it, to make it better by providing him with whatever it was that he required from her. I will refrain from commenting on the details of the "unforgiveable" manipulations[6] in this text which systematically construe Althusser as the victimized hero of this melodrama and Hélène as the villain (who allowed herself to be dragged down by her husband's destructive lucidity!) except to refer you to the opening lines of Audre Lorde's poem "Power" (which is cited in full in the epigraph to chapter 13):

> *The difference between poetry and rhetoric*
> *is being*
> *ready to kill*
> *yourself*
> *instead of your children.*[7]

Karol's tribute to Althusser, on the occasion of his killing of his wife let us not forget, ended with the following:

> For her we can do no more, except not to allow her to be erased from our memory, and remind ourselves of the role she played alongside Althusser. For him, however, we can still do something: we can make every effort to ensure that in addition to his despair, he does not have to suffer an internment that would not provide any conditions for a cure. We, his friends, who, in one way or another, for a long or short period of time, have known the benefit of his intellectual lustre and moral integrity, can only hope that beyond the tragedy itself inner peace will one day return to him.[8]

It was my anger and alarm in the face of this collective cover-up, this collusion of commentators and cognoscenti alike in Althusser's crime through their relentless and dogmatic refusal to cast a single doubt on the "intellectual lustre" and "moral integrity" of a man who kills his wife (if he happens to be a famous French philosopher that is)[9] and thus to cast a single doubt on their own philosophical and political correctness, that provoked the polemic which follows. In it I make links between the personal and the political and among science, patriarchy, and violence which are examined in greater detail in the chapters that follow.

"Why Althusser Killed His Wife"[10]

This is a polemical essay motivated by personal and political outrage—not at the fact that Althusser killed his wife, tragic though that may be (tragic for whom, I wonder), but at the response of the media to that event, and subsequent discussion of it among colleagues and cognoscenti. These have consistently taken the form of:

One. *Blaming the victim*, that is, the wife who, we are told, was "opinionated and argumentative" (unlike Althusser?), and "little liked by the couple's friends" (the *couple's* friends? Who constitutes a couple, I wonder. What constitutes a friend?)

Two. *Exonerating the guilty*, Althusser. Sympathy (and by implication identification) with Althusser is such that reports of the killing read like obituaries for *his* death, not hers. The tragedy is *his*, not Helen's. (Is this because he "lost his mind" [which of course he has not] and she "merely" lost her body?)

The truth we cannot afford to forget, however, is that it is only because Althusser had, and *still has*, the "mind" he had, that he killed his wife. We cannot afford to continue to separate the intellectual in a man (I choose my terms carefully) from the emotional: the depression from the ideas; or the political from the personal: the commitment to class struggle from the stormy marriage, the dead wife.

The truth is that the Althusser who killed his wife is Althusser, the revolutionary; the Althusser who is currently interned in a psychiatric hospital is the same Althusser who wrote *Pour Marx* and other books. His philosophical and intellectual practice cannot be separated from his personal and emotional practice: they are rooted in the same soil and have the same material, social, historical and ideological conditions of possibility and determinancy, and it is to these we must look to find the connection between the ideas and the man (between Althusser "sane" and Althusser "psychotic" or "depressed.")

Neither Althusser, "France," nor the world's intellectuals and revolutionaries will acknowledge *patriarchy* as the powerful, pervasive, and pernicious ideological state apparatus which it is; at the same time, none of them escape its effects. The specificity of *patriarchy* as a political ideology and as a practice was overlooked by Althusser and is consistently denied, negated, or trivialized by the academic and intellectual élite. But it was patriarchy that killed Helen and broke Althusser. Let me make some connections to clarify such a bald statement.

Althusser, like other left revolutionaries, was thrall to the ideology of science. After the fall of the family, science remains as the last (I hope) taboo: the last holy cow about which one cannot utter a doubt. And after the death of God, it remains as mythical a source of security as did the family; but more importantly, it is also a source of authority and legitimacy. But the ideology of science is historically, logically, materially, formally, and structurally inseparable from the ideology, practice and discourse of patriarchy according to which science is equated with knowledge, knowledge with power, and power with dominance.

Natural science has sought to dominate and control nature; social and political science to dominate and control human nature—man, humanity, society. The rhetoric of freedom, of human emancipation from the control of nature, has served to conceal and obscure the material base and conditions of possibility of both sciences: *real social relations of servitude, inequality and dominance*. This material base is constituted by the division of labor, private property, social stratification (hierarchies of control and authority), and the separation of Man from Nature. These structures, which are structures of both production and reproduction, are essentially structures of violence; they consist of some men violating others and violating nature. Women are violated as both other and nature. While only some men, in some historical periods, have been violated as nature—native Indians, for example, blacks, the insane, the diseased, the cretinous.

These social structures are the material foundation of science, and also of patriarchy. In other words science *is* patriarchal science.

Revolutionaries like Althusser, who appeal to science to authorize and legitimize their theories and practices as *social* scientists, authorize and legitimize violence at the same time; for that appeal itself enmeshes them in a bourgeois and patriarchal ideological apparatus—theory and practice—which is both relatively autonomous, that is self-determining, and inherently and intrinsically violent.

Some men escape the violence of patriarchy: in that they hold the dominant positions in the constitutive structures mentioned—the division of labor, private property, and social hierarchy (*all* men are the bearers of dominant positions in the Man/Nature split); for instance, scientists, students, artists, intellectuals, "professionals." These are men who live off the surplus of other people's labor and speak with the authority of specialized knowledge. But they escape patriarchy's violence only when they are its agents and perpetrators.

Moreover all men by virtue of being *men*, escape the violence intrinsic to the fourth structure: the separation of Man from Nature. But again, they escape it only to the extent that they perpetrate it, and *all* women are their victims. All women are de-vitalized and violated as *non-men* by virtue of, and often in the name of humanism: the split between Humanity and Nature which is intrinsic to both patriarchy (the systematic and socially sanctioned supremacy of men over women) and science, the systematic and socially sanctioned supremacy of man over nature.

The ideology of science has also required and sanctioned the *separation* of sexuality, reproduction, and women from the specifically human and the humanly significant (after all, they serve only the natural functions); together with their *privatization* and depoliticization within the family or personal life (*whose* functions, *whose* personal life, *whose* family?). This has happened to such an extent that, even today, demands by feminists for a systematic critique of patriarchal social relations are jeered out of the court of serious political praxis (*whose* court, *whose* jeers, *whose* praxis?); and feminism is admitted only at the very *margins* of philosophical and political discourse, if at all, as another pressure-group, another special-case, another special-interest, even minority group, another voice to be heard, synthesized, accommodated, included and *assimilated* within the present ruling structures of scientific and political discourse.

As long as this continues and men refuse to take the feminist critique seriously, they will continue to *reproduce the violent patriarchal social relations* which they have internalized, which have made them what they are, which they refuse to acknowledge and of which they are the undisputed beneficiaries—in the scientific, political, and philosophical praxis as much as in the so-called "personal" praxis of their so-called "private" lives (personal and private from whose point of view? From the point of view of the brotherhood, the patriarchy, of course). And philosophers will continue to kill their wives.

As a matter of fact, philosophers and political scientists have always killed their wives (sisters, mistresses, whores). The philosopher's wife as shrew was instituted together with the philosopher-king himself (Socrates); and as man's natural inferior and servant by Aristotle, the first great scientist we are told. Philosophers and political scientists have systematically destroyed women and the life they embody by denigrating and exploiting them, and by denying, refusing, invalidating, ridiculing, denouncing, trivializing and sometimes even asphyxiating, and always ultimately *silencing* ("and the *word* was made flesh—*whose* word, *whose* flesh, whose *logos*?) the authentic necessarily protesting ("opinionated and argumentative"?) voice of women.

We should not therefore be surprised by Althusser's "stormy relationship" (*whose* relationship, *whose* storm? At least there was life left in Helen to be taken), his "periods of severe depression," and his final destruction of his wife. *Theirs was no personal tragedy.* The violence, the contradictions, and the struggle that characterized this particular relationship are intrinsic to and constitutive of all patriarchal relationships and sexual relationships in particular because of their central structural position in the social "conjuncture."

They are also constitutive of science, which cannot therefore be looked to as Althusser and other revolutionaries do, for a solution to that violence which is its condition of possibility and realization. Because of this, science will always and necessarily obscure the real structures of violence because it is itself founded upon them by either mystifying them as did Darwin, reifying them as did Freud, or passing over them in silence as did Althusser and his principal inspiration, Marx. Meanwhile both the science and the politics continue to kill us.

NOTES

1. These phrases are paraphrases from back issues of *Newsweek*, *New Left Review*, and the London *Sunday Times*.
2. The expression of sympathy and compassion, and by implication exoneration, for men who kill their wives is common practice in our society. Althusser's crime against his wife and the response of our cultural authorities to it was not an isolated event but part of a syndrome. This is why it was so easy to cover-up its ideological and political conditions of possibility and effect, and why I thought it was so important to name them. For more on the collusion of the state and the media in the protection of men who kill and abuse women and children, see Geraldine Finn "Taking Gender into Account in the 'Theatre of Terror': Violence, Media and the Maintenance of Male Dominance," *Canadian Journal of Women and the Law* 3 (1989–90): 375–94.
3. K. S. Karol, "The Tragedy of the Althussers," *New Left Review* 24 (1980): 93–95.
4. Ibid., 94.
5. Ibid., 95.
6. Bryan Turner in a footnote to chapter 1 of his *Descent into Discourse. The Reification of Language and the Writing of Social History* (Philadelphia: Temple University Press, 1990), 234, invites readers to compare K. S. Karol's *New Left Review* article with "the unforgiveable discussion in Geraldine Finn's 'Why Althusser Killed His Wife.'"
7. Audre Lorde, *The Black Unicorn* (New York: Norton, 1978), 108.
8. K. S. Karol, "Tragedy of the Althussers," 95.
9. See note 2 above.
10. "Why Althusser Killed His Wife" was first published in *Canadian Forum* 61 (September-October 1981): 28–29.

Chapter 2 Two

Reason and Violence: More than a False Antithesis—A Mechanism of Patriarchal Power

I WROTE THIS ESSAY originally as the introduction to a daylong interdisciplinary symposium on "Reason and Violence: Feminist Perspectives," which I organized as part of the annual meetings of the Canadian Learned Societies in June 1982 while I was still smarting from the Althusser cover-up. The object of the symposium was to bring feminists together from across a number of different disciplines—psychology, sociology, politics, biology, law, history, social work, philosophy, and the visual and performing arts—to explore the connections between "reason" as traditionally interpreted and "violence" as traditionally practiced. Potential participants were invited to reflect upon what they had learned about "reason" in their efforts to theorize and/or combat violence. And the final selection of speakers was informed by my own conviction that *reason is an instrument of violence and not its antithesis* and by my desire to test this hypothesis against the "evidence." What follows is a preliminary and somewhat schematic account of how that thesis might be defended.

"Reason and Violence: More than a False Antithesis—A Mechanism of Patriarchal Power"[1]

It is commonly assumed though seldom actually argued that reason and violence are antithetical or mutually exclusive. It is further assumed though again rarely argued that reason is good (right and desirable) and violence bad (wrong and undesirable).[2] Those who challenge this presumed antithesis usually do so by pointing out that not all violence deserves to be dismissed as irrational and that in some circumstances the most rational thing to do is to act (or more commonly, to react) violently. In such cases (for example, in cases of self-defense), it would be contrary to reason to refrain from violence.

This weakening of the antithesis affects only one of the terms of the presumed polarization, however, by conceding that violence is not always exclusive of reason. The *key presumption* of the antithesis, that reason per se is right and its right to rule is sovereign, remains unchallenged.

It is rarely argued that reason itself may be a source of violence—and when it is, it is always presumed that there has been a historical 'falling away' from a more primordial and pristine 'higher' reason (which would necessarily exclude violence) to a 'lesser' instrumental or technical rationality, for example, which is the real root of the violence perpetrated in reason's name.[3] I know of no critique that suggests that *reason itself* and not just its historical forms and deviations may be a source of violence. It seems that Reason, like Science and the Family, is sacrosanct; an a priori good thing, which in itself can only benefit humanity—in spite of what would appear to be a wealth of evidence to the contrary. Any violence associated with Reason, like the violence associated with Science and the Family (one in ten wives in Canada battered, one in four girls incestuously assaulted) is attributed, again a priori, to particular and supposedly accidental features of a historical form of Reason, Science, or the Family, and never to Reason, Science, or the Family itself.

I maintain, by contrast, that Reason itself is constitutively and not accidentally violent[4] and that it is neither good nor even neutral (i.e., that its value depends on its use), but like Science and the Family, it is a constitutive part of a political ideology (a theory and a practice) and apparatus of violence which is used to keep subordinates in their place in a given social and economic order. I believe, furthermore, that this Reason is most fundamentally an instrument of specifically *male* power and violence, constructed in the image of men and rooted in a peculiarly male experience of powerlessness and alienation and that it is, perhaps first and foremost, an instrument of their particular alienation of women.

These are large claims and I cannot pretend to defend them adequately in the space of these few pages. What I will do, however, is indicate the general direction of my argument and some of the particular details by which it might be supported.

First no one can really say what Reason is.[5] But whatever it is (or is said to be), it is constituted in discourse and within that discourse has always been characterized as follows: as that by which we arrive at *Truth*; as that which always has its *Other* (what Reason is always contingent upon what it *is not*: it is not faith, for example, or emotion, or personal, or particular); as in some sense a function or faculty of the *mind*. These three characteristics of Reason, vague as they may be, are sufficient to render Reason both political and politically inaccessible (invisible, indefinable, intractable) and are the root of Reason's enormous power and Reason's violence. This is because, whatever it is (whatever precise content or denotation is attributed to Reason at any given moment in history) Reason is always exclusive and authoritarian, polarizing and law-making. *It always has its Other* over which it is sovereign, which it is entitled to control or destroy as circumstances demand. This is why I believe Reason to be constitutively violent.

Within the discourse of Reason, Reason as the locus of Truth plays the part of God. It is both the author and arbiter of the objective order of the world and of our knowledge of it, on the assumption that there is a single correctness about the world and Reason proves our sole access to it. As the norm of knowledge (i.e., as God) Reason is law-making and law-preserving. But law, as we learned from Walter Benjamin,[6] is itself "an immediate manifestation of violence" in that violence is a necessary condition of its possibility. (How we "define" violence will be considered later in this paper; the sense in which it is being used until then should be clear from the context.) For law is established and maintained only through force: the forced repression of dissent and the forced submission of dissenters. And indeed we have all been forced into "acknowledging" the various (and often changing) "truths of Reason": by failure, discipline, humiliation, or expulsion in our pursuit of knowledge in academia; by threats of hell and damnation in our pursuit of goodness in religions; by hospitalization, alienation, or incarceration in our pursuit of social and psychological health in our "private" family and social lives; by unemployment and homelessness in our pursuit of a living in our "public" and "productive" lives; by prison, death, or exile in our pursuit of justice and self-determination in our "political" lives—and so forth.

Again if Reason is Truth, then that which is not Reason (and there is always something which is not Reason, for Reason is essentially oppositional—it would be nothing were it not for that to which it is opposed) is False and a candidate for elimination or repression.[7] Since Reason itself has no real referent (or content) and is actually constituted as that which it is not, anything can be opposed to Reason depending on what it is politically expedient for the ruling-class spokesmen of Reason (i.e., of Law) to discredit, control, or repress at the time—nature, experience (both "subjective" and "objective"), faith, emotion, intuition, instinct—and even forms of Reason itself re-named and re-classified as "rationalism," "scientism," "instrumentalism," "objectivism," "subjectivism," and so forth. For Reason if it is Right is necessarily exclusive: of certain knowledges and certain subjectivities. It disqualifies most often knowledge acquired from particular practice and concrete everyday experience (i.e., *knowledge available to everyone*) at the same time as it diminishes those subjects who can only speak from these positions—historically women and those men who do physical labor—those who service a ruling class who claim to "know" and "rule" by virtue of their superior Reason miraculously untarnished by the "personal," "material," "practical," or "emotional" constraints that disqualify those over whom they rule from both knowledge and the good life.[8]

Thus Reason serves the ideological (always political) purpose of *ruling-out* as ill-founded and irrational and therefore untrue—the only knowledge available to members of certain social classes (the dominated). Since knowledge is power and truth a knowledge-effect, that is, an effect of power, the discourse of Reason effectively deprives members of these classes of social power and maintains and reproduces its concentration in the hands of a ruling and leisured élite.[9] Immediate truths which originate in and are verified by the actual practice of life are, along with those with access to them, ruled out of the court of Reason. They are in turn obfuscated, discredited, and repressed (as subjective, particular, and unverifiable, for example) in the name of a transcendent Reason whose "eternal" categories of thought are sanctified as sovereign.[10]

The identification of Reason with the Mind reinforces this polarization which I maintain is implicit in and necessary to the discourse of Reason, and reproduces it as a feature of reality itself. At its most primitive the dualism presumed by the discourse of Reason consists in the division of human beings into minds and bodies and the simultaneous association of Reason (Truth and Right) with the former.[11] It is man's Mind or Reason we are told that distinguishes him from the rest of the natural world and entitles him to sovereignty over it.[12] Knowledge is a function of the Mind, and knower and known belong to different orders of being. Man, the Mind, is the subject who knows; Nature, mere matter, the object known. The knower is active, the known passive. The knower is universal, the known "merely" particular. This fundamental dualism—part and parcel of the discourse of Reason—has generated a whole battery of dichotomies that are constitutive of male-stream thought at all levels—the political, economic, historical, scientific, or whatever—the most common of these being the supposed oppositions between mind and body, reason and emotion, culture and nature, universal and particular, abstract and concrete, sacred and profane, divine and mundane, absolute and relative, subject and object, order and disorder, real and apparent, self and other, light and dark, good and bad, true and false, and, of course, male and female.

I maintain that this division of reality is peculiarly and not accidentally male. It serves peculiarly male needs for a certain kind of power, needs that women do not experience as a result of their more immediate and concrete relationship to the species by way of their reproductive activity. These dualisms express at the ideological level men's experienced alienation from species continuity, creativity, and community at the basic material level of their relationship to reproduction—from which they are excluded. Consequently male thought emphasizes difference, separation, opposition, polarity, and conflict in its discourse about the world. For that is indeed how men experience their relationship to species continuity, creativity, community, and control: they are alienated from it.[13] At the same time male thought expresses men's desire for a unity, continuity, and community they do not immediately experience in their everyday lives, in its persistent aspiration to "oneness": to the universal, absolute, eternal, and unassailable knowledge and subjectivity of a transcendent and impersonal Reason.[14]

The dualism of male-stream thought, of which the discourse of Reason is a powerful and telling example[15] serves men's interests by mediating ideologically[16] their experienced alienation from the species. But it does so at the expense of women's lives. For women are men's Other; we therefore belong to that pole of the system of dichotomies that requires control and domination by the other pole consisting of Reason and Men. This identification of women with the irrational and inhuman pole of the mind/matter dichotomy persists to this day and serves to disqualify female knowledge a priori whenever it fails to conform to the norms and practices of male-stream rationality.

Representing the world in dualistic terms allows the knower to treat not only nature but also people as objects and to take no kind of responsibility for the uses and direction of his knowledge—which is declared Rational and therefore impersonal and objective.[17] It has enabled men, the knowers, to falsely abstract themselves from nature, as if they were not themselves historical, material, organic, and social beings. This abstraction of men from the rest of nature, and from women, is the root at one and the same time of both their *power*, for they can be ruthless with others with whom they feel no identification, and their alienation, from the world, each other and themselves. It is also a measure of their freedom, and, for them, of their "humanity"; the more they control the more free they think they are. But the more free they are in this sense, the more alienated they are from their real material roots in nature and intersubjectivity. Within the discourse of Reason, freedom and alienation are far from being antitheses: they are two sides of the same coin—gains in freedom perceived as control over nature only increase the alienation they are presumed to remedy.[18]

Reason and violence are far from antithetical, therefore. On the contrary Reason is constitutively violent, first because it is Right and therefore necessarily coercive, and second because it is most essentially part of a mechanism of power.

But what is this violence to which Reason is conventionally opposed? Just as there is "no universally agreed or uniquely correct sense of Reason,"[19] so it must be acknowledged, there is no universally agreed on or uniquely correct sense of violence. I follow Robert Paul Wolff's example[20] here in maintaining that what is perceived and conceived as violence varies according to expectations and to one's vital interests. When my peripheral interests are at stake, anything in excess of moderate force from others, whether mental or physical, will be perceived as violent, while I am inclined to forget that other parties to the dispute may find their primary interests challenged and thus have a different view of what is and is not violent. (Compare the "violence" of a husband's response to a scratch on the fender of "his" car, with the "violence" of a wife's response to a muddy footprint on the kitchen floor.) Basically, then, the concept of violence, like Reason "serves as a rhetorical device for proscribing those political uses of force which one considers inimical to one's central interests."[21]

The denunciation of physical force within the discourse of Reason, therefore, as irrational, immoral, and illegitimate as a way of resolving conflict, enforcing decisions, or achieving ends, serves an ideological function of ruling out the only instrument of power available to those social classes whose subordination it ensures and relies on. It is always *those who hold power*, that is, those who have the ability (the social power) to enforce decisions, who insist on the correctness of "rational methods" (husbands, fathers, university directors, department chairmen, property owners, teachers, doctors, etc.) for settling disputes and challenges to the status quo and who declare the use of physical force (though not the use of mental coercion, for that is a mechanism of *their* power and therefore serves their vital interests) to be violent and therefore irrational and inappropriate. (Except, of course, when it is named "counterviolence" as is done in the cases of prisons and asylums—more "rational" methods of social control.) This should not surprise us, for physical force is a means to power, ultimately that upon which all power, even the "legitimate," is based; and argument is not. Physical force must therefore be suppressed if present power structures are to be preserved.[22] Argument, on the other hand, is to be encouraged for it poses no direct threat to the ruling order. It merely postpones change indefinitely, distracting opposition, while maintaining prevailing power relations.

The appeal to argument, "rational methods" and Reason should be seen for what it is: an essentially *defensive* tactic, that is, a tactic of those who are defending their power. For they are not, in their turn, required to support their position or their stipulation against physical force with reasons. Their characterization of some forms of force as *physical*, and others as not; of physical force as *violent*, and others as not (e.g., the force of argument, the force of law); of violence as exclusive of Reason; of Reason as right and therefore the only permissible means to social ends . . . all these are a priori unsupported themselves by "rational argument"—for they cannot be. Their legitimacy and authority, like all legitimacy and authority, is founded in *Rule* not Reason, *Force* not argument, and *Power* not persuasion. Far from being the "precise opposite of power and violence" as Popper proclaims,[23] Reason is its equivalent, and one of the most effective means of its exercise and mystification.

NOTES

1. First published in the *Canadian Journal of Political and Social Theory* 6, no. 3 (Fall 1982): 162–68.
2. Karl Popper in his 1947 address "Utopia and Violence," reprinted in *Conjectures and Refutations* (New York: Harper and Torchbooks, 1968), 355–63, voices these assumptions about reason. "I am a rationalist," he says, "because I see in the attitude of reasonableness the only alternative to violence." "I believe that we can avoid violence only in so far as we practice this attitude of reasonableness when dealing with one another. . . . I choose rationalism because I hate violence." "Reason is for him the precise opposite of an instrument of power and violence; he sees it as a means by which these may be tamed." In "Reason and Revolution," *Archives Européenes de Sociologie XI*, 1970, 252–62, he reaffirms this commitment claiming that "reason is the only alternative to violence so far discovered." For a discussion of Popper's views, see Roy Edgley, "Reason and Violence" in S. Korner, *Practical Reason* (Oxford: Blackwell, 1974) 113–35.
3. I am thinking here, of course, of the Frankfurt School of thought.
4. I also believe that Science and the Family are constitutively and not accidentally violent. For a discussion of this claim with respect to Science, see my "Women and the Ideology of Science" in *Our Generation* 15, no. 1 (Spring 1982) chapter 3.
5. "There is then, no universally agreed or uniquely correct sense of 'reason.'" G. J. Warnock, *The Encyclopedia of Philosophy*, vol. 7–8, ed. Paul Edwards (New York: Macmillan, 1972), 84.
6. See "On Violence" in Walter Benjamin, *Reflections, Essays, Aphorisms, Autobiographical Writings* (New York and London: Harcourt Brace Jovanovich, 1978).
7. Reason rarely eliminates that which it is not for it usually requires the emotion (the caring of women, for example) or the physical strengths and skills of others (the labor of colonized people, for example), which it denounces and alienates from itself, in order to be at all. (Cf. the Master–Slave relationship in Hegel and de Beauvoir's elaboration of it in *The Second Sex*.)
8. Historically Reason emerged as the norm and law of knowledge, truth and right around the time of Pythagoras when the separation of knowledge and philosophy from the techniques of production kept pace with the rise of slavery and an increasing contempt for manual work. "It was found extraordinarily fortunate that the secret constitution of things should reveal, not to those who manipulated them, not to those who worked with fire, but to those who drew patterns on the sand." Indeed, it becomes difficult to hold any other view of the origin of knowledge—that knowledge could be arrived at by interrogating nature directly, for example—"when all the implements and processes by which nature is made to obey man's will" have become the province of slaves, subordinates and social inferiors, like women. See Benjamin Farrington, *Greek Science* (Melbourne: Penguin Books, 1953) from which these quotations were taken.

9. This is Michel Foucault's language. See his *Power/Knowledge* (New York: Pantheon Books, 1980) for example. The ideas in this paragraph are explored more fully in my paper on "Women and the Ideology of Science" cited in note 4 above.
10. Categories are like definitions. They oblige us to represent reality in predetermined ways and exclude us from knowledge and/or rationality (and power, of course) when we do not. They dictate unchanging patterns of both natural and cognitive events and processes, and they fix the truth—and therefore power. For a further critique of categories and definitions, see "Women and the Ideology of Science."
11. It is a historical question, whether the discourse of Reason coincided with the emergence of dualistic thinking. As far as I can tell it did—in the history of Western thought both appear along with Pythagorean idealism. But this point requires further consolidation. See Genevieve Lloyd, *The Man of Reason* (Minneapolis: University of Minnesota Press, 1984).
12. Just as God, the Almighty Mind or Logos of the world gets his entitlement to rule over man from his supposedly superior Rationality, uncontaminated as it is by any contact with the flesh or matter of any kind.
13. For a thorough and truly ovarian analysis of the thesis proposed here, see Mary O'Brien's *The Politics of Reproduction* (London: Routledge and Kegal Paul, 1981).
14. It is, in fact, an aspiration of godliness that the existentialists, in particular Sartre, have documented so well and transformed into a metaphysics.
15. It seems that all male thought is dualistic, including mythological thought. The extension of this analysis to so-called "prerational" or "prescientific" thought remains to be done. I am inclined to think that Reason replaced the phallus as the talisman of men's difference and power, as a symbol and expression of their alienation, and as an instrument of their control over women, nature, and progeny. But again this hypothesis requires further consolidation.
16. I use the term ideology here very much in Althusser's sense of the term whereby ideology is an apparatus of power that alludes to reality in an illusory way. Ideology represents the imaginary relationship of "subjects" to the world and each other, but it can be decoded to reveal the truth is mystifying and reifying and that is its condition of possibility.
17. I am paraphrasing Margaret Benston here. See her "Feminism and the Critique of Scientific Method" in *Feminism in Canada: From Pressure to Politics*, eds. Angela Miles and Geraldine Finn (Montreal: Black Rose Books, 1982).
18. This point is dealt with more fully in "Women and the Ideology of Science," where it is extended to include a critique of Humanism.
19. Warnock, *The Encyclopedia of Philosophy*.
20. Robert Paul Wolff, "On Violence," *The Journal of Philosophy* 66 (1969): 601–16.
21. Ibid., 613.
22. Not only physical force of course. The power of emotion and feeling must also be discredited for the holders of power are human after all, and powerful emotions as well as physical force are also capable of rocking the boat.
23. Popper, "Utopia and Violence," 363.

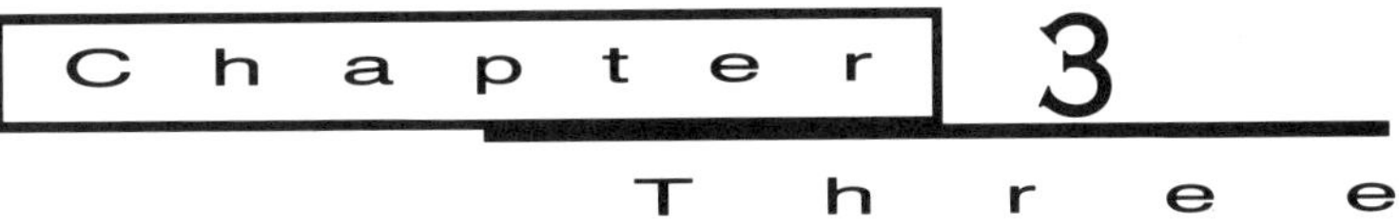

Women and the Ideology of Science

IN "WHY ALTHUSSER KILLED HIS WIFE," I argued that Science both presupposes and reproduces patriarchy and the social and political relations of violence upon which it relies and that Science cannot therefore be looked to, as Althusser and other political thinkers do, for a solution to that violence which, I maintain, is both the condition of its own possibility and one of its chief effects. "Women and the Ideology of Science" was written in response to requests for clarification and substantiation of these claims. It was originally prepared as an occasional lecture for an undergraduate class in sociology whose professor had invited me to discuss the issues raised in the original Althusser article in greater detail and to elaborate on its arguments. The principal organizing categories of my critical work, which are repeated and refined in subsequent chapters, are introduced and clarified here: the categories of patriarchy, science, ideology, violence, domination, objectivity, and dualism, for example. The critique of Science they are marshalled to perform, like the critique of Reason above and the critique of Pornography that follows, is uncompromising in that it does not allow for the possibility of a Science (a Reason or a Pornography) that is not violent: that does not, that is, presuppose and thereby reproduce the rationality and intentionality of dualism, and the politics of division, domination, and denial which is its condition of possibility and its end.

"Women and the Ideology of Science"[1]

INTRODUCTION

When Althusser killed his wife one year ago, I was not at all surprised. Not because of any special familiarity I have with Althusser, or Helen, or the details of their "personal life"—for I knew nothing about them other than what I gleaned from the reports of the killing, but because I had read Althusser and was therefore familiar with his "politics." It was clear to me that Althusser's "personal and private" tragedy, that is, his killing of his wife and possible insanity, was both consistent with and conditioned by his "scientific and political" theory: that they are, as he himself might say, part of the same social "conjuncture" and thus rooted in the same historical, material, and ideological conditions of possibility and determinancy. Consequently Althusser's theory—albeit sometimes in an illusory and allusive way—could (and indeed should) be used to illuminate his practice and vice versa. And this particular practice—his killing of his wife—seemed to me to render such a critical reflection on a rather fashionable mode of political theorizing more urgent.

According to Althusser ideology alludes to reality but in an illusory way; it represents "the imaginary relationship of individuals to their real conditions of existence."[2] I am suggesting that Althusser's own political theory could and should be treated as ideology in this precise sense and that the theory and the practice, therefore, can and should be used reflexively and critically to demystify each other. For example Althusser's theoretical understanding of ideology and science, of the role of the subject in history and ideology, and of the significance of class-struggle within capitalist social relations, could be carried over, almost verbatim—*mutatis mutandum*—to illuminate his own theory and his practice in this particular instance—which was indeed the "last instance" for Helen—within *patriarchal* capitalist relations. In other words Althusser can be hoisted on his own petard, so to speak; his own theory can be used as a tool against itself, to demystify itself of its own ideological content—as can the theories of Marx and Freud. This is part of their strength and contributes to their lasting and continuing ability to illuminate our understanding of social praxis. It is not a weakness of their theoretical contributions. Althusser's killing of his wife, illuminated by his own theory, discloses, for example, that which lies outside of his discourse yet provides it with its very condition of possibility—patriarchy, of course; that is, the rule of the fathers, which is only made possible by the institutionalized servitude and subordination of women. (Behind every great man is a . . . dead? sick? crazy? defeated? unhappy? . . . at best mystified, woman or rather a series of women, his sisters, his mother, etc.) The oppression and domination of women by men is the silent, unseen, and unacknowledged (suppressed and repressed, i.e., tabooed) material condition of possibility, not only of Althusser's particular theory and practice, but of all male-stream thought in whatever context or discipline.

Like all truths that are repressed at the conscious level, this one reveals itself to us at the level of personal and collective pathological practice: in the numbers of "sick" women, poor women, battered women, raped women, crazy women; in pornography and language; in entertainments and media and business practices; and in a mystified and illusory way even at the level of "intellectual" or "objective" ideas. Althusser's killing of his wife (like the wrangling over money and "possession" of children in divorce proceedings, which discloses the mystified reality of marriage, which is most fundamentally an economic and political social relation and not a romantic one) was a spontaneous expression at the level of practice of a truth that is systematically denied conscious acknowledgment in sexist society—the truth that men's lives are constituted by, predicated upon, maintained by, and maintaining of the servitude, oppression, and *silence* of women.

No one thought to ask why Althusser expressed his depression, his tension, his misery, his instability, in this particular and precise way—by killing his wife. We must ask what made her the appropriate and permitted object of his violence and destructive despair, and not himself, as in the case of Poulantzas, for example? Or the director of his university? His best friend? His students? Or why kill a person, rather than burn books, or destroy property? It is well known that we do not express our anger to those we fear or respect or need; we vent it on those we can afford to lose, or alienate, on those less powerfully placed than ourselves, on those who cannot harm us, on those we can replace. Not a pleasant thought to pursue, but the truth rarely is. And why asphyxiate? I found this powerfully symbolic, considering the significance of language in human being and being human and the predilection for gagging women in both soft- and hard-core pornography and "romantic" literature alike. For women are not supposed to speak in patriarchal society, to share in the word, or in the logos of thought; women must be silenced, especially the authentic voice of women, which is necessarily, if authentic, protesting and argumentative—if not by a kiss, then by less subtle and more final measures.[3]

Were these questions not asked because we all know the answers—deep down in our singular and collective historical consciousness? I think so. We know why Helen was killed. Like all women "the lady did protest too much" as ladies are wont to do; like all women she happened to be there when Althusser "broke." But wives do not just happen to be there—there in the so-called "private" realm, where men are permitted to abandon "reason" for "emotion" if circumstances demand. There is a whole institutionalized patriarchal state apparatus that puts and keeps women there—servicing men's "personal" and "emotional" needs.

This is the kind of critique Althusser's theory and practice suggested to me—the complete absence of which motivated the expression of outrage indicated here and articulated more polemically in "Why Althusser Killed His Wife" (chapter 1).

It enraged me that *none* of the subsequent discussions of the event among the so-called radicals and revolutionaries of the Left literati even mentioned the possibility of linking Althusser's theory with his practice, let alone considered it as a serious and urgent need, and male (though not female) colleagues, furthermore, expressed moral and political indignation at the very entertainment of such ideas. I was told it was "in bad taste" and taking feminism too far to suggest that Althusser's ideas, especially his commitment to Marxism, Science, and class-struggle, had any connection with his dead wife. In response to this I wrote a polemical essay called "Why Althusser Killed His Wife," indicating more precisely some of the possible connections between Althusser's political ideas and personal praxis and at the same time expressing my own outrage at this persistent refusal of the Left to explore this relationship systematically—not only in their response to the particular case of Althusser but in the generality of their discourse on politics.

I suggested there that science is both patriarchal and violent, not accidentally but constitutively, and that revolutionaries, therefore, like Althusser, who appeal to science to authorize and legitimize their theories and practices as *social* scientists authorize and legitimize violence and patriarchy at the same time. For their appeal to science enmeshes them in a sexist and (now) bourgeois ideological apparatus—theory and practice—that is both relatively autonomous, that is, self-determining and inherently and intrinsically violent. Here I shall develop these ideas more fully; arguing that science *is* ideology and not its Other as many, including Althusser[4] would claim, that science *is* patriarchal and sexist, and that as such science both presupposes as its condition of possibility and reproduces as its implicit intentional end, *unequal* social relations that are necessarily hierarchical and oppressive and fundamentally violent.

Ideology of Domination

By ideology I mean a representation of reality at the level of ideas that systematically conceals much of that reality first, by *mystifying* it, that is, by presenting a partial truth about reality as if it were the whole truth. For example science is assumed to be "progressive" because it increases our control over ourselves and nature and thus "liberates" us from the demands of necessity. There is certainly *an element* of truth in this—science has facilitated our control over the material world in *some respects*, but that control is limited to certain people and certain limited spheres of praxis. It is accompanied by increasing entropy and *disorder* in those systems beyond its immediate spheres of control and thus generates an ever-increasing demand for more "scientific" control of the material reality it transforms. Indeed some have even suggested that this scientific control over things is entirely illusory; for all that has been achieved is *conceptual mastery* of nature[5] and that, in fact, we have less control of our material destinies than people in prescientific societies. Furthermore this partial and very ambiguous "control" of science over "nature" has correlated negatively with our "control" over social reality, such that *social entropy* has escalated with the "advance" of science, along with disorder at the level of individual existence. I shall return to this example later.

Science is ideology therefore because it mystifies reality. It is ideology because it also *reifies* reality, that is, it presents these partial and historical truths as if they were not only the whole truth but also as if they were not historical but universal or "natural,"[6] and as if they were "objective" truths i.e. truths which are independent of the knower. For example science describes laws—universal laws of nature, we are told—which are said to describe how things *are* in some essential and "objective" sense; when in fact they describe how things have been perceived to be by particular social and historical individuals with particular interests and particular goals defined by their position in a particular "social conjuncture." And I shall return to the question of laws later.

When I claim that science is sexist, I mean that it serves men's interests at the expense of women's interests, that women are both excluded from and violated by science, and that this exclusion and violation is constitutive of science itself. By patriarchy I mean the following: a system of ownership and control of progeny, whereby men establish their rights over children and women. I believe, though I am not about to argue it here, that patriarchy is the first political institution[7]—both chronologically and logically—and the root of all social hierarchies, all authoritarian control, and all challenges to that control. It entails male ownership of children and women. For if paternity is to be assured, women's sexuality must be controlled; in fact *all* women must be collectively controlled by *all* men. Thus rule of the fathers entails the rule of men over mothers, daughters, and sons. History is the history of the various revolts of the sons against the fathers, of the sons asserting their right to rule against the ruling fathers—they are demanding their rights as patriarchs. This is true even in the case of class-struggle, for political and state power is but the institutionalized form of patriarchy. Revolutionaries, like Althusser, for example, can be seen as just another form of the same thing: the brothers fighting among themselves to wrest power from the ruling patriarchs. Their revolt, however, is structured in the image of the father—whether it be in the name of freedom, reason, justice, or science—for all of these values have been created within the patriarchy and therefore serve its interests. The ideology of science is historically, materially, formally, structurally, and logically inseparable from the ideology, practice, and discourse of patriarchy. Science grew up along with patriarchy; they nurtured each other and they share the same structures of male-dominance. Science is equated with knowledge, knowledge with power, and power with dominance—and that is why it is pursued.

> Natural science has sought to dominate and control nature; social and political science to dominate and control human nature—man, humanity, society. The rhetoric of freedom, of human emancipation from the control

> of nature has served to conceal and obscure the material base and conditions of possibility of both sciences: *real social relations of servitude, inequality and dominance*. This material base is constituted by the division of labour, private property, social stratification (hierarchies of control and authority) and the ideological separation of Man from Nature. These structures which are structures of both production and reproduction, are essentially structures of violence; they consist of some men violating others and violating nature. Women are violated as both other and nature. While only some men, in some historical periods have been violated as nature—native indians (in pre-scientific societies), for example, blacks, the insane, the diseased, the cretinous.[8]

Thus to promote science is to promote patriarchy, for their values are the same male values: control, authority, and domination; and their point of departure is the same condition of male alienation from the reproductive process.

I am not claiming that science has *become* ideological or patriarchal, or that science has been *used* to exclude, control, or violate women (though I am not denying this either), and could therefore, by implication be otherwise. I am making the much stronger claim that science is ideology and is sexist *constitutively*, not accidentally. It follows from this that there could be no socially "pure" or guiltless science and that transferring control of science, from the military-industrial complex, for example, to the "people," or from men to women or a community of both, would not challenge the destructive violence that I believe is intrinsic to science itself and that I will now try to disclose to you more systematically.

First let us consider science itself. To what does it refer? It refers to a practice, a set of theories, and a methodology,[9] though what goes under its name varies according to the historical demands of the ruling class of patriarchs. But it is always political, not only as a practice (vis-à-vis its control and controlling interests) but also as a methodology and in the choice of its concepts and terms of representation of the world. And there is violence at every level. There is violence at the level of practice for the practice of science is made possible by the economic and political oppression of others. Science is always conducted in the interests of the ruling class, and it is in their interests to maintain the political structures of dominance that make their rule possible. The rule of the fathers and their domination of women and children was formerly legitimized and authorized by appeals to a Divine or Natural Order (usually considered to be the same). Thus inequalities of social power and the domination of some men by others and all women by all men was neutralized and naturalized by the appeal to an objective order of the world. Since religious ideology no longer serves this purpose of legitimizing power, the ideology of science has taken it over. Scientists are the high priests of the bourgeois order which has *redistributed* patriarchal power among the fathers but maintained its precise distribution between the sexes. But science continues to serve the interests of the ruling class and is made possible by the subordination and servitude of those over whom it rules. This was made very apparent to me recently when I listened to Quirks and Quarks on C.B.C. Radio. Every item was lauded as an occasion for progress for either the military, business, or government; and at the end we were invited to listen in next week to hear about the newly discovered disease that afflicts homosexuals only, and the new research supporting the view that boys are physiologically constructed to be better at math than girls (and guess what science is based on?). It was clear to me whose interests science serves—and they are certainly not mine—they are the interests of the ruling patriarchy, of which I can never be a part. Thus it is quite appropriate that science should be investigating diseases of homosexuals and the lower-class brains of girls; science studies those it wants to control, and the increasing assertiveness of women and homosexual men threatens the rule of the patriarchs, which at its most fundamental level is rooted in their control of reproduction. Knowledge is control and scientific knowledge serves social control.

There is violence at the level of scientific theory, too, not only with respect to science's choice of paradigms and concepts (e.g., the hierarchical structure of the planetary system, the mechanical individualism of atomic theory, the aggressive and selfish gene, and survival of the fittest) but more fundamentally at the level of laws. Walter Benjamin in a difficult but excellent essay, "The Critique of Violence,"[10] observes that all violence as a means, rather than an end in itself, is either law-making or law-preserving and that "all lawmaking is to that extent an immediate manifestation of violence." And science, if anything, is about laws. Laws oblige others to observe them and exclude those who challenge them. They are a form of social control—in this case, of mind-control. They suggest nonhistorical and unchanging patterns of "natural" events and processes, and they fix the truth. They are authoritative and like definitions:

> They channel the imagination and deflect queries from what is actually going on. They are therefore inherently reactionary and conservative. They prevent us from thinking about the complexities of what is happening by covering it up in a category.[11]

Thus "from the point of view of violence, which alone can guarantee law, there is no equality." Just as there is no equality in the scientific community, but a rigid hierarchy of authority and control, and corresponding rites of passage, initiation, and legitimation.

Finally, there is violence in the method of science. It is a function of its required objectivity and abstraction. The scientist is encouraged and disciplined to regard the world as the object of his omniscient spectator gaze, and not as the medium of his existence, which it in fact is. This ensures the complete lack of identification of the scientist with his object of study—whether these be atoms and molecules or girls' brains and homosexual diseases. And this, in turn, enables him to intrude upon and manipulate his object of study, tear it from its contextual home, and reduce it to quantifiable units with a clear conscience—together with the assurance of his own superiority and power over the same object. In this way science kills what it studies.[12]

Patriarchal Practice

Of course not all science is the same. The precise contents of its practice, concepts, and methods change according to changes in historical circumstances and the social organization of power and resources. For science is a product of human praxis. It is produced, reproduced, consumed, and distributed within particular political and economic contexts that determine its particular content. But it is always directed toward "the acquisition of scientific authority in terms of prestige"[13] and toward the maintenance of control. And in all cases *what* counts as science is not determined by what is done, nor by how it is done, but by *who* does it. The abstract classification of natural phenomena was once considered the business of science,[14] but you can be sure that a peasant's detailed classification of plants, insects, leaves, and the stars never qualified as science. For science is done by the initiated, by an élite. It is essentially hierarchical, exclusive, authoritarian, and directed toward the control and domination of others. Peasants make pots and grow food from seed, protecting them from climatic damage and the possible ravages of animals and insects; farmers practice animal husbandry, build complicated fencing systems, and irrigate land; herbalists cure and prevent sickness; mothers reproduce (or not) the human kind, transform raw food into cooked and flour into bread, pieces of straw into baskets and sheep's wool into coats; and working men construct machines of all kinds in their yards, breed pigeons and greyhounds, train hawks, fix their cars, their plumbing, and their electrical devices—but none of these is granted the title of science, though their practices are skilled, systematic, repeatable, teachable, informed by understanding, and productive of truths that are objective by anyone's standards. These are not scientific practices, however, because they are not institutionalized, not hierarchical, and not authoritarian; and they are neither élitist nor exclusive but characteristically collective, communal, and social, and rooted in the lived realities and shared needs of ordinary people. Science, on the other hand, presupposes, maintains, and legitimizes social inequalities of power and privilege. It is parasitic and "pure", and practiced by an élite class who do not labor but acquire their leisure to pursue knowledge for its own sake" from the exploited labor of others.

Thus revolutionaries who appeal to science to legitimize their claim to lead and rule only challenge the bourgeoisie on their own terms. They are saying: We are scientists, too, and therefore fit to rule; in fact our science is superior to yours and therefore this entitles us to right rule. The familiar radical critiques of science are therefore inadequate, for they do not get to its root. For it is not the use of science that is oppressive but science itself. No one can be a scientist with a clear conscience, for science, as a practice entails: 1) *specialization* and therefore the division of labor which is always unequal and always alienating;[15] 2) *hierarchies* of control and decision making, for science is essentially institutional and professional (where there is no institutional control there is no science); and 3) *domination*, for knowledge is power and specialized knowledge gives power to an élite, that is, to a ruling class. Science does not just happen. Priorities are established in someone's interest and often in the name of others who are presumed not to know enough to know what is good for them. These others are traditionally women and members of subordinate classes.

In addition science's theory and practice embody male norms and thus exclude women almost a priori. The characteristics required to practice "normal,"[16] that is, institutionalized science, coincide with "normal" male characteristics, for example, being aggressive, strong, independent, logical, in control of physical environment, dominant, mechanical, handy with tools, good at abstract and rational thought, etc. Women, on the other hand, are characterized (and produced) as intuitive, emotional, dependent, loving and caring, respondent and passive, and not good at abstract and objective thought. The Catch-22 is, however, that at the same time as science is characterized as a male activity, it is characterized as *genderless* and "objective" with respect to both its methods and its concepts.[17] Thus the female half of the dichotomized reality is not only excluded but is also rendered invisible for male is defined by decree as the norm of the rational, scientific, and essential human "appropriation" of the world. Thus science assumes, reproduces, authorizes, confirms, and *reifies* the traditional dualisms of male-stream thought that have permitted men to separate both in theory and in practice their emotional life from their intellectual life and their personal from their public practice. At its most primitive this dualism consists in the assumption that human beings consist of minds and bodies and that it is "man's" mind, his Reason, that distinguishes him from his fellow creatures and entitles him to dominate them just as God, the Almighty Mind, was once thought to dominate Man. For this split between Humanity and Nature is hierarchical and presumed to entitle those who are members of the former class to dominate and control that which belongs to the latter—in the name of Humanism. This hierarchical split—or dualistic mode of thought and action—is intrinsic to both patriarchy, the systematic and society sanctioned supremacy of men over women, and science, the systematic and socially sanctioned supremacy of Man over Nature. And women, nature, and the vast majority of men have been and continue to be violated in its name—in the name of Reason, Progress, Science, Freedom, or Humanism.

According to the dualistic mode of thought, knower and known belong to different ends of an assumed polarity, indeed, to different orders of being. The scientist is the subject who knows; the world is the object known. The knower is active; the known is passive. The knower is universal; the known is the "merely" particular. The scientist, as Reason incarnate (but somehow untransformed by the incarnation), knows and studies the world "objectively," that is, as pure Reason, stripped of any emotional, personal, historical, political, or economic qualities or ties with that same world. This dualism is constitutive of male-stream thought at all levels—the political, economic, philosophical, historical, artistic, psychological, etc.[18] It is peculiarly, and not accidentally, male for it serves male needs for creativity, control, and immortality; needs which women do not experience as a result of their more immediate and concrete relationship to reproduction. Dualism expresses at the ideological level men's experienced alienation from species continuity and creativity and thus from human "first" nature. Male thought thus emphasizes difference, separation, polarity, and conflict and traditionally assumes the following dichotomies as givens and as universal and absolute: mind/body, rational/emotional, cultural/natural, universal/particular, abstract/concrete, sacred/profane, divine/mundane, subject/object, light/dark, order/disorder, real/apparent, self/other, good/bad, and, of course, male/female and scientific/unscientific (or true/false).

Dualism serves patriarchy by assigning women to that pole of the presumed dichotomy that requires control and domination by that identified as human. Pythagoras, one of the first to systematically articulate dualistic thought as philosophy and science, believed that there is a good principle that has created order, light and man and a bad principle that has created chaos, darkness and women. Plato identified nature and matter as female and ideas as male. Aristotle associated activity with maleness and passivity with femaleness. Form reigned superior over dead, passive matter.

> Socially Aristotle found the basis for male rule over the household in the analogy that, as the soul ruled the body, so reason and deliberation, characteristic of men, should rule the appetites supposedly predominant in women. Aristotle's biological theory viewed the female of the species as an incomplete or mutilated male, since the coldness of the female body would not allow the menstrual blood to perfect itself as semen.[19]

* * *

> The male provides the "form" and the "principle of movement," the female provides the body, in other words the material. Compare the coagulation of milk. Here, the milk is the body, and the fig juice or the rennet contains the principle which causes it to set. . . .
>
> Thus, if the male is the active partner, the one which originates the movement, and the female *qua* female is the passive one, surely what the female contributes to the semen of the male will not be semen but material. And this is in fact what happens; for the natural substance of the menstrual fluid is to be classed as "prime matter."
>
> Taking then the widest formulation of each of these two opposites, viz., regarding the male *qua* active and causing movement, and the female *qua* passive and being set in movement. We see that the one thing which is formed is formed *from them* only in the sense in which a bedstead is formed from the carpenter and the wood, or a ball from the wax and the form.[20]

Machiavelli concludes *The Prince* with the following exhortation:

> I hold strongly to this: that it is better to be impetuous than circumspect; because fortune is a woman and if she is to be submissive it is necessary to beat and coerce her. Experience shows that she is more often subdued by men who do this than by those who act coldly. Always being a woman, she favours young men, because they are less circumspect and more ardent, and because they command her with greater audacity.[21]

And Bacon treats nature as a female to be hounded and tortured through mechanical inventions and explicitly compares this process of dominating nature with the witch hunts that coincided with the scientific revolution in sixteenth- and seventeenth-century Europe—an apt and telling coincidence of theory and practice. In his "De Dignitate et Augmentis Scientarium" written in 1623, he has the following to say about the methods by which nature's secrets might be discovered:

> For you have but to follow and as it were hound nature in her wanderings, and you will be able when you like to lead and drive her afterward to the same place again. Neither am I of the opinion in this history of marvels that superstitious narratives of sorceries, witchcrafts, charms, dreams, divinations, and the like, where there is an assurance and clear evidence of the fact, should be altogether excluded . . . *howsoever the use and practice of such arts is to be condemned*, yet from speculation and consideration of them . . . a useful light may be gained, not only of the true judgment of the offenses of persons charged with such practices, but likewise for the further disclosing of the secrets of nature. *Neither ought a man to make scruple of entering and penetrating into these holes and corners when the inquisition of truth is his whole object*—as your majesty has shown in your own example.[22] (My emphasis.)

The strong sexual implications of the last sentence are not accidental to the scientific principles extolled by Bacon and are characteristic of the scientific revolution. "As woman's womb had symbolically yielded to the forceps, so nature's womb harbored secrets that through technology could be wrested from her grasp for use in the improvement of the human condition."[23] "Human" here could not possibly be held to include women or nature, since their subjugation is its condition of possibility.

Dualistic thinking can justify any social hierarchy, for it enables the knower to objectify and reify the "other," the known, and thus to act upon it, control, dominate, and violate it as mere object, as a threat to order, reason, and right rule, as that which conflicts with and contradicts "humanity's" higher interests. To perceive nature and women as Other is to objectify them and legitimize intrusion into them and their manipulation in the service of what can only be men's interests for, if they are other, they can be appropriated and possessed and they must be "mastered." We must not forget that the original meaning of "famulus" was "slaves" or "servants"; and "family" denoted men's possessions—their house, land, animals, children, and wife.

Representing the world in dualistic terms allows the scientist to treat not only nature, but also people, as objects and to take no kind of responsibility for the uses and direction of science, which is regarded, not morally, but politically as a source of power. It enables men to abstract themselves falsely from nature as if they were not organic and social beings themselves. This is the root at one and the same time, of both their power (for they can be ruthless with others) and their alienation from the world, each other, and themselves. Unfortunately it is also a measure of their "freedom" and "humanity" for the more they control, the more free they think they are, and the more free they are, in this sense, the more separated they are from their real material roots in nature, and thus the more they are alienated. And yet this is called Humanism.

Humanism, like science, is presumed to be a good thing, necessarily "progressive." But we must not forget its roots. The birth of science and the first dawn of Humanism coincided with Greek imperialism, colonization, and slavery. The European Renaissance coincided with European colonization, imperialism, and slavery and has been maintained only through the enslavement of their own citizens to wage-labor as the necessary condition of the industrial revolution and the rise of capitalism. Empire building and the enslavement of large populations must be accompanied by an ideology and a structure making control of such dominions possible. The rhetoric of Humanism and scientific progress toward an enhanced "humanity" provides that legitimation, justifying oppression and exploitation in the name of order, freedom, rational control, and progress, where there was previously, we are told, chaos, servitude (to nature), and stagnation.

The truth is, however, that neither Science nor Humanism have enhanced the lives of most of us. Both represent ideological, institutionalized, élitist, and hierarchical systems of ideas and values that distort and disguise human reality and social practice by mystifying it, that is, by asserting partial truths as if they were whole truths, and reifying it by asserting those partial, historical, and particular truths as if they were universal, unchanging absolutes. They function to authorize, legitimize, and reproduce unequal and oppressive social, political, and economic structures that are their only condition of possibility. The pursuit of humanistic ideals and scientific truth are the privilege of a ruling class though they are packaged as "our" ("everyman's") cultural inheritance. They are made possible only by the forceful appropriation of social labor and social wealth from the ruled by the rulers—in the name of "control" and "progress."

The rhetoric of Humanism recognizes the dignity of Man: his freedom, his rational autonomy, and his capacity to form his world and himself according to his needs, desires, and interests (though these values have seldom, if ever, been extended to women). This rhetoric is addressed to Man in general. While, as a matter of fact, the idealized reality that it represents—a life of freedom, dignity, and rational autonomy—is the privilege of an absolute minority, which entirely excludes women and the vast majority of men. The recognized humanities and sciences are likewise pursued and promoted for the glory and status, freedom and dignity, and wealth and control that accrue to *individual men* (and now sometimes individual women) and not for the benefit of some mysterious and vague "humanity" in general as we are led to believe.

In other words the so-called "civilization" of Man refers to the civilization or the humanization of some men; and this has been achieved by the dehumanization of men in general[24] and of all women. They have been systematically deprived of that dignity, freedom, and rational control which supposedly distinguishes the truly human from the merely natural or animal existence. Dualistic thought and practice—the separation of Man from Nature and Mind from Body—is intrinsic to both Humanism and Science and permits men to violate nature for the "greater glory of mankind" (formerly of God) and to extract physical labor from those who the same men declare "less rational," for the sake of "progress." The ideology of Humanism and Science has also:

> required and sanctioned the separation of sexuality, reproduction and women from the specifically human and the humanly significant (after all they serve only the natural functions); together with their privatization and depolitization within the family or personal life (whose functions, whose personal life, whose family?).[25]

It is thus that science violates women.

The scientific ideal is rational control—of the social and material conditions of human existence. The dream of ever-increasing control is the fire that fuels the continuing growth and development of science and technology and of social control through increasing government bureaucracies and institutions. The goal is presumably total control. But the dream of total control is an absolute fantasy, corresponding to no kind of possible reality. Our scientists are chasing an illusion. For though they be men, they, no less than the rest of us, are natural, organic, and material beings whose existence is necessarily and unavoidably constrained by that fact. They are a constitutive part of the world they are endeavoring to control, and they, no less than the rest of us, are social, historical individuals whose consciousness and perception is necessarily and unavoidably rooted in and produced by those social and material realities. No man can be God, not even a scientist. No man can transcend his situatedness in and of this world. No man can be sovereign subject, invulnerable, inpenetrable, or inviolate.

Science will not therefore solve our social problems for it is part of the problem itself. The scientific manipulation of things will not bring an end to social degradation, oppression, and political and economic exploitation. For science is made possible by them, needs them, reinforces them, confirms them, and reproduces them. We must, therefore, stop appealing to science—its methods, its concepts, its authority, its power, and its modes of legitimation and verification—as the desirable or necessary foundation of social revolution (as the revolutionary tradition invariably does). For one of the conditions of our liberation from oppressive structures of dominance will be our liberation from the mystifying and reifying oppressive social praxis of science itself.

NOTES

1. First published in *Our Generation* 15, no. 1 (Winter 1982): 40–50.
2. "Ideology and Ideological State Apparatuses" in *Lenin and Philosophy and Other Essays* (New York and London: Monthly Review Press, 1971), 162.
3. See chapters 4, 5, and 7 of this book
4. See especially *Reading Capital*, by Althusser and Balibar, N. L. B., 1970: "Science can no more be ranged within the category of 'superstructure' than can language . . . the relatively autonomous and peculiar history of scientific knowledge and the other modes of historical existence" (133); and *Lenin and Philosophy*: "Marx founds a new science i.e. he elaborates a system of new scientific concepts where previously there prevailed only the manipulation of ideological notions" (42). G. Cohen, the new darling of Anglo-American Marxist scholars in his recent *Karl Marx's Theory of History: A Defense* (Princeton, N.J.: Princeton University Press, 1978) claims a similar status for marxism: that is science and science is not superstructure and thus not ideological. For a thorough and devastating critique of Cohen and other "technological determinist'" interpreta-

tions of Marx, see Eduardo Saxe-Fernandez's unpublished Master's thesis, "Marxism, Revisionism and Technological Determinism," University of Ottawa, Department of Philosophy, 1981.

5. See W. Leiss, *The Domination of Nature* (New York: Doubleday, 1972), especially, chapter 6, Science and Nature: "The mastery of science is manifested in its ability to cast a 'veil of ideas' over the nature experienced in everyday existence, that is, to treat the phenomena of nature as if they were purely mathematical-geometrical objects" (139). Other points made in this paragraph are considered by Claude Lévi-Strauss throughout his writings, but in particular in his *Conversations with Claude Lévi-Strauss* ed. G. Charbonnier (London: Jonathan Cape, 1969). For example "in order to establish his ascendancy over nature, man had to subjugate man and treat one section of mankind as an object" (31); "any social field—if we call a society a social field—produces entropy, or disorder, as a society, and creates order, as a culture. It is this inverse relationship which, in my opinion, expresses the difference between peoples we call primitive and those we call civilized. Primitive people produce very little order by means of their culture. Nowadays we call them the underdeveloped peoples. But they produce very little entropy in their societies. On the whole, these societies are egalitarian, mechanical in type, and governed by the law of unanimity" (40–41). (By culture Lévi-Strauss means the organization of things and by society the organization of "men.")
6. In this respect any appeal to the "nature" of things, or to "natural" processes is always suspect for it reflects a desire for *stasis*, for absolutes, for unchanging givens.
7. For a systematic and powerful defense of this thesis, see Mary O'Brien *The Politics of Reproduction* (London: Routledge and Kegan Paul, 1981).
8. "Why Althusser Killed His Wife," p. 6 in this volume.
9. Margaret Benston, "Feminism and the Critique of the Scientific Method" in *Feminism in Canada. From Pressure to Politics*, eds. Geraldine Finn and Angela Miles (Montreal: Black Rose Books, 1982), 47–66.
10. In Walter Benjamin, *Reflections, Essays, Aphorisms, Autobiographical Writings* (New York and London: Harcourt Brace Jovanovich, 1978).
11. Geraldine Finn, "Feminism and Socialism: Towards a New Synthesis," unpublished paper, 9. Rousseau makes a similar protest against the intrinsic inequalities of laws in the last pages of *Emile* (London: Everyman, Dent), 457: "Where is there any law" he asks, "Where is there any respect for law? Under the name of law you have everywhere seen the rule of self-interest and human passion." And Michel Foucault has more recently expressed a view similar to that of Benjamin in claiming that "humanity installs each of its violences in a system of rules and thus proceeds from domination to domination. The nature of these rules allows violence to be inflicted on violence and the resurgence of new forces that are sufficiently strong to dominate those in power. Rules are empty in themselves, violent and unfinalized; they are impersonal and can be bent to any purpose. The successes of history belong to those who are capable of seizing the rules, to replace those who had used them, to disguise themselves so as to pervert them, invert their meaning, and redirect them against those who had initially imposed them; controlling this complex mechanism, they will make it function so as to overcome the rulers through their own rules" (*Language, Counter-Memory, Practice*, ed. Donald Bouchard [Ithaca, New York: Cornell University Press, 1977], 51).

12. Rachel Vigier makes a similar claim about philosophy—the original science, of course—in her unpublished paper "Philosophy in the Key of Life," read to the Canadian Society for Women in Philosophy (S.W.I.P.) at their annual conference in Toronto, October 1981. There she argues that philosophy "as a method of purification, becomes in effect the art of dying" (12); that "a true philosopher prepares for death from the moment he accepts the philosophical task. Half-dead, he deserves death which is the release of the soul from the body" (13); that philosophical abstraction is the "homicidal-suicidal agent of the philosophizing fathers" (1); that philosophy in this way "becomes the antidote to life" (15); that "philosophy is dead" (16) because only life gives the possibility of thinking, and the philosopher (and scientist, I would add) abstracts himself from life, "He himself withdraws from the object of thought and focusses primarily on death isolated from its range of life" (19), while "thinking is like dancing and only a thought which comes to you through your muscles is worth trusting" (20).
13. Pierre Bourdieu, quoted by Trevor Pinch in *The Social Production of Scientific Knowledge*, ed. E. Mendelsohn, P. Weingart and R. Whitley (Boston: D. Reidel Publishing Co., 1977), 178.
14. See, for example, Aristotelian science and the science of the Classical age, beginning midway through the seventeenth century in Europe. For a description of the latter, see Michel Foucault, *The Order of Things: An Archaeology of the Human Sciences* (New York: Vintage Press, 1973).
15. "The *division of labour* is the economic expression of the *social character of labour* within alienation . . . nothing but the *alienated* establishment of human activity as a *real species-activity* or *the activity of man as a species-being*.

    The economists are very confused and self-contradictory about the nature of the *division of labour* (which of course has to be regarded as a principal motive force in the production of wealth once labour is recognized as the *essence of private property*), i.e. about the alienated form of human activity as species-activity.

    The *division of labour* and *exchange* are the two phenomena which lead the economist to vaunt the social character of his science, while in the same breath he unconsciously expresses the contradictory nature of his science—the establishment of society through unsocial, particular interests." Karl Marx, in the Economic and Philosophical Manuscripts, in *Early Writings*, ed. T. B. Bottomore (New York: McGraw-Hill Paperbacks, 1963) 181, 187; original emphases.
16. See Thomas Kuhn, *The Structure of Scientific Revolutions* (Chicago: University of Chicago Press, 1970): "In this essay, 'normal science' means research firmly based upon one or more past scientific achievements, achievements that some particular scientific community acknowledges for a time as supplying the foundation for its further practice. Today, such achievements are recounted, though seldom in their original form, by science textbooks, elementary and advanced . . . these . . . serve[d] for a time to define the legitimate problems and methods of a research field for succeeding generations of practitioners" (10). "Men whose research is based on shared paradigms are committed to the same rules and standards for scientific practice. That commitment and the apparent consensus it produces are prerequisites for normal science, i.e. for the genesis and continuation of a particular research tradition" (11).
17. See Margaret Benston, "Feminism and the Critique," 47–66, for a discussion of the "maleness" of science, as well as Ruth Wallsgrove's "The Masculine

Face of Science" in *Alice Through the Microscope*. The Power of Science Over Women's Lives, by The Brighton Women and Science Group (London: Virago Press, 1980); and two papers presented at the Annual Meeting of the American Association for the Advancement of Science, in Toronto in January 1981: "Is Feminism a Threat to Scientific Objectivity?" by Elizabeth Fee, and "Women and Science: Fitting Men to Think about Nature" by Hilde Hein.

18. The designation "male-stream" thought originated with Mary O'Brien. I first became aware of it in her essay "Reproducing Marxist Man" in *The Sexism of Social and Political Theory*, ed. Lorenne Clark and Lynda Lange (Toronto: University of Toronto Press, 1979).
19. Carolyn Merchant, *The Death of Nature*. Women, Ecology and the Scientific Revolution. (New York: Harper and Row, 1980), 13.
20. Aristotle, *Generation of Animals*, quoted in *Not in God's Image*. Women in History from the Greeks to the Victorians, eds. Julia O'Faolain and Lauro Martines (New York: Harper Torchbook, 1973), 119.
21. Machiavelli, *The Prince* (Harmondsworth, Middlesex, England: Penguin Classics, 1961), 133.
22. Carolyn Merchant quoting from Bacon, "De Dignitate et Augmentis Scientiarum" 168.
23. Ibid., 169.
24. Lévi-Strauss makes this point in his critique of humanism, both aristocratic and bourgeois, in his "Answers to Some Investigations," chap. xv, in *Structural Anthropology II* (New York: Basic Books, 1976). He fails to notice, however, that his own elaboration of culture in his other works, especially in *The Elementary Structures of Kinship* (Boston: Beacon Press, 1969), in terms of the exchange of women—as the precondition and creation of culture—makes the objectification of women, as values to be exchanged, the means and condition of possibility of the humanization of men. He thus places patriarchy at the very root and base of "civilization" and "socialization." For a detailed analysis of his reification and mystification of patriarchal social relations, see Gayle Rubin's excellent essay, "The Traffic in Women: Notes on the 'Political Economy' of Sex," in *Towards an Anthropology of Women*, ed. Rayna Reiter (New York: Monthly Review Press, 1975), and my own discussion of Levi-Strauss's structural anthropology in "Understanding Social Reality: Marx, Sartre and Lévi-Strauss," unpublished Ph.D. thesis, University of Ottawa, 1981.
25. Geraldine Finn, "Why Althusser Killed his Wife," *Canadian Forum* (September-October 1981): 29; p. 7 in this volume.

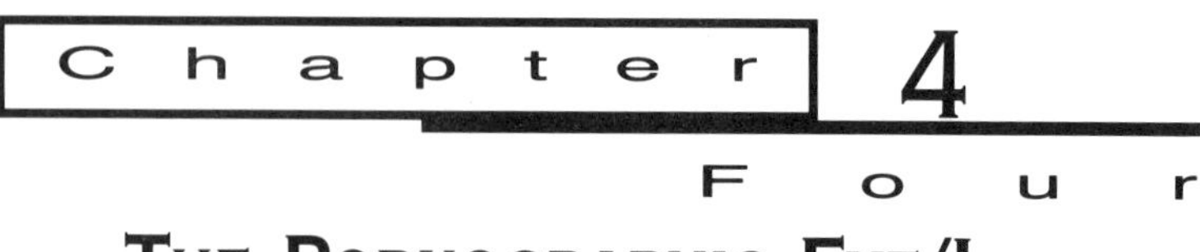

The Pornographic Eye/I

IN THE SPRING OF 1984, I was invited by the *Canadian Journal of Political and Social Theory* to prepare a paper on pornography for their symposium at the annual meetings of the Canadian Learned Societies and for publication in a subsequent issue of the journal. This chapter is that paper.

Sex and Pornography were hot political topics at the time, and although I had followed the debates and debacles conducted in their name, and devoted a considerable amount of research and reflection to their deliberation over the years, I had systematically avoided coming out in public on the issue. This was not because I had nothing to say that was not already being said, but because I felt I had rather too much, and that what I had to say could not be said, and certainly would not be heard within the terms of the vested interests that were organizing the debates at the time and polarizing all analyses into binary opposites and all arguments into positions for or against censorship or freedom of expression; pornography or erotica; sexual liberation or sexual repression; and homosexuals, heterosexuals, bisexuals, lesbians, the bourgeois family, perverts, pimps, prostitutes, and prudes. The urgencies of the sexual status quo at the time, which had forced the question of sex and representation out of the closet and on to the public agenda *as a question*—as a political question at that—kept forcing it back into the closet in the stampede for early closure that is, for settling the Sex question once and for all. Although there was much talk of "social construction" in these debates, it seemed to me to be selectively invoked and that Sex itself continued to circulate as a given. People just disagreed about *what* was given and what in fact you are entitled to do with it.

"The Pornographic Eye/I" intended to destabilize and displace the organizing and polarizing terms of these debates, especially their taken-for-grantedness of Sex, and thereby to broaden and deepen our understanding of the theoretical and political stakes at issue within them. It proved to be the most difficult essay I have ever written, seconded only by "No Bodies Speaking: Subjectivity, Sex, and the Pornography Effect" (chapter 7) for similar reasons. It was difficult because the material itself is hard to contemplate—the material realities of the pornographic eye/I (I kept wanting to turn away) and because its cumulative effect on one's own person, like the cumulative effect of the culture it authorizes on one's life, is also hard to bear. It was difficult because in my determination to let no one off the (sexual) hook, I had to cover so much ground and hold on to so many different threads of argument at the same time. And finally, and perhaps most importantly, it was difficult because I knew that what I wanted to say was not what people wanted to hear and that it would, if it were successful, leave no one secure in their sexual practices or beliefs.

As it happens the essay found its audience and remains probably the best known and most widely circulated of my publications. It certainly precipitated me into the Sex debate (see Finn 1986, for example, and chapters 5 and 7 below), but on my terms not theirs, as evidenced by the heretical title of the next chapter "Against Sexual Imagery. Alternative or Otherwise," which develops the arguments introduced below.

THE PORNOGRAPHIC EYE/I[1]

Pornography is about sex. It is one of the ways men and women are sexualized in our culture. It is both an expression of that sexualization as well as a powerful instrument of its production and reproduction.

The kind of sexuality presumed and promoted in pornography is not significantly different in its essentials from that which is produced in us elsewhere by discourses and practices not normally thought of as pornographic; by those which are not even explicitly concerned with sex as much as by those which are: by and through the discourses of history, religion, law, medicine, philosophy, pedagogy, art and literature, etc., etc., as well as by and through the discourses and practices of psychoanalysis, psychotherapy and sexology, the explicitly "erotic" arts and literature, and in modern advertising and the discourse of pleasure that a commodity economy requires. In fact pornography is nourished by the sexual orthodoxy (and vice-versa) and reinforces its most fundamental "truths" or truth-effects as Foucault would say.[2] Pornography, in this sense, is neither deviant nor perverse nor subversive of an authoritarian repressive sexual régime articulated from elsewhere, as those who deplore or defend it would sometimes have us believe. It is rather just another instrument of that régime, which incites sexuality far more than it represses it,[3] and is a further propagation of its powerful effects.

This régime of sex which dominates our culture is one that both naturalizes sex, on the one hand, by constituting it in discourse (and therefore in practice) as if it were a universal, a spontaneous finality or a unified, causal principle of action—an instinct, a drive, a need, Eros or desire; and sexualizes nature, on the other, by tying sexuality as difference, the difference between masculine and feminine, to the difference of the sexual organs.[4] This discourse of sex actually constitutes the sexualities it purports to describe, exploit, explain, or modify. And, of course, it constitutes male and female sexuality differently. In fact I would maintain that this is the whole point of it: to mark that difference, "epitomizing a whole system of difference"[5] that is, in my opinion, the key political and ideological foundation of our social order.[6] The sexes are separated only "in order to establish the absolute privilege of one over the other."[7] Why insist that there be two sexes if not so that one may be subjected to the other? "Indeed, why differentiate if it is not to form a hierarchy?"[8]

Pornography expresses and reproduces the hierarchical difference between masculine and feminine that is produced (and produced as "natural") everywhere else in our culture: in the family, in school, in the marketplace, in church, in the universities, the libraries, museums, galleries and concert halls, in science and medicine, and in industry and entertainment. Both the form and the content of pornography (the medium and the message inextricably and mutually determining), for example, constitute women as objects available for the use and/or contemplation of a subject that is male. It thus objectifies the feminine and feminizes the object as Woman, while subjectifying the masculine and masculinizing the subject as Man; tying femininity to objectivity and immanence and masculinity to subjectivity and transcendence, just as the philosophers, the artists, the scholars, the scientists, and the storytellers have done for as far back in our history as we have been allowed to remember. What I want to emphasize in this chapter, however, is not so much pornography's objectification and sexual passification of women, which has rightly received the critical attention of feminists in recent years, as its *subjectification* and sexual incitement of men. For although pornography is ostensibly about sex objectified in Woman and woman objectified in Sex, the principal protagonist in pornography is, after all, the male-spectator-owner for whom the whole performance has been arranged. "Everything is addressed to him, everything must appear to be the result of his being there."[9] It is men, after all, who produce and consume pornography; it is, therefore, their subjectivity rather than ours that is most immediately effected by it. How then shall we characterize this masculine subject as constituted in and by pornography?

Pornography literally means writing about prostitutes (from the Greek πõρυη, porne meaning harlot, and γράφειυ, graphein meaning to write). If we consider those discourses and practices most readily identified as pornography today—magazines, movies, burlesques—we will see that this original etymological sense of the term (extended to include images and visual representations) captures much of what is distinctive about pornography and the way it constructs and "marks" the masculine-feminine distinction, as well as much of what pornography shares with other cultural representations of that distinction. In the first place pornography constructs Man (i.e., masculinity as subjectivity and subjectivity as masculinity) as an *observer* of women; and Woman, correspondingly (i.e., femininity as objectivity and objectivity as femininity) as the *observed* of men. In this respect pornography merely continues a practice immortalized, if not instituted, in the mythology of ancient Greece—it was, after all, the face of Helen that launched a thousand ships—and replicated since then in our cultural processes, both sacred and profane.

Our current visual environment, for example, is saturated with images of women presented specifically as *sights* for the viewing pleasure of a spectator who is presumed to be male and is thus constituted as male in the very production and reproduction of these images.[10] Publicity is obviously one of the biggest manufacturers and distributors of these sights. But publicity did not invent Man the observer-subject or Woman the object-observed. It merely continues an older, more respected tradition of post-Renaissance oil painting, which also presented sights for the viewing pleasure of the spectator-owner: sights of what he might possess—commodities, merchandise, objects of exchange, property—including, of course, sights of women's naked bodies conventionalized as nudes.[11] And like the images of modern publicity (and the objects of which they are images)[12] these sights in oil painting did not so much reveal themselves (i.e., the truth of the objects they represented) as designate and individuate the spectator-owner as a Man—of wealth, stature, and power—as a man to be envied. The oil painting presented images of objects but only in order to designate a social relationship: that of the spectator-owner to the real objects of which these images were but representations. Pornography does the same thing. It presents images of women but only to designate men and the social relationship between them and the object-woman-viewed. Paradoxical as it may seem, pornography does not reveal Woman, though in it Woman reveals all, because Woman does not disclose herself in pornography. On the contrary, it is Man who is revealed in her objectification. For the Woman he observes is the objectification of *his* idea. She is, after all, Man-made: not a real prostitute, but a product of the masculine imagination, the Word made Flesh and inevitably bearing the mark of her creator.

These same structures of male-subjectification and female-objectification also characterize regular movies. They, too, designate the spectator-subject as male and the male as spectator-subject and Woman as the object of his petrifying gaze. Feminist filmmakers and film critics have done valuable work exposing this structural relationship in recent years.[13] And Stanley Cavell has explored aspects of the same structure—in his case the condition of the viewer—from a somewhat different perspective in his book about film titled *The World Viewed*.[14] He claims there that the "ontological conditions of the motion picture reveal it as inherently pornographic,"[15] in that it constructs a world from which the spectator-subject is necessarily "screened" and over which, therefore, he can feel he has mastery and control. Given that the "body of a woman is culture's time-honoured and conventional victim"[16] we are not surprised to hear Cavell go on to describe the history of film as "a history of the firmament of individual women established there." "Remarkable directors," he suggests, "have existed solely to examine the same woman over and over through film. A woman has become the whole excuse and sole justification for the making and preserving of countless films."[17] He cites Garbo, Davis, and Dietrich as examples, but I am sure you will have no trouble bringing his list up to date: Liv Ullman in Bergman's films, Diane Keaton in Woody Allen's, and Hanna Schygulla in Fassbinder's come easily to mind, as well as these words of François Truffaut, uttered in 1958 and reiterated recently in the *Manchester Guardian Weekly*: "The cinema is the woman's—that is to say the actress's—art. The director's job is to *get pretty women to do pretty things*."[18]

It is certainly no secret that many movies are made today simply and solely as vehicles for displaying particular women to the world: those women with whom the director is "sleeping," as we so coyly put it. In this respect the social relationships immortalized on film—between men and women, spectator-owners, and objects of possession respectively—are fundamentally the same as those designated in paintings of the classical nude (sacred) and in the photographs of modern pornography (profane). In each case particular men—a Polanski, a Manet, a Huge Hefner—put "their" women on display so that other men will recognize their power, their wealth, and their social stature and envy and respect them for it.

So men are constructed in pornography (as elsewhere) as the spectator-owners of women. What kind of women do men enjoy looking at and possessing? First of all the women observed in pornography are *not real*. Real women appear in pornography but never as themselves. In fact they are referred to as "models"—an ambiguous term that can mean "something to be copied, pattern; example; small scale reproduction; three dimensional plan," as well as "one who poses for an artist or photographer," and, most apt of all I think, "*one of a series of varying designs of the same type of object*."[19] For the real women who appear in pornography are always disguised as objects, usually as exotic objects in improbable settings that emphasize their unreality: surrounded by furs and feathers and satin and lace, for example; or alternatively, whips and chains and knives and leather; hanging like pieces of meat from hooks in the ceiling or strutting around like "undulating vamps with gigantic cigarette-holders."[20] What men see, therefore, when they look at pornography (or indeed any public image of women) are not women but women made over into *artifacts*. They gaze at a man-made object, not a woman; at a body "eviscerated of its substance and history"[27] and not at the living flesh:

> abstract, impeccable, clothed with marks [By "marks" Baudrillard means things like lipstick, jewelery, boots, which mark women as cultural products and appropriate objects of desire.] and thus invulnerable; "made-up" (*faict* and *fainct*) in the profound sense of the expression; cut off from external determinations and the internal reality of its desire, yet offered up in the same turn as an idol.[22]

For this pornographic woman (i.e., the artificial woman that is the product of pornography) is simultaneously produced as an object of male desire and is addressed to the male spectator precisely to solicit from him some sort of sexual response. She is in fact produced as both idol and idolizer.[23] For her desire is constituted as his desire for her. Indeed the whole point of her construction is to call forth *his* sexuality and the experience of sexual potency and control that his penis is supposed to confer upon him "naturally."

Hence the appropriateness of the etymological meaning of pornography, that is, writing about whores. For, from the point of view of the male client, the prostitute, like the pornographic woman, has also only one way of being-in-the-world and that is as a sexual object-for-him, not for-herself. But, of course, it must be difficult for a man to maintain this illusory belief in the objectivity of Woman when he is actually engaged in some sort of sexual activity with a real one, especially if she insists on talking or if she is the one that takes the money and not some other man. This threat of encountering the Other as subject and in particular of encountering Woman as Other as subject (the threat of measuring their penis power according to the reality principle) can be circumvented in pornography; which substitutes an image of an unreal prostitute for an interaction with a real one, and an exchange between men (money for access to female artifacts) for a relationship between an individual man and a real woman—that most dangerous of all encounters.

Thus pornography offers men a certain kind of security. In the first place, it protects them from "prostitutes," that is, from Woman as subject of her own sexuality, by killing her off; by petrifying the prostitute in print as other-than-herself and reducing her there entirely and solely to a sight/site of men's sexuality not her own, and men's control. For she now belongs completely to those who buy and sell her. It also establishes the spectator-subject of pornography in the community of men by allowing him to participate, if only symbolically, in the exchange of women, which, if Lévi-Strauss is to be believed, is at the very foundation of culture: "The fundamental step because of which, by which, but above all in which, the transition from nature to culture is accomplished."[24] Men it seems must exchange women to realize themselves as men, that is, establish their gender-identity as masculine and earn the recognition and, more importantly, the allegiance of other men.

Our modern Pygmalion, who can only desire that which he has made over as a site/sight of male sexuality, is not so very different from his prototype, who also shunned the society of real women, disgusted as he was by the conduct of the Propoetides. These were "girls," according to F. Guirand, who "rashly denied the divinity of Aphrodite. To punish them Aphrodite inspired in them such immodesty that losing all sense of shame, they would prostitute themselves to all comers. In the end, they were turned to stone."[25] It is important to understand who and what these "girls" were rejecting when they denied Aphrodite to appreciate the moral of this tale. According to Homer, Aphrodite, the goddess of love, rose spontaneously out of the foam produced on the sea by the castrated genitals of Uranus. She was, that is, the product of Man, not Woman. The gods were apparently so struck by her beauty when they saw her that each "wished in his heart to take her as a wife and lead her to his abode." Guirand comments that it was "natural" that they should be thus moved "for Aphrodite was the essence of feminine beauty. From her gleaming fair hair to her silvery feet everything about her was pure charm and harmony. . . . Aphrodite exuded an aura of seduction. To the perfection of her figure and the purity of her features she added the grace which attracted and conquered." And, finally, quoting Homer, he adds, "On her sweet face she always wore an amiable smile."[26]

For her beauty, Aphrodite was rewarded with an apple in the famous Judgment of Paris (archetype of the modern beauty contest). She in turn rewarded him by offering him as "his own" the most beautiful of mortal women. He chose Helen, who unfortunately had already been claimed as "his own" by Menelaus. The theft of Helen from her original owner unleashed the famous Trojan Wars—an orgy of bloodshed and devastation more commonly blamed on mortal Helen's beautiful face (as Mankind's original sin is blamed on Eve) than on the men who quarreled over possession of it or the goddess (of love, let us not forget) who gave Paris rights to it.

These Propoetides then, who were so despised by Pygmalion that he shunned the company of *all* women and so uncompromisingly punished by Aphrodite, that smiling goddess of love, were abjured precisely because they rejected the feminine ideal that Aphrodite represented and that continues to be prescribed for women in the mythology of our time—an ideal, I would remind you, that is entirely man-made. For, Aphrodite, like that other much favored goddess Athena, sprang full-grown from Man: she had no mother and owed all she was and could be to him. Since she was neither born nor nurtured by women (as real women are), she had been protected from their influence and could therefore be made completely to the specifications of her male creator: to be the sight/site of smiling beauty, flattering and obsequious, and the passive recipient of the desire such sights called forth in men, in this case, "to take her as a wife and lead her to his abode." (I leave it to you to consider the nature of the desire called forth by modern pornography—I suspect it may be a little racier than this, though not on that account any more or less distasteful.)

The first Pygmalion was a sculptor "only happy in the silent world of statues which his chisel had created."[27] And although he was disgusted by real women, like the modern pornographer, this did not mean that he wasn't interested in Women, that is, in turning his gaze upon them—as long as they were artifacts, of course. In fact, he fell in love with an ivory statue he had made; moved, of course, by the extraordinary beauty (he had created there). Aphrodite, goddess of this sort of love, eventually took pity on him and brought his beloved statue to life that she might return his kisses. (We are not so far away from Sexy Suzy with the "movable parts.")

What can we learn from this about sex and the differential sexualizing of men and women in our culture? Well it doesn't tell us much about women's sexuality, other than how it is regarded by men, but it does say rather a lot about men's. Most fundamentally it establishes male sexuality (and male subjectivity therefore) as *voyeuristic, fetishistic*, and *narcissistic*. For it is the *artifact* that is the object of men's desire; the body is made over into a perfect object and "marked" with signs of its cultural appropriation, its colonization:

> Tattoos, stretched lips, the bound feet of Chinese women, eyeshadow, rouge, hair removal, mascara, or bracelets, collars, jewellery, accessories: anything will serve to rewrite the cultural order on the body; and it is this that takes on the effect of beauty.[28]

And it is the *sight* of these artifacts (their beauty) that elicits the sexual response in men. And finally, that which is "adored," endowed with magical qualities, and fetishized in pornography, is not at all the object signified, "the body's wildness veiled by make-up,"[29] for example, but the *signifier* itself, that is, the system, the code, the cultural order made manifest in the fetishized object. It is the power of patriarchy, *men's will inscribed on women's bodies*, which excites the pornographer and at the same time refers him to his penis, the biological alibi of his difference and of his membership in the sex class that rules, as well as the symbolic instrument of his domination. Which explains why power is "sexy" for men; for their power refers them directly to the sexual organ that is the only excuse for it, as well as why men's sexual pleasure is so often limited to the "phallic orgasm" since "potency is man's pleasure."[30]

Men take pleasure in looking at women, therefore, only to the extent that women designate them as men. These "marked" women (lipstick, high heels, tight clothes) they call "real women."[31] What they really enjoy and at the same time reproduce for themselves and for others in this practice of looking is the system of differences that marks them as men, that is, as dominants in a sexually bifurcated and hierarchized social order. This explains why men whistle at women (suitably inscribed with the culturally determined indicators of sexual submission) to impress other men and not to impress women. The whistle establishes the whistler's membership in the male sex class while exercising and inscribing the power of that class in the continuing reproduction of the patriarchal cultural order.

> This fetish-beauty has nothing (any longer) to do with an effect of the soul (the spiritualist vision), a natural grace of movement or countenance; with the transparency of truth (the idealist vision); or with an "inspired genius" of the body, which can be communicated as effectively by expressive ugliness (the romantic vision). What we are talking about is a kind of anti-nature incarnate, bound up in a general stereotype of models of beauty, in a perfectionist vertigo and controlled narcissism. . . . It is the final disqualification of the body, its subjection to a discipline, the total circulation of signs.[32]

It is in this sense that pornography is about power: the power of culture/men over nature/women. As long as men have this power, or feel they do, they don't need pornography. When they don't, they do.

Pornography, however, only exacerbates the condition it attempts to remedy—absence of desire, of the pleasure in potency. For it perpetuates an ideal of masculinity that cannot be realized in practice, that is, with real women in the real world. It thus increases the pornographer's isolation, frustration, deprivation, and resentment. Hence the escalation in pornography—both quantitative and qualitative—and the desperation of those of us who would end it if we could. For there is no built-in limit to the pornographer's need, nor to the pornographic imagination its needs must call forth. For both the need and its imaginary satisfaction in pornography are the effects of the very same power structure they attempt to recreate and they are determined elsewhere in all those apparently nonpornographic discourses and practices of our culture which cooperate in the social construction of an ideal of maculinity that is instrinsically contradictory and therefore necessarily unattainable.

For this masculine subject constituted as observer (of the feminized object and the objectified feminine) is not, of course, original to pornography. He is the traditional Subject, Man, of our culture—of its rationalism, humanism, and individualism. We can trace his ancestry back at least as far as Plato (and perhaps even further in some respects as my brief reflections on Greek mythology would suggest), who was one of the first to identify subjectivity with rationality, knowledge and thought, and these with the abstraction of a (masculine) self from concrete involvement in the lived world.

This splitting-off of Man from the material world (of nature) and of his intellect from his personal experience was reaffirmed during the Renaissance in the philosophy of Descartes and the science of Francis Bacon, for example, and was a necessary condition of possibility of the scientific and industrial revolutions that followed.[33] The same divided subject remains with us still as the model of our education, our science, our government, our arts, and our leisure, etc.[34] It is perhaps the cornerstone of patriarchal power. For, from the very beginning of this tradition, the thinking, knowing, observing, and emotionally detached subject was always constituted in discourse and *in practice* as male, and the object known, nature, matter, as female.[35] This "has enabled men, the knowers to falsely abstract themselves from nature, as if they were not themselves historical, material, organic and social beings. This abstraction of men from the rest of nature, and from women, is the root at one and the same time of both their *power*, for they can be ruthless with others with whom they feel no identification, and their alienation from the world, each other, and themselves."[36]

The desire to view, which is incited in the subject-Man from all directions in our "society of the spectacle,"[37] not only by pornography and publicity but also by science for which "objective observation" is absolutely constitutive—is really a *desire for the condition of viewing*[38] that is, for the "ontological status of separation" of Sovereignty. For the viewer is external to the world-viewed and therefore unaffected by it. The world is present to him and visible, but he, like God, is absent from the world and invisible. He cannot be objectified by the gaze of another subject for he is not part of the world his gaze objectifies. In pornography he looks at her looking back at him, but she cannot see him. He is Sovereign. The world-viewed appears in response to his will, and he has only to close his eyes or turn away and the world-viewed will cease to be. He is judge, spectator-speculator, owner, and controller, with no responsibility for or to that which he observes. He conjures it both in and out of existence. He is the one who knows, while he himself is inscrutable and is not known.

Now this condition of viewing (voyeurism) may be a secure one. But it is certainly ideal, that is, false and therefore full of contradictions. For Man, after all, is in and of the same world which is the object of his gaze. The flesh and blood and guts he objectifies on the screen and takes so much pleasure in revealing and reviewing (in print, in the laboratory or on the battlefields of sport and war) always come back to haunt him. For they are his own blood and guts—denied, objectified, and projected onto the Other, onto Nature, Woman, and Enemy, but never by that means exorcised.[39] They cannot be for they are the very conditions of his own possibility to be at all. Subjectified, sexualized Man has to work harder and harder to overcome this contradiction which is at the very heart of his project to maintain his illusion of Sovereignty and thus his "holy virility."[40] In fact I would say that this is the hidden motor of our history, driving men ever onward in an endless search for that final and unambiguous experience "of freedom" that will confirm their (transcendent) masculinity once and for all.

Since masculinity—the ontological condition of viewing—requires the objectification of the world, which it imagines is "external" to its seeing eye/I, we should not be surprised, therefore, at the violence that is perpetrated in its name (in the name of God, Reason, Freedom, Progress, History, Humanity, Science, Art, or, as in the case of pornography, in the name of Sex). For you can only objectify the living by taking away its life, by killing it either in fact or fantasy. And the latter is just as violent as the former. For fantasy "is precisely what reality can be confused with. It is through fantasy that our conviction of the worth of reality is established"[41]; it teaches us how to see the world. We act according to our desires, and we desire according to what we see.[42] The hoardings on the street, the newspaper stands and corner stores, the movies, the television, our stories, and our art show men sights of women against which they are encouraged to measure their subjectivity and their sexuality—since male gender-identity leans on sexuality—on the penis as the mark of their difference and their power. "The sight of it as an object stimulates the use of it as an object":[43] fragmentation, separation, manipulation, abstraction, mutilation, possession, consumption, elimination, and so forth. Little wonder Peter Sutcliffe, the "Yorkshire Ripper" who killed thirteen women before he was apprehended in 1981, thought he had a divine mission to kill prostitutes. As pornography makes clear, sex and violence go hand-in-hand in our culture, and the desire to kill women is virtually built into men's sexuality.[44]

A subjectivity that is external to its world, as the observer-subject is, deprives itself of the nourishment that only the world can supply; and as a result becomes increasingly impoverished, isolated, and estranged from itself, from others, and from the reality of the world it aspires to know and control merely by looking. Sights, appearances pried away from their meanings (their contexts and their history) are silent. Dead objects are mute. In the world of the voyeur, therefore, there is no dialogue; no relationship, no speech, and no response and therefore no understanding, neither of self nor of the objects "known." For only that which narrates can make us understand, and the voyeur's world is that of the eternal present.[45] "The world complete without me is the world of my immortality"[46] and, therefore, an unreal world. For we are all mortal and so visible and present to each other and the world outside the defined space of the pornographic spectacle; beyond the covers of the magazine, the doors of the darkened booth, the exotica of the nightclub, which screen the spectator-subject from that which is made visible to him. "As in Plato's cave," however, "reality is *behind* you.

It will become visible when you have made yourself visible to it, presented yourself."[47]

We will not fight pornography by censoring it, therefore; nor by flooding the market with alternative sexual imagery as is often argued by those who oppose present pornography and the traditional discourse of sex in the name of "sexual freedom," desire, and the right of individuals to "take their pleasure and make their own lives."[48] For it is precisely the politics of "taking one's pleasure" and "making one's own life" (of rational individualism) that is at issue here. Objectification and abstraction, emotional detachment, isolation and estrangement from the Other belong to the *voyeur-subject* of sexuality itself, that is, to the "ontological condition of viewing" and not to the world-viewed. Tinkering with the latter does nothing to challenge the sexual régime articulated through the former. Censorship merely suppresses the voyeur-subject in some of its ugliest manifestations, while the introduction of alternative sexual imagery actually generalizes and diversifies its incitement. Neither strategy challenges the sexual régime itself—its form, its logic, its code, its mode of production of truth, knowledge, pleasure, need, people, practices, and sexuality—as a "complex political technology"[49] administering life (of both individuals and the species) through the subjugation of bodies (under the sign of sex) and the control of population.[50]

Patriarchy requires such a régime and thrives on sexual incitement: on the identification of self with sex, sex with pleasure, and pleasure with potency (dominance and submission). For sex, the possession of a penis, is patriarchy's only excuse; the sign and symptom of men's domination of women. It must therefore be constantly called forth as evidence of the régime and of the legitimacy, by right or by might, of its rule. The real penis, however, is hardly a symbol of power. It is fragile and vulnerable and compared with the sex organs of women, which bring forth new life and feed it, scarcely an indicator of strength or superiority. So the real penis (like real women) does not feature in the mythology of Man. It is not the penis that is objectified and fetishized in our culture, but the phallus, symbol of the power which possession of the penis confers on men. The real penis does not appear in the world-viewed lest its truth be revealed and the alibi of male-supremacy be disclosed for the fraud that it is. The real penis is not present to the world which men rule in its name despite the fact that the whole world designates it in its absence. Masculinity therefore is not constructed on the basis of men's *real* identity and difference as located in the real penis but on an *ideal* difference constituted most essentially in the cultural differentiation of Man from his Other, from that which lacks the (elusive) penis and is on that account declared to be "ontologically lacking." Masculinity, under patriarchy, needs an Other from which a Man can distinguish himself; for masculinity resides completely in what *she*, femininity, is not.

Since real women do not designate Man and his genitals as their "natural" superior, Man is obliged to construct an Other that does. The sexual régime, what Gayle Rubin has called the sex-gender system,[51] by which male and female are differentiated by sex and *identified* with that sexual differentiation in both discourse and practice, is the mechanism by which patriarchy, that is, male-subjectivity, creates its Other precisely to designate itself as its superior: its creator-spectator-owner-judge.

We must not think therefore that by saying yes to sex we say no to power. For it is just this "agency of sex we must break from":[52]

> If everyone is led, by this controlled structuration to confuse himself with his own sexual status, it is only to resign his sex the more easily (that is, the erogenous differentiation of his own body) to the sexual segregation that is one of the political and ideological foundations of the social order.[53]

The idea of sex, like the idea of Reason or Science, makes it possible for us to evade what gives power power, that is, the very hegemony of a discourse: "the way it passes for truth and . . . the way its premises and logic are taken for granted."[54] We should aim at *desexualization* of pleasure, bodies, persons, relations, needs, and not at sexual specificity. "If female sexuality is now inhibited," as some have argued who opposed Women Against Pornography because they seem to be also against "sex," "male sexuality is driven and cannot serve as a model."[55] Repression is surely a relative term that presumes some norm both of what constitutes sex and what constitutes a "healthy" frequency or quality of sexual activity. Repression must, therefore, be demonstrated, not assumed, and should certainly not be measured against the yardstick of male sexuality, past or present, which like male rationality and male science is more an indicator of Man's/compulsive drive for power than an expression of his freedom.

No man is immune to the sexualization depicted in pornography for pornography only makes explicit the differential structure of masculine-feminine produced elsewhere in our culture. Every man embodies the power celebrated and reproduced in pornography by which masculinity subjugates women, even he who chooses not to exercise it. For the woman walking behind you in the street does not know that; she fears and mistrusts you as much as she does the pornophile or the rapist you might well be. Sexual liberation, therefore, does not consist in the liberation of that sexuality which has been induced in us by the various mechanisms of patriarchal power but in our liberation from it. We must refuse the sexual codification of our identity, our pleasures, our frustrations, and our freedoms; stop looking at and appraising each other like commodities, "objects" of "desire," and start presenting ourselves to the world and others in all our ambivalence and ambiguity. Rebellion (freedom) consists in the rejection of the code, "the austere monarchy of sex."[56] not in its appropriation; in the upsurge of particular, localized *speech*—truths and knowledges "incapable of unanimity"—and not more public discourse combining the "absolutely explicit with the completely unspecific."[57] "When it comes to abolishing patriarchy the problem for men is not for them to create 'a new man,' but on the contrary, to destroy that 'man' from whom, as males, we have *all* been created, and who, in one way or another, we have *all* reproduced."[58] Real men do need pornography, unfortunately, just as patriarchy needs real men. Our rejection of one, therefore, necessarily entails a rejection of the other two; they stand or fall together.

NOTES

1. First published as "Patriarchy and Pleasure: The Pornographic Eye/I," *Canadian Journal of Political and Social Theory* 9, nos. 1–2 (1985): 81–95.
2. Sexuality is the set of effects produced in bodies, behaviours and social relations by a certain deployment deriving from a complex political technology." Michel Foucault, *The History of Sexuality*, vol. 1, trans. Robert Hurley (New York: Vintage Books, 1980), 127. For a detailed discussion of discourse as an instrument of power, both productive and constitutive of its objects, see the writings of Foucault generally, and *The History of Sexuality*, vol. 1, and *Power/Knowledge* (New York: Pantheon Books, 1980) as this relates to sexuality in particular.
3. See Foucault, *The History of Sexuality*, vol. 1.
4. See Jean Baudrillard, *For a Critique of the Political Economy of the Sign*, trans. Charles Levin (St. Louis, Mo.: Telos Press), 99.
5. Ibid., 93.
6. Here I strengthen Baudrillard's suggestion that sexual segregation is "one of the key political and ideological foundations of our social order." Baudrillard, *For a Critique*, 99.
7. Ibid.
8. Emmanuel Reynaud, *Holy Virility. The Social Construction of Masculinity*, trans. Ros Schwartz (London, England: Pluto Press, 1981), 10.
9. John Berger speaking of the classical nude in *Ways of Seeing* (London, England: BBC and Pelican Original, 1971), 54.
10. Ibid., 47, for a discussion of the criteria and conventions by which women have been judged as sights in the context of European oil painting.
11. Ibid., 83–112, for a discussion of oil painting as the celebration of status and wealth.
12. See Baudrillard, *For a Critique*, for a discussion of the object a sign.
13. See E. A. Kaplan, for example, *Women in Films. Both Sides of the Camera* (London and New York: Methuen, 1983). See Laura Mulvey, *Visual and Other Pleasures* (Bloomington and Indianapolis: Indiana University Press, 1989), Teresa de Lauretis, *Alice Doesn't: Feminism, Semiotics, Cinema* (Bloomington and Indianapolis: Indiana University Press, 1984), and *Technologies of Gender: Essays on Theory, Film, and Fiction* (Bloomington and Indianapolis: Indiana

University Press, 1987), Constance Penley, *The Future of an Illusion: Film, Feminism, and Psychoanalysis* (Minneapolis: University of Minnesota Press, 1989).

14. Stanley Cavell, *The World Viewed. Reflections on the Ontology of Film* (Cambridge: Harvard University Press, 1979).
15. Ibid., 45.
16. Susan Griffin, *Pornography and Silence. Culture's Revenge Against Nature* (New York: Harper Colophon Books, 1981) 19.
17. Cavell, *The World Viewed*, 48.
18. *Manchester Guardian Weekly*, September 11, 1983 ("Le Monde" section). My emphasis.
19. *Penguin English Dictionary* (Harmondsworth, Middlesex, England: Penguin Books, 1965) edition, 455.
20. Roland Barthes, *Mythologies*, trans. Annette Lavers (England: Paladin Press, 1973): 84.
21. Baudrillard, *For a Critique*, 93.
22. Ibid., 95.
23. "Professor Higgins is the Frankenstein of modelers, creating not an idol but an idolizer," Cavell, *The World Viewed*, 235.
24. Claude Lévi-Strauss, *The Elementary Structures of Kinship* (Boston: Beacon Press, 1969), 24.
25. In Felix Guirand, ed., *The New Larousse Encyclopedia of Mythology* (London and New York: Hamlyn Publishing Group, 1982), 131.
26. Ibid., 130–31.
27. Ibid.
28. Baudrillard, *For a Critique*, 94.
29. Ibid.
30. Reynaud, *Holy Virility*, 66.
31. Ibid., 27–28. "It is not very difficult to borrow the accessories of femininity: clothes, shoes, wigs, make-up, hair removers, and even padded bras, hormones, silicone, electrolysis or plastic surgery; man only has to use the same means as woman to become a 'real woman.'. . . In fact the problem of the transvestite who does not want to be recognized as such, is not how to transform himself into a woman, but how to avoid overdoing it."
32. Baudrillard, *For a Critique*, 94. See also Reynaud, *Holy Virility*, 21. "When a woman takes off her pinafore she must be 'beautiful': it is out of the question for her to be natural—she is supposed to be natural enough as it is. She must wear make-up, be deodorized, perfumed, shave her legs and armpits, put on stockings, high heels, show her legs, emphasize her breasts, pull in her stomach, paint her nails, dye her hair, tame her hairstyle, pierce her ears, reduce her appetite and, without making a single clumsy gesture, or uttering one word too many, she must seem happy, dainty and original."
33. See chapters 2 and 3 in this volume.
34. For an excellent discussion of how this objectifying attitude conditions our music as well as our pedagogy, see Christopher Small, *Music—Society—Education* (New York: Schirmer Books, A Division of Macmillan Publishing Co., 1977).
35. See chapters 2 and 3 in this volume.
36. From "Reason and Violence. More than a False Antithesis—A Mechanism of Patriarchal Power," chapter 2, in this volume.
37. Guy Debord, *Society of the Spectacle* (Detroit, Mich.: Black and Red, 1977).
38. Cavell, *World Viewed*, 102.

39. See Susan Griffin, *Pornography and Silence. Culture's Revenge Against Nature* (New York: Harper Colophon, 1981).
40. See Reynaud, *Holy Virility*.
41. Cavell, *World Viewed*, 85.
42. "I can only choose within the world I can *see* in the moral sense of 'see' which implies that clear vision is a result of moral imagination and moral effort." Iris Murdoch, *The Sovereignty of Good* (London: Routledge and Kegan Paul, 1970), 37. "As moral agents we have to try to see justly, to overcome prejudice, to avoid temptation and curb imagination, to direct reflection" (40). Murdoch is the only ethical theorist I know who makes *selfless attention to particular realities* central to the moral life and a necessary condition of goodness, knowledge, and truth, that is, the indispensable antidote to the natural enemies of goodness: "the fat relentless ego" and "personal fantasy." Murdoch goes some way to providing us with that "ethics of seeing" that Susan Sontag calls for in *On Photography* (New York: Delta Books, 1973).
43. Berger, *Ways of Seeing*, 54.
44. In "'I just wanted to kill a woman!' Why? The Ripper and Male Sexuality," *Feminist Review* 9 (October 1981), Wendy Hollway analyzes the newspaper reports of Peter Sutcliffe's trial showing "men's collaboration with other men in the oppression of women" in that the trial "refused to recognize the way in which Sutcliffe's acts were an expression . . . of the construction of an aggressive masculine sexuality and of women as its objects. This 'cover-up' exonerates men in general even when one man is found guilty" (Hollway, 33).
45. See Sontag, *On Photography*, for a discussion of these structures as they relate to photography.
46. Cavell, *World Viewed*, 160.
47. Ibid., 155.
48. As in Ann Snitow, Christine Stansell, and Sharon Thompson, eds., *Powers of Desire. The Politics of Sexuality* (New York: Monthly Review Press, 1983), 41.
49. Foucault, *History of Sexuality*, 127.
50. Ibid., 139–159.
51. Gayle Rubin, "The Traffic in Women: Notes on the 'Political Economy of Sex'" in *Toward an Anthropology of Women*, ed. Rayna Reiter (New York: Monthly Review Press, 1975), 157–210.
52. Foucault, *History of Sexuality*, 157.
53. Baudrillard, *For a Critique*, 99.
54. Hollway, "I just wanted to kill a woman," 33.
55. Ethel Person, "Sexuality as the Mainstay of Identity: Psychoanalytic Perspectives," *Signs. Journal of Women in Culture and Society* 5, no. 4 (Summer 1980), 605–30.
56. Foucault, *History of Sexuality*, 159.
57. See Cavell's characterization of pornography. Cavell, *World Viewed*, 55.
58. Reynaud, *Holy Virility*, 15.

Chapter 5 Five

AGAINST SEXUAL IMAGERY. ALTERNATIVE OR OTHERWISE

THIS CHAPTER EXTENDS THE analysis of the Pornographic Eye/I to argue that there can be no sexual imagery in the present context that is not at the same time complicit with and therefore reproductive of patriarchy, that is, of the system of male dominance which is built on, by and for the sake of sexual difference upon which the pleasures and provocations of sexual spectatorship rely. It was written for a symposium on "Images of Sexuality" organized by the Artists' Centre d'Artistes (Gallery 101) of Ottawa in the spring of 1985. This was an intellectual and artistic assembly of national scope and character that brought together artists, writers, critics, and intellectuals from across Canada to address the issue of sexuality in art and the media. A month-long curated exhibition on the theme of sexuality was held in conjunction with the symposium and in defiance of the Ontario Censor Board, which had been especially vigorous at the time in its surveillance and suppression of publications, exhibitions, and expressions of gay and lesbian sexuality in particular.

Not surprisingly "Against Sexual Imagery. Alternative or Otherwise" was not a big hit at this symposium, since it threw into question two of the most dearly held (and otherwise unchallenged) premises of the conference and the artists and individuals whose interests it was intended to serve: the premise of an artist's right to freedom of expression in general and the premise of the individual's right to freedom of sexual expression in particular. One of the speakers was so incensed by my presentation that he was moved to criticize its arguments in the version of his own paper that was published in the conference proceedings after the event. I was invited to respond to those criticisms by the editor of the proceedings and that reply appears in the Afterword to this chapter. "Against Sexual Imagery" assumes the arguments of the Pornographic Eye/I to build its case against sexual imagery in general. Since I could not assume a familiarity with those arguments on the part of its audience, some of the analyses from the first essay are repeated or paraphrased in the second. I have decided to leave those repetitions in, in part for emphasis and further clarification, but also to preserve the flavor and flow of my original argument.

Against Sexual Imagery. Alternative or Otherwise[1]

The argument of this chapter is that the production and dissemination of alternative sexual imagery, which continues to celebrate sex, sexual identity, sexual desire, and sexual pleasure, albeit a "sex-positive" and pluralistic sex, as Varda Burstyn and others suggest,[2] strengthens rather than weakens the dominant regime of sexual representation and sexual practice that it purports to undermine: a régime that is heterosexist and sexist, depersonalizing and objectifying, and productive and expressive of male power and a masculine sexuality which is essentially voyeuristic, narcissistic, and fetishistic. This is because the production and dissemination of images of alternative sexual pleasure do not challenge the two most fundamental strategic premises of the dominant discourse which are constitutive of both its power and its perversity: its volarization of *sex* as the primary source of personal identity, pleasure, and power, and its incitement and authorization of visual *representation* as the means and ends of its achievement, of the achievement of that identity, pleasure, and power that sex is supposed to rightfully and naturally confer upon us.

The dominant sexual regime dominates, that is, organizes persons and social relations under the law of men, by way of its code rather than its content; by the form of its discourse rather than by any particular meanings that are spoken in its terms. In other words the sex/representation code itself constrains and limits what can be said within it and therefore what can be done in its terms, it enables some truths and the realization of some truth effects and excludes others.[3] It is my opinion that the modern discourse of persons, power, and pleasure, which organizes our experience and identity "under the sign of sex" and produces the truths of sex through diverse systems of representation (from the religious and medical to the economic, the political and the pornographic), systematically excludes the possibility of any genuine alternative to the depersonalized, objectified, and impoverished social-sexual relations of male dominance and female subordination with which we are so familiar and so dissatisfied. This is because the power dynamic, the binary relationship of dominance-subordination which positions men as dominants, is constitutive of and constituted by the very terms of the discourse—sex and representation—and not by any particular messages constructed by their means. In other words there is something about sex and something about representation that positions us, inexorably, on the polarized axis of power, either up/dominant or down/submissive, and forces us into social-sexual relationships that are intrinsically sadomasochistic.

I will try to show how this is so by considering each of the two terms of the sexual discourse in turn, beginning with sex.

SEX: WHAT IS IT WE WANT TO REPRESENT AND WHY?

When we speak of sex as something other than real sexual practices (gender)[4] or real sexual organs (reproduction)—as, for example, something we can "repress" or "reclaim as a force for social change and to empower us" as Burstyn suggests, we treat sex as if it were a natural given of a human being: as an instinct, a drive, a need, a unified causal principle, a mysterious secret force within us, which we could, in principle, realize (or not) more or less as we wish, were it not for social and political structures that confine or coerce us into repressive or oppressive sexual positions. It is as if sex were a natural essence, a good, which gets perverted and distorted, manipulated and exploited, in societies like our own which are divided by gross inequalities of economic and political power across class, race, and gender lines. This view, I think, both mystifies and falsifies the complex and contradictory truths of our sexual experience by naturalizing and idealizing its social origins and political purposes. For this notion of sex, apparently undivided by male and female difference, is an entirely abstract and speculative notion, "an ideal point made necessary by the deployment of sexuality and its operation," according to Foucault, and not the natural and universal given it claims to be. "Sex," I am suggesting, is not the biological root cause of sexuality, but one of its ideological effects that masquerades as "natural" to veil its social and political origins. This is why we are so mystified by sex, as we are not by real penises and real vaginas, whose real material and social being is entirely inadequate to the sexual mystique that is built up around them under the sign of sex. Unlike the body, the flesh, real penises, and real vaginas, sex is an ideal category of thought, a fictional unity of representation, and not a real datum of experience. In this respect we can compare sex to the soul—an equally mystified, fictional unity in which men have invested their personal happiness and salvation, their status as sane, and their worth and dignity as human beings and members of the human community.[5]

Like the soul sex is an entirely discursive object, one that is known and realized *only* through its various representations. It is the effect in us of representation—and nothing else. "The increasing organisation of gay sexuality around male images testifies to this," according to Frank Mort, to the "highly constructed nature of sexual identities and pleasures."[6] But in doing so it also mirrors and reinforces the code (though perhaps not the specific contents—which are only, after all, variations on a theme) of *heterosex*, which constructs sexual desire as an essentially voyeuristic, narcissistic, and fetishistic desire, for an object that is both other than self and yet entirely self-referring: a man-made object that mirrors the desire of the spectator-subject as both its idol and idolizer. It is certainly well recognized anyway that alternative sex requires alternative sexual imagery if it is to be actualized and realized in practice. What concerns me, however, is just how alternative can sex be, given that it must rely on the same means and, to a large extent, the same relations of production, that is, representation, as that which it purports to subvert or at least challenge?

Obviously those who control the means of representation will control our experience and understanding of sex and so our experience and understanding of the worth of sex, self, and others. This means that sex is an essentially *political* issue, for it is an effect of power and therefore an inevitable site of political struggle. It also means that sex is always, in some sense, imposed upon us by those who control discourse. And we cannot escape or ignore its imposition, for the apparatus of sex *claims* us (like the Jesuits once claimed our souls) well before we are old enough to resist and whether we like it or not. We cannot take it or leave it because, like the soul, sex is not really ours: it is a kind of manna from heaven, a magical transcendent power, a moral agency (masquerading as biology rather than theology these days) invested in us from elsewhere by others. We can only submit to its rule and definition or struggle against it, but we cannot escape it. Our sexual status, our status as *sexed* that is, as bodies entirely positivized by sex, is not under our control, not a matter of choice. We cannot throw it off. For whatever we do or say to escape, it can always be recuperated under the "austere monarchy of sex" within the dominant discourse that organizes social life and persons by its means. Both sex and the soul masquerade as natural or divine givens, gifts to the human being, but neither of them really designates an "it" at all, a unified and universal essence, an autonomous and opaque animus deep within the individual self. What they really signify is a set of *social relations* that produce us as particular kinds of subjects (dominated and divided subjects) and at one and the same time conceal the history and direction of that process of production (the process of our subjectification) by referring our identities, pleasures, desires, conflicts, and needs to an imagined *internal agency*, an abstract, privatized, objectified, *impersonal* principle—once the soul, nowadays sex.

Like the soul sex is necessarily and essentially divisive. The soul split each one of us into two opposing but inexorably connected parts, body and soul, and at the same time authorized one pole of the opposition, the soul, to dominate the other, the body. Sex splits the self into masculine and feminine (self and other) and at the same time institutes the dominance of the masculine over the feminine (of the self over the other). "Indeed," states Emmanuel Reynaud, "why differentiate if it is not to form a hierarchy?"[7] In fact I think this is the whole point of such discourses which set up dichotomies as oppositions and contradictions: they relocate, ideologically, social divisions of dominance and subordination *within* the individual, providing the social hierarchy with its natural alibi and at the same time converting the pain and conflict that hierarchy generates from a social and political issue into an individual problem with one's personal identity—with one's God, or in this case, with one's sexuality. Just as the soul, the most elusive and ideal pole of the divided self, was constituted as the essential Man, and the body, the more easily known and concrete pole, repudiated as passive and recalcitrant matter, which must be subordinated to that Man's will, so is masculinity (the self) the more elusive and ideal pole of sexuality, constituted as the essential human subject, and femininity (the other), that which we all know concretely and immediately by virtue of the circumstances of our birth and nurture, correspondingly repudiated as passive Nature to be subordinated to the will and desire of an essentially masculine sexual agency. It seems to me, therefore, that as long as we identify ourselves, our pleasures, and our pains with our sexuality, we are destined to swing between these two poles.

This is the sense in which "sex is destiny" is true. Biological males need not assume the masculine position in the polarity, of course, just as biological females need not assume the feminine. But there is no position available between the two poles in a sex-gender system that bifurcates human beings into self and other, and into two discrete, exclusive, and unequal sexes, and reduces all ambivalence, ambiguity, and difference to a binary differentiation of self and other, of male and female and ultimately of sex organs. In such a system, which binds each one of us to our sex, sex to gender and gender to organs of reproduction, all differences get coded as sexual and all desire for wholeness, therefore, for reparation of that sexual split, as the refusal of sex difference, that is, as the desire for unity and Oneness rather than as a desire for community in diversity. The Other, the body of the sexed other, appears to have a wholeness, a coherence, a sexual identity, an identity with his or her sex, that I lack. As a sight, an object-seen, she or he does not appear to be split by sex as I am—or at least, I project my desire for closure, for sexual wholeness, onto the Other. Her apparent wholeness is experienced, therefore as both an object of fascination and desire and as a threat. On the one hand I desire her wholeness to heal the split in myself; on the other I fear the power her closure represents: her seamless phallic objectivity excludes me—is, was, or will be, the instrument of my own division by sex (castration). The pleasure of anticipated possession/identification is always, therefore, haunted by the threat of loss. I want to possess and be possessed by the phallic other, but I want it so much that I at the same time hate and fear the Other for having this power over me. Besides, if I claim his phallus to complete me, then he will no longer be desirable. So we are stuck on the sexual seesaw, swinging between acquiescence and assertion, dominance and submission, masculinity and femininity, self and other (the phallus and the cunt), seeking our sexual identity from others who are seeking theirs, locked in the illusion of sex and the perverse desire for the perfect phallus that it calls forth.[8]

This split in human beings and the pattern of sadomasochistic sexual relations that it sets up, seems to me to be implicit in any account of persons that identifies and differentiates them by sex, by *their* sex, as "man" or "woman," that is. For, however sex is characterized, as a drive, a need, an instinct, a spontaneous finality, a unified causal principle of action, a gift of God, a human right, as eros or libido or whatever, sex, like the soul, is always alien to me—in-me-but-not-of-me. It is always an effect produced in my by discourse/power, by institutions and technologies, by others: an intruder in the flesh that divides me from myself and sets up within me an insatiable (because illusory) desire for sexual closure; for the coincidence of self with self, of sex with self, of masculine with feminine, of self with other, which I believe we all once knew (pre-Oedipally) before our bodies and our consciousness were systematically divided by and within the discourse of patriarchy under the sign of sex and in the name of the Father. We must not think, therefore, that by saying yes to sex, we say no to power, on the contrary, as Foucault states,

> One tracks along the course laid out by the general deployment of sexuality. It is the agency of sex that we must break away from, if we aim—through a tactical reversal of the various mechanisms of sexuality—to counter the grips of power with the claims of bodies, pleasure and knowledges, in their multiplicity and their possibility of resistance.[9]

Sex and Representation and the Reproduction of Male Power

I have argued that sex cannot be separated from representation; that it is an entirely discursive object, the effect in us of what Foucault calls an apparatus or technology of sexuality, which far from repressing sex, systematically incites, extracts, induces, titillates, and indeed coerces us into placing ourselves, our identities, our pleasures, our pains, and our politics (viz. the new Right) under its sign; that, for this reason, sex cannot be understood apart from power: that we are, as it were, colonized by sex, by *heterosex*, one that depends on gender division and hierarchy and subjected to its regime long before we reach the point of making sexual choices, which choices, being sexual, do nothing to subvert the rule of heterosex itself.

In this section I want to argue that the visual representation of sex, again by virtue of its form rather than its content, reproduces, reinforces, and generalizes the same social-sexual effects of male dominance and female subordination that seem to me to be constitutive of sex itself. In other words male power is reproduced by visual representations of sexuality as one of their effects, regardless of the particular narrative represented.[10] This is, in part, because images of men and women, however they are depicted, have "overdetermined codified meanings": male-dominant-active, female-subordinate-passive, which attach to them regardless of individual intentions; and because man and woman are signs that represent something in the personal unconscious of each one of us, as well as in the collective consciousness articulated in the dominant discourse. But it is also because visual representation itself, especially those forms which systematically conceal the facts of their process of production, like most films and photographs, construct, produce, and reproduce the viewer as *male* or, to be more precise, in the masculine position, that is, as one who enjoys the power that masculinity confers. Visual representations of sexuality structure the gaze of the spectator as a male gaze.[11] The act of viewing itself, therefore, actually reproduces male power positions. In fact it is one of the principal modes of production of masculinity and its power, which explains why men, more than women, need and desire to take up the spectator position especially if they are "screened" from the world viewed as they are in the cinema, before television sets and computers, behind cameras, wind-screens, telescopes, microscopes, and two-way mirrors, in laboratories, libraries, and operating rooms, etc.[12]

Historically in our culture men have been the producers, purveyors, and consumers of images, sexual or otherwise. The images they have enjoyed and exchanged tell us more about them, their aspirations and ideals, their sexuality, and their masculinity, than they do about the objects or people represented, for there has been no reciprocal sighting/siting of the male-spectator-owner from the point of view of the object viewed. I would even go so far as to suggest that this is the whole point of the historical enterprise of representation, considered as a ritual or institution. Sights are produced for the viewing pleasure of the spectator-owner precisely to designate him (his wealth, stature, and power) and not what is represented: to distinguish him from other men (and women, of course) as a man to be envied and respected. He enjoys the sights of what he might possess or control: sights of the Other. These sights, whether they be codified as sexual or not, do not reveal themselves or the truth of the world represented by them but designate and individuate the spectator-owner as a man with power over others. Oil paintings, for example, once presented images of things, material things, that could be possessed—commodities, merchandise, animals, property, bodies conventionalized as "nudes," and so forth. But what they signified and celebrated was a *social relationship*: that between the male spectator-owner and the real objects depicted in the paintings and that between the spectator-owner and the painting itself, which testifies to the power the former has over others to organize, direct, and alienate the labor of others for his own pleasure and gratification.[13]

Pornography does the same thing. It presents images of women, but only to designate men and the social relationship between them and the object-woman-viewed. Paradoxical as it may seem, pornography does not reveal women, though in it Woman reveals all. On the contrary it is Man/men who is revealed in her objectification. For the woman he observes is the objectification of his idea, his desire. She is, after all, Man-made: not a real woman at all but the product of masculine imagination and masculine power.[14] (This, of course, is also true of the male-object-viewed in male homosexual pornography.) And it is this that produces the pleasure in the spectator of pornography, this self-indexing effected by the image and not some "nostalgic return to the unwritten body,"[15] as Mary Ann Doane puts it, which the imagery calls forth. The same social relationship of dominance and control is celebrated in mainstream films, of course. They, too, designate the viewer as the male-spectator-owner of the world-viewed, and Woman as the object of his gaze, his desire, his will, his power, and his control. The social-sexual relationship immortalized on film is fundamentally the same as that signified in paintings of the classical nude (sacred) and the photographs of modern pornography (profane). In each case, a particular man—a Polanski, a Manet, a Hugh Hefner—puts his woman on display so that other men will recognize his power, his wealth, and social stature, and above all, his "holy virility" and respect and envy him for it—indeed, pay him for the illusion of access to the same relationship. Thus the illusory power given the male viewer in paintings, photographs, and films translates into and produces "actual male power positions."[16] These forms of representation constitute the active subject as male and as an essentially spectator-subject, and his sexual pleasure as an essentially voyeuristic, narcissistic, and fetishistic pleasure. For it consists in enjoying the sight of an other only inasmuch as that sight designates the masculine self as the spectator-owner-producer of the image, the object represented by the image, and perhaps most importantly of the *signifying system itself*, the code by means of which the object is made-over into a cultural artifact and an object of desire.[17] Representations of sex thereby express and reproduce the hierarchical difference between masculine and feminine, between self and other, and between subject and object, which is produced as "natural" simultaneously everywhere else in our society; a whole apparatus of representation that subjectifies the masculine and masculinizes the subject under the sign Man, and objectifies the feminine and feminizes the object as Woman—tying femininity to objectivity and passivity, and masculinity to subjectivity and agency, just as the philosophers, priests, artists, scholars, scientists, and storytellers have done for as far back in our history as we are allowed to remember.

For the masculine subject constituted as observer is not, of course, unique to sexual discourse. He is the traditional subject, Man, of our culture: of its rationalism, humanism, and individualism, as well as of its science and sexuality.[18] We can trace his ancestry at least as far back as Plato. The human subject has since then been identified with the seeing-subject and the spectator-consciousness rather than with the doing-subject and the participating or touched-and-touching consciousness and with a subject and consciousness essentially detached from the world it claims to know and control merely by looking at it. Thus constructed, the subject desires and needs to view to fulfil himself precisely as subject and as *him*self. This desire to view is incited in the subject-Man from all directions in our own society, not only by publicity and pornography, but also by science itself for which objective observation is absolutely constitutive. It is really a desire for the *condition of viewing*, not a desire for the object or person viewed. It is a desire for the "ontological status of separation" and the experience of identity and individual sovereignty that this confers. It is, therefore, an entirely self-referential, onanistic, existential position from which one may then proceed to "jerk off the universe," as Susan Sontag once said of the project of philosophy in general and Jean Genet in particular.[19] The viewer is external to the world-viewed and therefore unaffected by it. The world is present to him and visible, but he, like God, is absent from the world and unseen. He cannot be objectified by the gaze of another subject, nor implicated in all the ambiguities and insecurities of a reciprocal relationship, because he is not part of the world his gaze objectifies. In pornography, for example, he looks at her looking back at him, but she cannot see him. He is sovereign. The world-viewed appears in response to his will, and he has only to close his eyes or turn away and the world-viewed will cease to be. He is judge, spectator-speculator, creator, owner, and controller, with no responsibility for or to that which he observes. He conjures it both in and out of existence. He is the one who knows, the one with the power, while he himself remains inscrutable, concealed, and unknown.

The ontological condition of viewing, however, which I am ascribing to subjectivity as masculine and masculinity as subjectivity, requires the objectification of the world that it imagines is external to its seeing eye/I. We should not be surprised, therefore, at the violence that has been perpetrated in its name—idealized, mystified, an reified as the name of God, Reason, Freedom, History, Humanity, Science, Art, or, in the case in point, of Sex. For you can only objectify the living by taking away its life, by killing it, either in fact or in fantasy. And the latter is *just as serious as the former*, for fantasy is "precisely what reality can be confused with. It is through fantasy that our conviction of the worth of reality is established."[20] It teaches us how to see the world and others. We act according to our desires, and we desire according to what we can see (in the moral sense of see). Seeing others as objects stimulates their use as objects: fragmentation, separation, manipulation, mutilation, experimentation, possession, exchange, alteration, elimination, etc. The hoardings on the street, newspaper stands and corner stores, movies, television, and literature and art show men sights of women (or sometimes suitably feminized men) presented as objects of and for masculine desire, against which men are encouraged to measure their subjectivity and sexuality. As pornography makes clear and as I have tried to indicate above, sex and violence and the treatment of women as objects of male desire go hand-in-hand in our culture. The desire to kill is virtually built into masculine sexuality.[21]

A subjectivity that is external to its world, as the observer-subject is, deprives itself of the nourishment that only the world can supply. As a result it becomes increasingly impoverished and isolated and estranged from itself, others, and the reality of the world it aspires to know, possess, and control merely by looking. Sights, appearances, prized away from their meanings (their contexts and their history), are silent. Dead objects are mute. In the world of the voyeur, there is no dialogue, no relationship, no speech, no response (and, therefore, no responsibility), and so there is *no understanding*, neither of self nor of the others viewed. Only that which narrates can make us understand, and the voyeur's world is that of the eternal present. It is, apparently, a world complete without me, and therefore it is a false and falsifying world.[22]

I think this is why many of us feel anxious, assaulted, excluded, angered, confused, and at the same time fascinated by sexual imagery, whatever its character. For, it is not so much what is represented that disturbs and fascinates us, but the *fact/act* of its representation that affects us in our very being. It recalls us to our own sexual division, our own "confused sexual views," to the lack of sexual wholeness and identity in our own lives and, at the same time, obliges us to take up a position (indeed, positions us) vis-à-vis the seamless image of totalized sexuality represented as "natural." We can choose between the active, dominant position of the masculine spectator-owner, for whom the image has been arranged, or the passive position of the object or person viewed, which is the subordinate and essentially feminine position. This is a much more difficult and compromising choice for women to make than men, for in both cases *women as women disappear*. There is no place in this code of sexual representation for the presence of women as women, as subjects in their own right or as subjects of a desire or sexuality that is not called forth by and for and with reference to men. If we identify with the object or person viewed, we subordinate ourselves to the rule of the Man-made artifact, made to serve his desire and to be both the idol and idolizer for him. If we assume the place of the masculine spectator-owner, we also align ourselves with his desire and therefore his subjectivity, and we once more negate and displace ourselves as women—as female, rather than male, subjects.

We will not fight pornographic sex, therefore, nor its reproduction in pornographic imagery, by producing more alternative "sex-positive" images. The pornographic sexual subject is tied to the code of sex and representation itself, rather than to anything that is said in its terms. Heterosexism, sexism, male-dominance, objectification, emotional detachment, isolation, estrangement, and violence belong most essentially to the *voyeur subject of desire*, to the condition of viewing, and not to the world viewed. Tinkering with the latter, with the contents of the world-viewed, does nothing to challenge the sexual régime articulated through the former: the construction of sexual difference, desire, pleasure, and power through spectatorship. Censorship may suppress the voyeur sexual subject in some of its uglier manifestations, but the introduction of alternative and supposedly "sex-positive" imagery just adds fat to the fire of pornographic sexuality by legitimizing, generalizing, and diversifying its incitement. As I have tried to show, it does nothing to challenge the heterosexist régime itself, which is a complex political technology presently administering the life of both individuals and the species through the subjugation of bodies and the control of population under the mystifying sign of Sex. Even sex-critical imagery reproduces the dominant sexual régime even as it attempts to demystify and subvert it, for it also exploits and explores the same sexual code. It positions us as spectator-owners of a desire we may wish to repudiate. But when we reproduce the code, we reproduce the system.[23] The pornographic fascination with the violence of patriarchal sexuality is not diminished by presenting sexuality in a historical or critical mode—as the films of Fassbinder and *Not a Love Story* have demonstrated. While celebrations of sex, no matter how "alternative" they purport to be, do not even cast doubt on that which gives the dominant sexual regime its power: sex itself and its incitement and production through representation. Our sexual liberation depends not on the liberation of that sexuality, which has been induced in us by the various mechanisms of patriarchal power, but our liberation *from* it. To that end we must refuse the sexual codification of our identities and pleasures and begin, for example, to present ourselves to the world and others as far as possible without sexual boundaries and in all our ambivalence, ambiguity, contradiction, and incompleteness. Resistance to sexual domination consists in the rejection of the dominant code, not its appropriation, and in the elaboration of a political aesthetic that is sex-critical and not an "alternative" representation of sexuality which continues to identify, individualize, and positivize the body and its pleasures under the oppressive régime of a sexuality that is always *engendered*, divisive, and hierarchic. Sex cannot be separated from gender, nor gender from oppression. The endorsement of the one entails the endorsement of the other. The separation of sex from gender is one of the patriarchy's strongest ideological tools. It falsifies the reality of lived sexual experience and mystifies the oppressive social relations that structure and determine it, and it keeps us all imprisoned within those internalized relations. The struggle against patriarchy must include, therefore, the struggle against our own sexuality and a sexual ideology that falsely autonomizes and naturalizes both the means and ends of our oppression.

AFTERWORD

In his paper on "The Political Importance of Sexual Images," Bob Gallagher suggested that my use of the term sex in "Against Sexual Imagery" was confused and failed to recognize the important distinction between "gender" and "sexuality":

> In this analysis there is a slippage in the use of the concept of sex. The original observation of inherent inequalities in the categories of males and females was an observation concerning the construction of *gender*. (Similarly, one could have said this about the social or scientific meaning of *biological* sex: i.e. male and female.) However, the conclusion concerning the political dangers inherent in sexual representations is referring to the representation of *sexuality* meaning the representation of the erotic—of sexual practices. Such a transition is completely inappropriate.[24] (Emphases in the original.)

Gallagher also disagreed with the uses I made of Michel Foucault's account of the relationship between sexuality and power. Where I use Foucault to support a strategy of *less* sexual imagery, Gallagher uses him to support a strategy of *more*, implying that this is indeed the correct interpretation of the practical implications of Foucault's theoretical ideas:

> If we want to use Michel Foucault's concept we need to engage in the desexualization of pleasure, that is to say, the breakdown or demystifying (if you want to call it that) of sex as the bearer of our essence; to become conscious of, and act on, the constructive character of our sexuality. I think we need to create images of sexuality which subvert the normal as much as possible; that is to say to recognize the perverse. The perverse, it should be made clear, is not just the rejection of normalcy, but also the perception of pleasure. As Foucault says, "Modern sexuality is perverse, not in spite of its puritanism or as if from a backlash provoked from its hypocrisy; it is in actual fact, and directly, perverse."[25]

Gallagher goes on to marshall more citations from Foucault, including one from his own interview with him, to clinch his argument that what follows from Foucault's analysis of sex and power is his own strategy of more (perverse) sexual imagery, not my strategy of less.

As I argue below in my response to these criticisms, Gallagher is absolutely right in attributing to me a position that does not distinguish gender from sexuality. Indeed that is the whole point of my argument! Gallagher's a priori refusal of that point and his corresponding effort to insulate sexuality from the political critique of gender seem both incoherent and implausible as presented and in the context of my own argument and especially so when framed within the terms of Foucault's analysis which is invoked in its defense. No amount of citation will convince me that a strategy of more sexual imagery rather than less—perverse, or otherwise—follows from Foucault's account of the relationship between sex and power. And that is not the issue anyway. For what matters to me and my argument is not whether a form of resistance is true to Foucault's analysis, interests, or intentions but whether it actually reproduces or resists the relations of patriarchy. And for the reasons outlined above and reiterated below, I continue to believe that sexual representation in the present context does not resist those relations and the divisions and denials which organize male dominance but relies on them and reproduces them in turn as one of its effects.

Reply to Bob Gallagher[26]

Bob Gallagher objects to my paper on two counts: he thinks we disagree about the nature of power and the role and character of resistances, and he does not like the fact that I refuse to separate sex from gender in my analysis of sexual representation. He is right on the second count but quite wrong on the first.

Like Gallagher, I, too, understand power to be constitutive, "co-existent with the social body," and constantly reproduced at the level of social relations. This is precisely what my analogy between the soul and sex is meant to demonstrate: the social processes of the reproduction of patriarchal power in particular, that is, of the power of male over female. Sexuality relies on gender, which marks human beings as masculine or feminine and builds a whole system of (polarized) differences on the basis of genital organs. These come to stand for that difference and become the focus for the acting out of the repressions, oppressions, and desire for the Other that the production of human beings as either masculine or feminine, man or woman, relies on and in turn reproduces. I also recognize that subordinated subjects are active in the processes of production, reproduction, and transformation of social power and that they resist, oppose, and refuse as well as submit to the relations of dominance within which they are subjected (created as subjects). That is why I am so anxious that those who are opposed to patriarchy *resist* the ideological separation of sex and gender which is constitutive of patriarchal power in general and its dominant sexual regime in particular. It is sex that gives power power while concealing it under the category of the natural and/or neutral: the separation of sex from gender does precisely that. It is false and falsifying separation.

Like Gallagher I believe that sexuality is socially constructed (through imagery for example) and the site of power relations. But he assumes that because power is *presently* always part of sexual relations, "*It always will be*," and he slips thereby into that essentialist position he is so rightly quick to detect and denounce in others. He presumes that the necessary relationship between sex and power, which we both recognize as true *now*, is an *essential* (ahistorical) relationship. He thinks it cannot be *transcended* but only transformed and transgressed to create new sexualities, new power relations, and new pleasures. I see the present conjuncture of sex and power as a *historically specific* function of patriarchy and a *historical contingency* that *must* be transcended if we want to undermine, diffuse, and refuse that particular order of dominance. Gallagher calls for the creation of new "perverse" sexual imagery to "subvert the normal as much as possible" and I for the subversion of sexual imagery itself, whether "normal" or "perverse."

To advocate the subversion—or suspension—of all sexual imagery that is not critical of that which it shows is not to ignore the social and specific aspects of sexual representation and meaning, or to reduce all meanings, subjects, and sexualities to a homogeneous, unambivalent, unidimensional, and reified "essence," as Gallagher charges. It is rather to insist on the fact that we *cannot stand outside the social*—either as producers or consumers of sexual imagery; that the particular (my sexuality, for example, even if it is "perverse") is always informed and determined by the general (what Gallagher perhaps is referring to as the "normal"): that context (a gallery or a magazine) structures, informs, and transforms text (a personal photograph of a loved one, for instance); and that displays of sexual imagery in the *present* context, dominated and determined as it is by centuries of sexist practice and representations of sexuality which normalize, legitimize, and naturalize it, only add to the strength of an already constituted series of sexist images—even if this is not the intent of the image maker. And according to this already constituted series, *he* is always on top, even when *he* is not—even when he is not even a he! For the meaning is not constituted by *what* is actually represented but by the act of representation itself and the *social relations* that make it possible, plausible, and desirable—and productive of a pleasure that is designated as sexual. And those social relations are and remain patriarchal, which is why we cannot afford to reproduce or endorse them by creating more, supposedly alternative, sexual imagery.

NOTES

1. Originally published in *Parallelogramme* 12, no. 1 (Autumn 1986), no pagination.
2. See Varda Burstyn, ed., *Women Against Censorship* (Vancouver and Toronto: Douglas and McIntyre, 1985), and Varda Burstyn, "Censorship. Problems and Alternatives," *Parallelogramme* 9, no. 3 (February/March 1984).
3. "Sexuality is a set of effects produced in bodies, behaviours and social relations by a certain deployment deriving from a complex political technology." Michel Foucault, *History of Sexuality*, vol. 1, trans. Robert Hurley (New York: Vintage Books, 1980), 127. My understanding of sex as a discursive effect and site of power leans heavily on the work of Foucault. I would like to emphasize, however, that I am using Foucault's work rather freely to serve my own ends and not appealing to its authority to legitimize my arguments, nor am I claiming to have the correct line on its implications or meanings.
4. Sex is not, as Burstyn suggests, the "raw material" of gender (Burstyn, *Women Against Censorship*, 171), but one of its effects, which has become a pertinent fact in our society and hence a perceived and hallowed category of thought and practice precisely because of gender. (Here I paraphrase Christine Delphy, *Close to Home, A Materialist Analysis of Women's Oppression* [London: Hutchinson, 1984], 144.) In other words sex relies on socially constructed gender divisions and not vice-versa. The extent to which sex (i.e., sexuality) is gendered is constantly obfuscated by those who would have us fight fire with fire, that is, sexist sex with "alternative" sex—whatever that might be. (For example, Anne Gronau, "Censorship Caught in the Crossfire," *Parallelogramme* 9, no. 3 (February/March 1984). For more on this, see Geraldine Finn, "Women Against Censorship: A Response," *Canadian Dimension* 20, no. 4 (July/August 1986): 34–36; and Geraldine Finn, "Sexual Representation and Social Control," *Perception* 9, no. 4 (March/April 1986): 24–26.
5. According to Foucault the bourgeoisie "subordinated its soul to sex by conceiving of it as what constituted the soul's most secret and determining part." Foucault, *History of Sexuality*, 124.
6. Frank Mort, "Sex, Signification and Pleasure," Formations of Pleasure, Routledge and Kegan Paul, London 1983: 41.
7. Emmanuel Reynaud, *Holy Virility. The Social Construction of Masculinity*, trans. Ros Schwartz (London, England: Pluto Press, 1981), 10.
8. This account of the sexual dynamic draws on the work of Lacan. As with Foucault I use Lacan's work freely to serve my own ends. I am not appealing to its authority nor am I claiming to have the correct Lacanian line on sex and representation.
9. Foucault, *History of Sexuality*, 157.
10. "The representation of the male and the female, and the situating of the male and female viewer *in* representation, and the depiction of male and female sexuality (whatever that is) is the ideological mode of reproducing dominant relations, no matter what the "actual" narrative ostensibly is. Because the seen, and the scene, that we re-witness, is the reproduction of positions of secure perception as to the sexualized body, that body as always the *other* against which the sexual identity of the 'I' is reproduced, in the interests of patriarchal relations as much as the reproduction of the labour power necessary for capitalist relations. We see a man and a woman on a screen and we can begin at that first stage of perception to identify what is, and then identify with/through

representation." Peter Gidal, "Against Sexual Representation in Film," *Screen* 25, no. 6 (November/December 1984), 28.

11. See Laura Mulvey, "Visual Pleasure and Narrative Cinema," *Screen* 16, no. 3 (Autumn 1975).
12. See Stanley Cavell, *The World Viewed. Reflections on the Ontology of Film* (Cambridge: Harvard University Press, 1979) and chapter 4 above for a more detailed discussion of the moral and political implications of the subjectivity of the spectator-position screened from the world viewed.
13. Up to this point the ideas expressed in this paragraph are taken more or less unchanged from John Berger, *Ways of Seeing* (London: BBC and Pelican Original, 1972). After this point I use his ideas to develop my own argument about pornography, sex, and representation.
14. Chapter 4 in this volume.
15. Mary Ann Doane, "Women's Stake: Filming the Female Body," *October* 17 (Summer 1981), 24.
16. Peter Gidal, "Against Sexual Representation," 27.
17. Chapter 4 in this volume.
18. Chapters 3 and 4 in this volume.
19. Susan Sontag, *Against Interpretation and Other Essays* (New York: Delta Books, 1966), 99.
20. Cavell, *The World Viewed*, 85.
21. See Wendy Hollway, "'I just wanted to kill a woman!' Why? The Ripper and Male Sexuality," *Feminist Review* 9 (October 1981).
22. See Susan Sontag, *On Photography* (New York: Delta Books, 1973), for a discussion of these structures of spectatorship as they relate to photography in particular.
23. See Charles Levin's Introduction to Jean Baudrillard, *For a Critique of the Political Economy of the Sign*, trans. Charles Levin (St. Louis, Mo.: Telos Press, 1981).
24. Bob Gallagher, "The Importance of Sexual Images," *Parallelogramme* 12, no. 1 (Autumn 1986): n.p.
25. Ibid.
26. Originally published as "Geraldine Finn Replies to Bob Gallagher," *Parallelogramme* 12, no. 1 (Autumn 1986): n.p.

Part 2 Two

On Postmodernism

Chapter 6 Six

Beyond Either/Or: Feminism and the Politics of Postmodernism

THIS ESSAY WAS ORIGINALLY written for an interdisciplinary conference on Feminism, Critical Theory and the Canadian Legal System organized by the Faculty of Law at the University of Windsor as part of the annual meetings of the Canadian Learned Societies in June 1988.

Postmodernism as both a category and a practice was in ascendancy at the time among the cultural cognoscenti of North America. Authorized in part by the publication of Jean-François Lyotard's *The Postmodernism Condition* (1984) and the extensive scholarly debates that followed in its wake, and fueled by the enthusiastic and increasing familiarity of North American scholars with the work of French intellectuals like Lacan, Derrida, Barthes, Foucault, Baudrillard, and Deleuze and Guattari. My own critical analyses of "Science," "Reason" and the "Pornographic Eye/I," which make up Part I of this volume and which were written in the early eighties, were very much informed by the arguments of these thinkers who were not generally known at the time by the audiences for whom the essays were originally intended. As North American academics became more familiar with the work of these French thinkers, however, heated and informed debates ensued over its meanings and its intellectual and political implications. And Postmodernism moved quickly into center stage *displacing Marxism alongside and against Feminism* as the privileged, authorized, and authoritative category of contemporary male-stream critical political thought. It was within this context that the organizers of the conference invited me to present a feminist perspective on Postmodernism for a session on "Critical Theory and Feminist Theory."

"Beyond Either/Or: Feminism and the Politics of Postmodernism" identifies two dispositions within postmodernism that reproduce the political intentionalities and ends of the discourses and practices of the modernism that postmodernism purports to have displaced or at least distanced itself from. The two dispositions are designated as "lyrical nihilism" and "nostalgic rationalism," and the political intentionality they share with modernism as a politics of "final solutions," of "genocide." My identification, analysis and criticism of these tendencies is not directed at (nor inspired by) any particular theory, authority, text, or spokesman of postmodernism but at (and by) the discourse of postmodernism in general: at (and by) postmodernism *as discourse*, and the taken-for-granted terms and relevancies that organize its arguments and ends and that have come to define the specificity of the thought of the "postmodern condition." Subsequent chapters in this section continue this feminist dialogue with and against the politics of postmodernism *as discourse*, each one taking a different aspect of that politics as its specific focus: its systematic objectification and silencing of the body (even as it purports to speak from it) (chapter 7), its reconstitution of (white) male hegemony (even as it announces the end of its History) (chapter 8), and its status and function as ideology (chapter 9).

Modernism and postmodernism are contested categories, categories of contestation (see chapter 13). I take them up here and in subsequent chapters on their own terms, as they circulate in the discourses that invoke them and organize their meanings and effects (as I took up the categories of Reason and Science, and Pornography and Sex in previous chapters). Each essay offers a different specification of the meaning and scope of postmodernism according to the context within which it is addressed, and the object and objectives of its analysis. Although the term is never fixed, a preferred meaning does emerge in these discussions which is articulated more precisely in the last chapter of this book titled "The Future of Postmodernism."

BEYOND EITHER/OR: FEMINISM AND THE POLITICS OF POSTMODERNISM

In this chapter I use the terms modernism and postmodernism rather loosely to refer to those ideas and movements which Michaelis and Misgeld,[1] following Habermas,[2] designate by the term Modernity.[3] By *modernism* I mean that movement of thought and action which coincided with the Enlightenment and the emergence of modern Science and which still organizes the intentionalities and ends of our society and its dominant culture. It includes a commitment to Reason, that is, to rational analysis as the authorized mode of access to Truth, to rational control as the privileged means of human freedom, and to Progress as the Telos inherent in Humanity and History, of which there is presumed to be but One: one History, one Humanity, one Progress, one Telos—and one Science that will accomplish it by way of its ever increasing technological control of Nature. Modernism is thus a praxis that assumes, requires, and organizes the bifurcation of human experience and being, of epistemology and ontology, into a hierarchical system of Either/Or: either for or against Progress, Reason, Man; either Man or Nature, Rational or Irrational, Free or Unfree; and so on.[4] I use the term *postmodernism* to designate contemporary movements of thought and action which to one degree or another have lost faith in modernism: in Science and Technology and Enlightenment Reason and in the project of Emancipation that supposedly motivates, inspires, and directs them.[5]

The spokesmen of both modernism and postmodernism rely on "master narratives"[6] of Man, Society, History, Reason, and Civilization to articulate their respective theories and practices, which, like all narratives, have quite specific political implications. The *politics of modernism* is an instrumental politics of means and ends, of means subordinated to ends: of intervention, manipulation and control (of Nature, for example); of appropriation, domination, and regulation (of Man). The *politics of postmodernism* is both less unified and less transparent since it is still under contestation. But it tends to cluster around two divergent dispositions toward the modern in its most visible and authorized versions, which I shall characterize here as the "*French*" and the "*German*."[7] The tendency of the "French" dispositions is toward a politics of "*lyrical nihilism*": a praxis of fiddling-while-Rome-burns premised on the assumption that in the postmodern condition—where social meanings are both arbitrary and self-referring, social realities mere simulacra, and where we are all prisoners of language anyway—politics is no longer possible. The tendency of this version of postmodernism is to a sort of political quietism at best and cynical opportunism at worst. It is a politics that looks to the "Germans" (and to myself, though for different reasons) as the abdication of politics in the name of its impossibility. The "Germans" by contrast are not ready to give up on the project of modernity. The disposition of this tendency is toward a politics of "*nostalgic rationalism*": a praxis of reform and renewal of critical Reason for the sake of the familiar intentionalities and ends of modernism's project of Emancipation.[8]

The appeal of the "German" dispositions is its refusal to abandon a discourse of values and ends, and its corresponding commitment to the development and articulation of a political rationality that will enable their realization. Habermas and Gadamer, for example, clearly *care* about something other than themselves and the surfaces of modern life. (Though precisely what they care about is not so clear: Reason, Civilization, Freedom, Humanity? Whatever concrete realities they cherish, the terms of their respective rationalities remain too abstract for me.) The appeal of the "French" disposition is the antithesis of this. It lies precisely in its renunciation of the traditional repressive, oppressive, dogmatic, and totalizing practices of European Reason—of Reason *en tant que domination*—and in the abandonment of its ethical and political rationality in favor of aesthetics. (What often seems to me to be little more than commodity fetishism with a clear conscience.) Having announced the death of the subject and the social, the "French" invite us to dance at their wake and indulge our tastes at the trough of their simulacra—forgetting the exploitations and oppressions and systematic violations that continue as the conditions of possibility of this particular strategy of "play" and "jouissance," of a would-be *post*modern aesthetic.

It is interesting to note—though I cannot pursue the observation here—that those who are dancing on the grave of the social are "French" and those who are trying to revive it are "German."[9] And that in both cases the body is dead—or at least irrelevant. For it *is the soul*, the spirit, the rationality, the subjectivity, the sovereignty of Man that is at stake in these debates, not the body. And of course all the primary definers are men. I think the postmodern condition—the collective disaffection of Western man from modernism and modernity—is very much about men's relationship to nations and nationalism(s): a symptom of challenges to European hegemony from those it has traditionally constituted as its Other(s)—from women, for example, from Blacks in the United States, and from the indigenous peoples of Europe's former colonies. At some fundamental level, "the postmodern condition" articulates a crisis in European patriarchy; in the white man's privileged relationship to his tribe and to power and—since the power of that tribe is now in question—to his own very particular body: that white male body which once entitled him to power and authority over the Other(s) and now does not.

If this is the postmodern condition and these are the political tendencies of its authorities, what is—or should be—the relationship of feminism to it and to what Michaelis and Misgeld call modernity?[10] I will begin by clarifying the specificity of feminism as a politics in terms of its objectives, orientation, and methods and then go on to consider its relationship to modernity. At its most general and at the same time most fundamental, the specific political project of feminism is to identify and dismantle the exercise and organization of male privilege wherever it occurs, that is, to disempower men and empower women. The task is both a theoretical and a practical one, the one informing the other in a continuing praxis of critique, reflection, evaluation, and change.[11]

Feminist theory is theory developed from and for the standpoint of women: a standpoint outside the discursive and institutional frame that organizes and legitimizes male dominance by constituting the subject of the social—of its Culture, History, and Humanity—as male, that is, as Man.

> To begin from such a standpoint does not imply a common viewpoint among women. What we have in common is that organisation of social relations which has accomplished our exclusion.[12]

Feminism's critique of modernism will always be an immanent one therefore, because we can only take it up from where we are and who we are—which is always *in* patriarchy and *as* women constructed by and for the social and political intentionalities of male dominance. Feminist critique is always reflexive and turned upon ourselves inasmuch as we, too, are the bearers, the reproducers, the subjects of the structures, and relations of male dominance. Feminists seek to develop new theories and new practices (from the standpoint of women in the given sense) out of the old. We dip into the collective tool-kit of male-stream history and take from it what seems useful to us at the time, reshaping the tools to suit our purposes and discarding them when they are no longer useful.[13]

This plundering of male-stream history and social and political theory is perhaps what Michaelis and Misgeld are referring to when they speak of feminism's "ambivalent relation to the history of modernity" and insist that we resolve that ambivalence by choosing for or against the Emancipatory project: choose, that is, either Us or Them:

> Our argument is meant to make clear that a choice has to be made between one or the other position, the pursuit of emancipation as entailing an anticipation of the possible completion of modernity, on the one hand, or, on the other hand, the self-limitation of feminist politics and cultural and social innovation to radical subcultures which reject participation in the further transformation of modern institutions.[14]

This ambivalence toward male-stream theory and practice is, however, *precisely* what defines feminism and the specificity of its struggle against male dominance. Insisting that feminists resolve that ambivalence in favor of modernity as Michaelis and Misgeld do is tantamount, therefore, to insisting that feminists give up their feminism—that they trade in the feminist project of the identification, critique, and elimination of male power for the modernist project of its reconstitution, its reorganization, under a new description ("communicative rationality," for example).[15] It is asking feminists to give up the (ambivalent) standpoint of women inside/outside the circle of men, for the (unambivalent) standpoint of the (white) Man at its increasingly dead center.

So the first thing to say about the relationship between feminism and modernity is that it is and must remain a *critical* one, which is not the same thing as saying that we must reject it and all it stands for and against. On the contrary feminism must engage with modernity critically and creatively because it is *the* principal force shaping contemporary consciousness, culture, and social and political praxis. Just as we must engage with the law, the state, the church, the media, science, technology and so forth, all of which are instruments and manifestations of modernity. Modernity is so to speak the problem; it will therefore have to figure in the solution. But feminist engagement with modernity will always be ambivalent because it will always be critical. We may—indeed we must—participate in contemporary political movements that are not solely motivated by concerns with women or what Michaelis and Misgeld (disparagingly, I think) refer to as "subcultures." But inasmuch as we are feminists, we can never be party faithful. It is precisely this position of being *outsider on the inside* that defines political struggle. It is not a comfortable or easy position to occupy, and there is certainly nothing seductive or playful about it, as the lyrical nihilists would have us believe. As feminists here will no doubt bear witness to, *doing feminism is doing without*: without the guarantees, certainties, and ends—without the final solutions, that is—of traditional politics (indeed, insisting on these securities is the heart of the problem); and more particularly, doing without the comfort and consolation of the unambivalent, of an epistemological and political Either/Or—either with us or "agin" us; either sink or swim.

The relationship of feminism to postmodernism is, in fact, more nuanced than this, in that postmodernism has (to a degree yet to be determined) been shaped and formed in response to, or even in reaction against, feminism. The various theories and practices of postmodernism are, at least in part, an attempt by (predominantly white) male artists and intellectuals to reclaim the theoretical and political initiative and authority they have lost to feminism over the last twenty-five years in the name of all the old (modernist) universals—History, Humanity, Freedom, Reason, Western Civilization—on behalf of which postmodern Man still presumes to speak. From the standpoint of feminism, therefore, it is the relationship of postmodernism to feminism that poses itself as a question and not vice-versa. This I will now attempt to clarify.

Both the lyrical nihilist and nostalgic rationalist tendencies of postmodernism manage feminist difference and the difference feminism makes the same way.[16] The way they manage all differences that: by refusing its political specificity, that is, by appropriating, assimilating, subordinating, diffusing, dissolving, and reducing feminism to their own political project, which is *not* in either case and by any stretch of the imagination, the project of feminism—the project of the systematic disempowerment of men. Both tendencies present themselves as the *only* rational choice available to Humanity, as *the* (chrono) logical conclusion of History (as illustrated by Michaelis and Misgeld above). On the strength of which, each accuses the other (and all its Others—feminism, for example) of political and epistemological idealism: of disappearing the historical complexities of concrete reality into the abstract universals of totalizing theory. And in both tendencies, feminism assumes the place of Woman: the place of the hypostasized Other, which must be contained *or* excluded, contained *as* excluded. That is, feminism appears for both dispositions as an Otherness to be managed by precisely the same strategies of containment and exclusion by which the Otherness of Woman has been and continues to be managed within the modernist praxis postmodernism purports to displace: by denial, division, and domination; by exclusion and thereby inclusion precisely as the excluded, the abjected, Other; and by the reduction of its specificity, alterity, and difference to the Same—the recurring Sameness of the Other.

Because feminism has developed such a complete critique of the ideology and politics of both classical and renaissance Humanism, the lyrical nihilists who see no hope in the postmodern condition simply try to bring feminism on board the sinking ship of Humanity and drag us down with them into the socially and sexually undifferentiated mausoleum of hyperreality. The body being dead. Still firm in their belief, however, that their vision of Humanity, History, Reason, Emancipation, Subjectivity, and Man is the only One and that there is, indeed, only One History, One ship of Humanity, etc. And since that History has now come to an end and that ship is now sinking, we might as well bury our differences (i.e., our bodies) and go down together.[17] The lyrical nihilist version of postmodernism disappears feminist challenges to male power into a fatalistic discourse of pleasure, desire, and an anonymous, undifferentiated "the body," within which resistance and political subversion are constituted as individual transgressions of social norms. According to this view, the liberated "pomo" woman both exhibits and accomplishes her liberation, (her subversion, resistance, and difference) by assuming the social and historical inevitability of sadomasochistic (hetero)sexuality as her identity, destiny, pleasure, and power. (I am thinking of films like *Winter Tan*, *Fatal Attraction*, *9 $\frac{1}{2}$ Weeks*, and *Blue Velvet*, for example, and novels like *The White Hotel*.) Gender is *depoliticized* in this discourse of bodies, sexuality, and the masculine/feminine difference; functioning as an arbitrary abstraction or floating signifier somehow separable from the local, specific historical and concrete bodies marked by it.[18] So that if she wears a tie and yields a phallus, we are supposed to be persuaded that she has somehow single-handedly and by fiat transgressed the political organization of gender and demonstrated that the sexual fix[19] can be unfixed as easily as changing your underwear.[20] This "the body" circulates *in abstracto* in the lyrical nihilist tendency of postmodernism, where everyone seems to be speaking *about* it and *to* it but still never *from it*. There is still, that is, No Body speaking in this discourse. (And since the subject is dead, from whence the enunciation?) Like sex, gender, and power, the body continues to be objectified and depersonalized as it has always been in male-stream theory where the body does not speak but is spoken. It is a praxis that I have characterized elsewhere as pornographic.[21]

The nostalgic rationalist tendency of postmodernism—of those who believe the ship of Humanity and Reason can and must be salvaged and rebuilt—likewise tries to bring feminism on board if and when they notice us that is. In this case it is because we have been so effective in locating the weak links in modernism and can, like the little Dutch Boy, be put to good use blocking the leaks in the dyke of Reason with the materiality of our particular bodies while Noah and the boys get on with the real political work of building the new ark of universal theory that will transport us all to salvation.

What neither tendency admits, however, is that there is not and never has been just one ship of Humanity: one History, one Reason, one Telos, one Man; that their vision of History and Humanity is just one among many; and that there are hundreds of thousands of lighter craft out there on the ocean they cannot see. This is because they will not look and because when they do look they are blinded by the glare of their own superior Reason to what lies beyond its range and within its shadow—where they presume there can be only nothing or chaos. Both the infrastructure and superstructure of their privileged spectator consciousness is so large and so unwieldy and so alienated from their own flesh that they have no sensitivity to what lies outside it or within its interstices, that is, no sense organs with which to perceive or respond to others. The postmodern body is indeed without organs as some of our "French" brethren have argued[22] (though hardly with the same political intentionality as myself).

In this respect neither the lyrical nihilist nor the nostalgic rationalist tendency of postmodernism moves beyond the limits of the binary terms that organize the Enlightenment project they claim to differentiate themselves from. It is still, in both cases, a project of all or nothing—of sink or swim (of sink or sink for the nihilists). It is still a question of teleology of what Michaelis and Misgeld, following Habermas, refer to as *completion.* A project of ends, of *final solutions*, with all the social and political consequences such programs entail: the totalization of people, histories, and ideas; the obliteration of particularity, contingency, and difference. In a word it is still a project of what Brian Fawcett has called *genocide*, entailing the liquidation of "particularity, direction, local memory, creating in its stead a single focus on the monadic truth":[23] one Telos, one Humanity, one History, one Project of Emancipation—one Apocalypse. And universal abstract Reason remains as the implicit if not explicit privileged term in these increasingly authorized versions of postmodernism, beyond which lies the chaotic, meaningless disorder of particularity, contingency, and chance of the Body eviscerated of the Mind (history, agency, vision, understanding, wisdom, freedom, creativity, virtue, value, vitality, etc.), which the Reason of modern Man has systematically expropriated from it to and for its fantasy of the disembodied Self.

For the lyrical nihilists Reason, like God, is dead. It has imploded on itself and is in ruins, scattered irrevocably across the decaying social body over which its harbingers hover like vultures competing for the juiciest morsels. For the nostalgic rationalists Reason is dying but not yet dead and can still be given the kiss of life. We are not yet, for them, reduced to the condition of mere bodies. Nevertheless for both tendencies within postmodernism there is no way of adequately fulfilling one's Humanity outside the rule of a very traditionally conceived Rationality, one that is fundamentally at odds with and humiliated and compromised by its own embodiment: its own particularity, concreteness, finitude, fallibility, uncertainty, vulnerability, dependency, temporarility, mortality, etc. In short by its own *contingency*. It is for this reason that each tendency is in fact correct in its characterization of the other as a form of epistemological and political *idealism* (though not for the reasons offered). For neither the "French" nor the "German" tendency, neither the lyrical nihilist nor the nostalgic rationalist version of postmodernism, speaks *from* the body but rather *against* it, in a discourse within which Body and Woman are metonymic. Correspondingly in both tendencies, feminism—which displaces the intentionalities of binary thinking and refuses its bifurcation of Body and Mind, Reason and Unreason, Universal and Particular, and its corresponding project of Final Solutions—functions as an Other to be excluded and contained, as the Other of a Reason that is dying or dead, as the chaos of a "the" Body without Mind, as the non-sense (*non sens*) of Woman without Man; as *the* sign of the death of the Subject, the End of History, and the abandonment of the Project of Humanity. Thus feminism takes over the role of Woman in the political economy of these tendencies in postmodern thought. The lyrical nihilists welcome us as fellow travelers in hyperreality. (We are, after all, *all* Women now, now that the Subject, the Social is dead.) The nostalgic rationalists think we are throwing out the baby (of Enlightenment Reason and the project of Emancipation) with the bathwater (of its institutionalized violences)—overlooking the fact that it is the dirt from the baby that soiled the water! And both tendencies continue to judge us from the standpoint and perspective of a very traditional, and systematically, and dogmatically disembodied Subject, which they seem incapable of thinking beyond: incapable, that is, of thinking and speaking from their own sexually and racially specific and historically and spatially particular concrete bodies.

Conclusion

Postmodernism is both a symptom and response to a crisis in legitimation: in the legitimation of the Emancipatory project of modernity and of Enlightenment Reason that I have now come to see as embodying a politics of Final Solutions. This crisis in legitimation has not, however, led its spokesmen to question the modernist project or its presuppositions about Humanity, Freedom, Reason, and Man. Nor, therefore, to seek out alternative visions of the possibilities of being human or alternative political projects for their achievement. On the contrary it has led to what we have just seen: to a frantic search for alternative legitimations for the same vision of History and Humanity and for what is basically the same political project articulated by and in the name of the same Universals (Freedom, Reason, History, Man) on the one hand. Or, to the complete abandonment of vision, legitimation, and politics on the other and likewise in the name of (the impossibility of) the same universals. It is precisely the presupposition and praxis of these universals, and of the non-specific, non-concrete disembodied Subject of Humanity and History that coincides with it, which assumes no responsibility for the position from which he speaks nor for that which is spoken from it, that feminists have identified as the signature and mechanism of power, and patriarchal power, in particular. It hardly makes sense, therefore, to call on feminists to join a movement—the continuing project of modernity—committed to its re-member-ing and re(s)erection.

NOTES

1. Loralea Michaelis and Dieter Misgeld presented a paper on "Critical Theory, Feminist Theory and Modernity" at the same session of the conference for which this essay was originally prepared. My references to their work are based on an abstract of the paper that was made available to participants before the conference.
2. As, for example, in Jurgen Habermas, "Modernity—An Incomplete Project," in *The Anti-Aesthetic: Essays on Postmodern Culture*, ed. Hal Foster; trans. Seyla Benhabib (Port Townsend, Wash.: Bay Press, 1983), 3–15; and Jurgen Habermas, *The Philosophical Discourses of Modernity: Twelve Lectures*, trans. Frederick G. Lawrence (Cambridge, Mass.: MIT Press, 1987).
3. "By modernity we mean the emergence of new principles and forms of organizing society and politics which emerged together with the political, social and cultural revolutions and transformations since the eighteenth century in Western Europe and North-America. These principles and historical changes can be said to have political, social and cultural emancipation as their content. They entail, inter alia, the institutionalisation of universal suffrage and the formation of modern law, the emergence of emancipatory social movements and of welfare state legislation, industrialization and the employment of science in social policy, the creation of international institutions and the emergence of new forms of social and private morality as well as the emancipation of artistic production from comprehensive, frequently religious, world views" (Michaelis and Misgeld, "Critical Theory.")
4. Thus chapters 1 through 5 in this volume offer a systematic and sustained critique of the premises and practices of modernism though not under that description.
5. This description of postmodernism is addressed to postmodernism as it circulates in what has come to be known as "theory" and in the various discourses premised on the Lyotard-Habermas debate. A feminist engagement with postmodernism as it circulates in the discourses and practices of the Arts (in

architecture, literature, and the visual and performing arts) would require a somewhat different set of specifications. Although it is not sufficiently different, I believe, to insulate it from the general criticisms of postmodernism *as discourse* articulated here and in subsequent chapters.

6. Jean-François Lyotard, *The Postmodern Condition. A Report on Knowledge* (Minneapolis: University of Minnesota Press, 1984).
7. These are intended as *characterizations* not descriptions (of the origins or aspirations) of the two tendencies and dispositions under discussion, based on the observation that French thinkers (like Barthes, Lacan, Derrida, Foucault, and Baudrillard) are most likely to be invoked in those discourses of postmodernism, which tend toward one disposition, and German thinkers (like Gadamer and Habermas) in those that tend toward the other. I am not *reducing* French thought to one tendency and German thought to another, nor am I suggesting that *all* French thinkers are disposed one way and all Germans disposed another. I am simply pointing to *tendencies* in postmodern discourse more or less present in its local and particular articulations and perhaps sometimes not present at all.
8. Again I am not *reducing* postmodernism to these two tendencies but merely identifying them as implicit or explicit ends of its discourse, more or less present in its various realizations. I am not saying that this is *all* there is to postmodernism or that postmodernism always tends in one direction or the other or that postmodernist thinkers can be consistently summed up under one description or the other. On the contrary individual writers and texts often vacillate between both dispositions.
9. See note 7 this chapter.
10. See note 4 this chapter.
11. See Geraldine Finn, Introduction to *Limited Edition. Voices of Women, Voices of Feminism*, ed. Geraldine Finn (Halifax: Fernwood Publishing, 1993), 1–11.
12. Dorothy Smith, *The Everyday World as Problematic* (Toronto: University of Toronto Press, 1987), 78. See also Finn, *Limited Editions*, for further explication of the relationship between feminism and the standpoint of women.
13. Feminist invocations of the discourses of Rights and Freedoms, and Labor and Production, as ways of both clarifying and transforming the political realities of women's lives, are examples of this strategic and limited use of male-stream thought and practice. As I argue in chapter 12, feminists cannot *not* make use of the political categories of male-stream praxis. This does not mean that we have to believe in them, however, or swear allegiance to the traditions and institutions that have empowered them. (See chapter 12.)
14. Michaelis and Misgeld, "Critical Theory."
15. Habermas's privileged term. See Jurgen Habermas, "Modernity," and *The Theory of Communicative Action*, 2 vols., trans. Thomas A. McCarthy (Boston: Beacon Press, 1984).
16. See Geraldine Finn, "Managing the Difference," *Canadian Journal of Political and Social Theory* 10 no. 3 (1986): 176–84.
17. An exemplary text in this respect would be Arthur Kroker and David Cook, *Excremental Culture and Hyper-Aesthetics* (Montreal: New World Perspectives, 1986).
18. The authority of Derrida, Lacan, and Foucault is most often invoked (mistakenly, I believe) to legitimize this depoliticization of sex and gender.
19. See Stephen Heath, *The Sexual Fix* (London: MacMillan Press, 1982).

20. As appears to be the argument of Berkeley Kaite, for example, in "The Pornographer's Body Double: Transgression is the Law" in *Body Invaders. Panic Sex in America*, eds. Arthur and Marilouise Kroker (Montreal: New World Perspectives, 1986), 150–68.
21. Chapters 4 and 7 in this volume.
22. Gilles Deleuze and Felix Guattari, *The Anti-Oedipus: Capitalism and Schizophrenia*, trans. Robert Hurley, Mark Seem, and Helen Lane (New York: Viking Press, 1977).
23. Brian Fawcett, *Cambodia. A Book for People Who Find Television too Slow*, (Vancouver: Talonbooks, 1986), 63.

Chapter 7

Seven

No Bodies Speaking: Subjectivity, Sex, and the Pornography Effect

The argument of this chapter[1] is that the discourses of postmodernism within which sex, gender, and the body are currently being spoken collaborate with contemporary pornography in the maintenance and reproduction of women's silence; in the continuing social construction of the knowing, seeing, and speaking Subject of our culture as abstract, universal Man, and his corresponding Object as concrete, particular Woman; in the identification of the generic cultural Subject with mind, men, and transcendence (of the body and the world) and the generic cultural Object with body, women, and immanence; and in putting into play, that is, the hierarchical division of Man over Woman, Subject over Object, and Mind, the seeing and speaking (generic) mind of the masculine subject (the subject as masculine) over Body, the silent, seen, and spoken (generic) body of the feminine object (the object as feminine).

THIS CHAPTER WAS ORIGINALLY prepared for a session on Gender and the Body at the annual meeting of the Society for Phenomenological and Existential Philosophy which met in Chicago in October 1988. It continues the reflection initiated in the last chapter on the relationship between the speaking subject of postmodernism, "the" body spoken in its discourse, and feminism.

A sophisticated discourse of "desire" (i.e., a systematic exchange of clever but false propositions about "sex"), deriving most of its authority and substance from Bataille, Lacan, Derrida, and the Marquis de Sade, had recently penetrated the formerly and dogmatically "sexless" halls of academia, exploding at what seemed to be an exponential rate of (re)production. At every conference I attended and in every journal I consulted, there was Oedipus and the Phallus, intoned and recited with monotonous regularity by gentlemen of scholarly repute (or would-be scholarly repute) in tweed jackets and suits, in a *melancholy* but at the same time *triumphant* and *naturalizing* discourse of seduction, castration, frustration, masturbation, ejaculation, defecation, invagination, fragmentation, dismemberment, and lack. By means of which feminism's sustained and systematic *hard-earned* critique(s) of patriarchy, gender, sex, and science—which had put the question of the sexed body on the intellectual agenda in the first place—was steamrollered off the theoretical scene/seen.

The scene/seen of postmodernism and its discourse of sexed bodies in particular was in the process of being hijacked before our very eyes away from women and the project of feminism, by and for the Brotherhood. By this new alliance of the same old men accomplished by the same old means: the exchange of bodies (in this case, the discursive body as sign) and the collective and systematic obfuscation of the sexual specificity of the (subjects and objects of the) narrative that achieves it, that is, the narrative of Oedipus and the Phallus that organizes his entry into language and culture and determines his destiny and desires. This essay speaks from this experience of erasure (the erasure of women and the erasure of feminism) to the discourse of postmodernism that accomplishes it, applying the theoretical insights and analyses of the Pornographic Eye/I (see chapter 4) to postmodernism's discourse of "the" body.

This was one of the hardest papers I have ever written, even though I never had any doubt about what I wanted to say in it. Postmodernism rendered me speechless. That is what I wanted to say, and what I wanted to do was show how this was accomplished in its routine discourse(s) of "the" body. But how could I do this? How could I demonstrate the truth of my silence with speech? Or the mechanisms of my exclusion in terms of the discourse which accomplishes it? I was in a Catch-22 position: damned if I do (speak, that is, or remain silent), and damned if I don't. I finally resolved my dilemma by speaking about pornography in order to speak about postmodernism; by speaking of and to pornography and postmodernism in parallel and in turn. Until the two voices and their respective discursive objects converged into one, demonstrating in practice what followed from but could not be demonstrated in theory: the complicity of postmodernism's discourse of "the" body with pornography in the constitution of the knowing, speaking Subject of our culture as disembodied Man and its corresponding Body/Object, known, silenced, and bespoken, as Woman.

In this demonstration the two dispositions of postmodernism (described in the last chapter) toward nostalgic rationalism on the one hand and lyrical nihilism on the other assume the character of soft- and hard-core postmodernism respectively, according to the

> coolness of the gaze which contemplates the truth of the violence which patriarchy inflicts on women (which) marks as *absolute*, constructs as absolute, the boundary between his humanity and mine, his free speech and my silence.

Thus the tendency of those of the lyrical nihilist disposition to put "the" postmodern body into discursive play precisely as a dead and disappearing, fragmented and frenzied body in ruins and without organs, emerges here as the scholarly equivalent of hard-core pornography.

"No Bodies Speaking" what written for a specialized audience, that of the Society for Phenomenological and Existential Philosophy. It uses categories of phenomenology that would be familiar to that audience but not necessarily to readers of this volume. I have therefore added some explanatory footnotes to the original text to clarify some of those key terms. All my writing is in fact grounded in and informed by the phenomenological tradition in general and the existential phenomenology of Maurice Merleau-Ponty, in particular. This becomes more obvious in Part III where the philosophical foundations of the earlier (critical) essays addressed to (post)modernism are made explicit in my efforts to affirm the possibility of an alternative politics, ethics, spirituality, and future, which will not repeat the past nor therefore abandon us to either Nothing and NoBody, or more of the Same.

"No Bodies Speaking: Subjectivity, Sex, and the Pornography Effect"

> There are not one but many silences, and they are an integral part of the strategies that underlie and permeate discourses.[2]

The argument of this presentation is that the discourses of postmodernism within which sex, gender, and the body are currently being spoken collaborate with contemporary pornography in the maintenance and reproduction of women's silence; in the continuing social construction of the knowing, seeing, and speaking Subject of our culture as abstract, universal Man and his corresponding Object as concrete, particular Woman; in the identification of the generic cultural Subject with mind, men, and transcendence (of the body and the world) and the generic cultural Object with body, women, and immanence; and in putting into play, that is, the hierarchical division of Man over Woman, Subject over Object, and Mind, the seeing and speaking (generic) mind of the masculine subject (the subject as masculine) over Body, the silent, seen, and spoken (generic) body of the feminine object (the object as feminine).

To demonstrate *in writing* how these two very different sets of discursive practices collaborate in the production of the same truth effect—the masculine-feminine difference as a hierarchy of speaking over spoken, subject over object, which is what I mean by the "pornography effect," proved more difficult than I anticipated however.[3] For, although, pornography and postmodernism organize the same effect, that is, the silencing of women and the hegemony of disembodied male speech, they do not follow the same discursive route to that end nor share the same discursive point of departure. Their contents are divergent and discrete and those who occupy the position of subject in one do not recognize themselves as the subject of the other. The terms and relevancies of each discourse are exclusive of the terms and relevancies of the other. One consists of images (defended as speech), the other of words. More importantly, though, the effect of the two discourses, their convergence in the pornography effect, is not observable to those to whom the discursive structure assigns the position of agency, of speaking subject, since it is the effect of the structure rather than the contents, of representation. And like the eye/I of the beholder, the determining structures of the pornography effect of postmodernism and pornography are visible only to those outside the respective discourses that produce it: those who do not occupy the designated speaking position, and those whose exclusion the discourse actually organizes. (Just as the labor that produces the object as object for the Master is observable to the Slave and part of his consciousness but not to the Master, who as a consequence can entertain the illusion of the subject/object distinction and the separation of mind and body.)

The continuity of effect of postmodernism and pornography appears to me from this position of exclusion. What I discovered, however, as I set about writing this paper was that I can identify the symptom from this position, but I cannot *demonstrate* it. I can speak *of* the collaboration of pornography and postmodernism in the production of the same effect (my silence) as I do in my introductory paragraph, but I cannot speak *to* it. I cannot assume the position of speaking subject within the discourse that organizes my exclusion. I cannot demonstrate my exclusion from within the discourse that achieves it. I have been framed by these two discourses—boxed into a position where my silence is both real and visible (to me) but unspeakable. I could not enter into either discourse from this position, the only position from which the effect I want to demonstrate can be observed: the silencing effect.

Breaking the silence in ways that can be heard, as something other than a cry or a scream,[4] by those whose subjectivity and speech is organized by it, that can be heard, that is, by the hegemonic speakers of discourse, is always a tricky business: a question of moving in and out of a power discourse at two speeds, in two directions, and with double-vision[5]: using the terms that organize and conceal your silence and exclusion to reveal it to those whose interests it serves. And each discourse demands a different strategy. For there are as many ways of being wrong, being silenced, being excluded, of being an object as there are discourses that organize it. It is for this reason that I could not speak to postmodernism and pornography at the same time and expect to be heard by the discursive subjects of either. I had to pick my terms of entry according to the terms of the respective discourses. While to speak at all I had to abandon my point of departure—the position of the convergence of postmodernism and pornography in my silence. What I found myself doing, therefore, was intervening first in one, then in the other, vacillating between two mutually exclusive points of entry into the common problematic of how male discourse organizes my silence and the dominance of the masculine voice. What follows then is a juxtaposition of these two interventions, a demonstration in parallel and in turn of the collaboration of postmodernism and pornography in the continuing reproduction of male dominance and female subordination.

* * *

Gender is a political category (and practice) that rests on the sighting/citing/siting of genital difference: a sighting citing/siting that positions each one of us from birth on the appropriate side of a hierarchical set of masculine/feminine difference. The sighting/citing/siting of sexual difference, and by implication of *every and any body* (for everybody is sexually differentiated, Male or Female, in gendered society) is therefore always a political act, a gesture for or against the gender hierarchy articulated there.

Pornography is clearly a vote in favor of gender hierarchy: for a sexuality organized by, from, and on behalf of genital difference and of the exclusive and discrete sexual identities of Man or Woman that is built upon them. Pornography literally means "whore—painting." In pornography men represent women-in-general (that is, Woman) as whores for the viewing pleasure of men-in-general (that is, Man). That is, men who do not know each other address each other in their shared sexual identity *as men*—amuse and arouse, flatter and reward, communicate and bond, and speak with each other—through, across, and over against the sexually differentiated bodies of a series of anonymous women marked as whores for men, as all and only sex-for-men. In pornography as elsewhere in our culture, women are the means to the enterprises of others; they are the exchange objects par excellence by means of which social bonds between men are established.[6] In pornography women are the organs of men's speech; the body without organs is thus marked as male in this discourse.[7]

* * *

The discourse of postmodernism is just as clearly both a male and a master discourse: a lament by the masters for their lost mastery: loss of the subject, loss of the social, loss of the real, and loss of the meaning that pornography attempts to recover for men. The postmodern lament is also at the same time an effective collective effort of its reconstitution and recovery. I say this not simply because the spokesmen of postmodernism are predominantly if not exclusively men, though the significance of this fact could never be overestimated; but because the presumptive subject for whom postmodernism appears as a condition, the subject who speaks of it to other similarly placed subjects, is the traditional discursive subject of our culture:

the universal, nonspecific and implicitly, if not explicitly, disembodied subject of Plato and Descartes who aspires to mastery and control of both his environment and his body (body as environment). It is a subject marked by its position in discourse (in the sentence as well as in the "grand récit") as both external to the diegesis (abstract) and male. As the Subject of history and culture and as Man the subject of the grammatical sentence: he not she. (Gender-neutral = Not-Woman = Man = Universal. Woman = Not-Man = gender-specific = particular.)

This subject, Man, "the subject" of postmodernist discourse, has recently discovered "the body." More precisely the spokesmen of postmodernism have recently put "the body" into discursive play, specifically as a seductive (seducing and seduced) body of pleasure and desire: of "jouissance" and death, of death as jouissance and jouissance (le petit mort) as death.[8] Within the frame of its discourse, within the diegesis, that is, this "the" body of postmodernism is as undifferentiated and generic as "the" subject that speaks it: neither old or young, rich or poor, black or white, master or slave, man or woman. An indifference that marks "the" body of postmodernism as *male* (the body of Man) just as securely as it does the subject who speaks it. At the same time this undifferentiated (and therefore male) body circulates in postmodern discourse in the traditional position of the feminine as Object, as Other, as Sex, as Death; as that of which the subject speaks but not yet the place from which he speaks, as that against which the subject constantly asserts both his difference and his dominance (in speaking *of* it and *about* it, but not *from* it); as that which threatens the subject with its overwhelming powers of seduction and destruction, seduction as destruction, threatens him with his own death as "the" subject, that is.

What then are we make of this? This sudden irruption of "the" body marked in its indifference as male but positioned as female, the feminized male body, the masculinized feminine body, as an object of concern in the discursive self-consciousness of postmodern Man? The female body, the body feminized, has always circulated in discourse and practice as the penetrated, colonized, invaded (and invading) body: body eviscerated of mind as a sign of death, chaos, and disintegration. The contemplation of the dying, disappearing, and disciplined female body (body as the sign of the feminine) has never thrown our intellectuals into a panic before. On the contrary they have welcomed it into their discourse as the Other against which the (male) subject defines his subjectivity, difference, and transcendence. What are we to make of this? Why "the" body? Why not my body, or myself as body? Himself as body? Why now? Why dead? Why undifferentiated? Whose body are postmodernists really in a panic about?

* * *

The pleasure men take in viewing women as whores in pornography is rightly experienced as sexual in that it is aroused in them by the sighting/citing/siting of the sex of the subordinated other—the sexual difference on account of which she is subordinated to he, to him. It is a pleasure taken in the sighting/citing/siting of Woman reduced and subordinated to sexual difference, to Sex, to whoring for men.

Pornography thus reifies and displays, objectifies and make real, makes visible and fungible, the politics of the sexual relation that the respectable discourses of our culture conceal or deny even as they collaborate in its reproduction: the discourses of religion, science, and art, for example, as well as the more recent and supposedly oppositional discourses of postmodernism which is the focus of this presentation. Pornography is not therefore transgressive of the social-sexual order as those who defend it would have us believe. The only boundaries pornography breaks are those of acceptable sexual *speech* (hence the legal definition of pornography in terms of obscenity), not the boundaries of acceptable sexual *truth* (or reality). Pornography lifts the veil of sexual decency, which cloaks respectable sexual speech with the rhetoric of the family romance,[9] (of freedom and choice, identity and desire, pleasure and need, culture and nature) to expose and perform the political relation of men and women that supports it. That is the masculine-feminine difference as a practical hierarchy of power that systematically privileges men at the expense of women (expends women for the sake of men): a hierarchy of difference which sets men up as the collective subject of sight and speech (the free speech of the pornographer's vision) and women as the collective object of this vision, this speech. Man as sexual spectator-speculator and Woman as the prescribed social sight/cite/site of male spectatorship and speculation.[10]

* * *

The body-object, which circulates in postmodern discourse, has the same function as the body-object of pornography. It designates the same phallogocentric subject (Lyotard's hero of knowledge and liberty);[11] the same logic of domination that slips so seamlessly between desire and destruction, pleasure and power, jouissance and death; and the same "world-operating table" upon which "the strong-box"[12] of women's bodies are eviscerated of mind, speech, history, and value by being displayed, interrogated, mutilated, penetrated, and destroyed.

> I undress her, I bathe her, I stroke her, I sleep beside her—but I might equally well tie her to a chair and beat her, it would be no less intimate.[13]

* * *

Pornography merely reinforces and repeats ad nauseam and with overstated graphic detail one of the key structural and practical truth/effects of the ruling régime of representation: opening up positions for a seeing and speaking subject who is posited like God as both *male* and *absent* from the world of objects he puts into play; a subject not, therefore, implicated by what he sees and speaks, nor responsible for it neither for the status of the object *qua* object—*qua* woman *qua* sex *qua* object in the case of pornography—nor for his own relationship to the object *qua* subject *qua* Man.

Pornography thus simultaneously subjectifies men and masculinity and masculinizes subjectivity (agency, will, desire, speech, sight) and objectifies women (silences, passifies, and frames women) and feminizes objectivity separating thereby Subject from Object (Man from Woman), Mind from Body (masculine from feminine), and the Eye/I of the beholder from the observable world he speaks and sees and offers up as object for the collective pleasure and perusal of other similarly positioned subjects. There is of course nothing new about this. And this is really the point I want to make about pornography. The presumption of the position of the disembodied Eye/I is the esteemed and prescribed method of scientific objectivity and has been the mark of rationality and Reason since at least the time of Plato. Perhaps even earlier, for as I have argued elsewhere,[14] it is tempting to regard Pygmalion, who was disgusted by real women and only happy with the statues created by himself in his studio, as the prototype of the pornographer, of what I called there the Pornographic Eye/I.

The Pornographic Eye/I is a spectator-subject who, implicitly if not explicitly, disowns his own relationship to the flesh and to the local and historical specificities of his own socially privileged sex, gender, and body; who denies and disavows his plenitude, that is, what he *is* and *has*, rather than what he lacks; by not acknowledging the specificities of the particular place, the particular body, the particular history, and the particular interests from which he sees and speaks, and the connectedness of these with what is spoken, and by externalizing, reifying, and circulating his own facticity as and onto the objectified Body of the Other, of Woman, with which there can be and is no reciprocal sighting/siting or speech.

* * *

The postmodern condition comes into focus from the perspective of this seeing but unseen Eye/I, this Pornographic Eye/I, from the perspective of the traditional Subject who is no longer in control of the symbolic, of meaning, of hegemonic discourse; whose unity and identity have been disrupted and dispersed across several different competing organizing discourses (medicine, bureaucracy, mass media, technology) which position Man, the traditional unitary Subject, hero of knowledge and freedom, as Woman, that is, as the fragmented, undecidable, unstable Object of a series of discursive (power) practices articulated from elsewhere (everywhere and nowhere), beyond his mastery and control. The traditional Subject of our culture has lost his position of privilege outside the frame of the ruling apparatus. His words no longer articulate power or organize social relations, nor shield him from the particularity and contingency of what he knows and says. He is thus thrown back on his body, the traditional sign of contingency and particularity, of powerlessness and determinacy. And because he no longer rules this body, the body that is taking the place of the Subject in his discourse appears in his imaginary as dead, dying, in ruins, seducing and seduced—as total immanence eviscerated of Mind (the Subject).

* * *

The difference between hard-core and soft-core pornography—between rape and seduction, the interrogations of the torturer and the entreaties of the lover—is one of degree not kind: the former merely makes explicit the implicit intentionalities, meanings, and structures which inform and determine the possibilities and pleasures of the latter. Hard-core pornography is more chilling to me because the coolness of the gaze which contemplates the truth of the violence that patriarchy inflicts on women, marks as *absolute*, constructs as absolute, the boundary between his humanity and mine, his free speech and my silence.

* * *

I have the same experience of chill in the presence of what I have called elsewhere the "lyrical nihilist" tendency in postmodern discourse,[15] what we might call in this context the hard-core of postmodernism. This is the tendency which puts the body into discursive play precisely as a body on its way out: as a dead or dying body, a disappearing body, the body in ruins, the body without organs, the body-simulacrum penetrated by the various technologies of disciplinary power, and contaminated by all "the invading antigens of hypermodern culture."[16] This tendency in postmodernism is as compulsive and repetitive and as fetishistic (as narcissistic) as hard-core pornography in its insistent performance and display of the dominated body as feminine, as Body. Hard-core postmodernism *tells* in words what hard-core pornography *shows*—the expendability of women—as if it had already been accomplished, as if we women had already disappeared and died.

* * *

This then is what I mean by the pornography effect: the occlusion of the specificity of Man's speaking body by speech itself, by the speech that issues from it: the objectification of the "corps propre"[17] in and as the alienated and silent Body, Other than and external to the Subject, the knowing, seeing, and speaking Eye/I, which is posited as disembodied, as "le conscience de survol,"[18] and at the same time implicitly, if not explicitly, male.

Traditional discourses, which include contemporary science and sexology as well as pornography, achieve this effect—this occlusion of subject and object, of mind and body, of knowing and being, of Man and Woman—by naturalizing sex, gender, and the body and the divisions that have been built upon them as if sex, gender, and the body were objective necessities to which we must all submit and as if sexual identities, relationships, and practices flowed naturally and spontaneously from the configurations of the body—*including female immanence* (passivity, facticity, determination, subordination, embodiment) *and male transcendence* (agency, dominance, freedom). Postmodernism achieves the same effect—the alienation of the supposedly gender-neutral but nevertheless male subject from the specificities and particularities of his body, thereby guaranteeing the continuing social construction of male dominance, masculine transcendence, by *idealizing* sex, gender, and the body: turning them into floating signifiers, abstract symbols, and arbitrary signs that claim us in a second nature in the prisonhouse of phallocentric language.

In both cases (the pornographic and the postmodern, the naturalist and the idealist) the relationship and responsibility of the speaker to and for the spoken body is obfuscated. Pornography is more honest in its explicit designation of the speaking subject as male, as Man, and its recognition of sex, gender, and the body as *realities*; but more naive in its representation of those realities as *natural*—as objectivities confronting an "innocent" male subject. Postmodernism is more sophisticated in its systematic project of denaturalizing sex, gender, and the body, recognizing their discursive origins (formation) in a social construction articulated to the motivations and necessities of power. But postmodernists are less honest than pornographers in their systematic obfuscation of the masculinity of the subject and in their readiness to assume that because sex, gender, and the body are socially constructed and discursive, they are, therefore, *unreal*—and likewise the power articulated there. The unstable referent becomes no referent at all in this discourse. And the (disembodied, speaking) subject slips out of the picture once again.

Postmodernism, like pornography, is spoken by a subject who has no tolerance for ambiguity, undecidability, or difference, for the *contingency*[19] of being and knowing, for the particularity and instability of his own specific (sexual) identity—by a subject who thinks like a Master, that is, a subject who is still under the spell of the transcendental illusion which is constitutive of power and which he reconstitutes for himself every time he puts "the body" into play as a dead body, as "the" speechless body of an Other. The discourse of postmodernism expresses the same desire as that of pornography: the desire for (sexual) identity at any price, including the death of the differentiated body (of Woman, of the feminine, of female difference which announces male difference) if need be. It is a project of elimination which Lyotard rightly recognized in another context as terrorist.[20]

Postmodernism is in the process of erasing sexual difference by sleight of hand in its totalizing discourse of the undifferentiated, generic body, and in its co-option of women's bodies, of the feminine position, as the privileged figure for the instability and undecidability of postmodern Man. It thereby repeats and reinforces the strategies and effects of pornography: reconstituting the centrality and authority of male discourse, of the discourse which issues from the disembodied masculine position (external to the diegesis), and the corresponding silence of women: of the feminine difference that postmodernism is currently wiping from the discursive slate. Postmodern Man presumes to occupy all the discursive positions now. Now that the objects of the traditional Subject have started to talk back—women and previously colonized/feminized men, he moves in to claim their speaking voice for himself and as his own. Speaking of and on behalf of both femininity and feminism, he continues to marginalize, colonize, and silence our difference and our opposition, performing a "metaphysical cannabalism"[21] equivalent in its violence to the technological cannabalism of women's reproductive bodies and the pornographic cannabalism of our "sex."

From the point of view of the discursive object—of "the body," of the feminine, of feminism, of myself as Woman, as a woman—nothing much has really changed in the discursive organization of power, of subjects, and objects. Man is still thrown into a panic by the knowledge of his own embodiment—his own immanence, facticity, particularity, contingency—which he continues to disavow and project onto an Other: onto the discursive body-object (the feminine) of his speech. A body-object that he must always kill, one way or another, since its speaking back (its reciprocal sighting/citing/siting of he who speaks, of the body of he who speaks) threatens the integrity, authority, identity, and totality of the discourse in which it is spoken and the voice (the masculine voice) that speaks it. Hence the collaboration of postmodernism with pornography in the continuing social construction of male dominance in and through a discourse in which no body speaks.

NOTES

1. "No Bodies Speaking: Subjectivity, Sex, and the Pornography Effect" was first published in *Philosophy Today* 33, no. 2 (Summer 1989).
2. Michel Foucault, *History of Sexuality*, vol. 1 (New York: Vintage Books, 1980), 27.
3. See the "Rough Sex Defense" in *Time*, 23 May 1988, 44, for an illustration of how this discursive effect of pornography and postmodernism translates into very concrete, immediate, practical acts of objectification of the female body: in this case, seduced to death under the sign of "sex."
4. The cry of pain of the unwilling victim, the scream of orgasmic pleasure of the willing libertine. See Kaja Silverman, *The Acoustic Mirror. The Female Voice in Psychoanalysis and Cinema* (Bloomington & Indianapolis: Indiana University Press, 1988) for a discussion of Chion's argument that the cinema is "a machine made in order to deliver a cry from the female voice" (in Michel

Chion *La Voix au Cinéma*, Paris: Editions de L'Etoile, 1982). What cinema demands from women, Silverman argues, is "involuntary sound, sound that escapes her own understanding, testifying only to the artistry of a superior force" (77). I am suggesting that this is the effect, the demand, of all male-stream discourse, which is articulated from a position outside the text, outside the diegesis of theory.

5. See the discussion between Alice Jardine and Paul Smith in Alice Jardine, ed., *Men in Feminism* (New York: Methuen, 1987), 250–51. Also Naomi Schor, "Dreaming Dissymetry: Barthes, Foucault, and Sexual Difference" in the same volume (98–110).
6. See Claude Lévi-Strauss, *The Elementary Structures of Kinship*, trans. James H. Bell, John Richard von Sturmer; ed. Rodney Needham (Boston: Beacon Press, 1969).
7. For the "body without organs," see Gilles Deleuze and Felix Guattari, *The Anti-Oedipus: Capitalism and Schizophrenia*, trans. Robert Hurley, Mark Seem, and Helen Lane (New York: Viking Press, 1977).
8. As, for example, in Jean Baudrillard, *De la séduction* (Paris: Editions Galilée, 1979), and Arthur and Marilouise Kroker, eds., *Body Invaders. Panic Sex in America* (Montreal, New World Perspectives, 1987).
9. I was disappointed to see John O'Neill resort to "familism" in his discourse on *Five Bodies. The Human Shape of Modern Society* (Ithaca, New York: Cornell University Press, 1985). This is another text that illustrates all the strategies of postmodernism vis-à-vis feminism, femininity, and the undifferentiated body discussed in this chapter.
10. See chapters 4 and 5 for a discussion of this relationship between pornographic and would-be nonpornographic discourse of our culture.
11. Jean-François Lyotard, *The Postmodern Condition. A Report on Knowledge* (Minneapolis: University of Minnesota Press, 1984).
12. From Milan Kundera, *The Unbearable Lightness of Being* (New York: Harper Colophon, 1985), 234. This is another example of a postmodern text that laments the loss of meaning, loss of the social, loss of the real, of and for a subject who is clearly male but conveniently forgetful of that fact, and who, like the pornographer and the postmodernist, totalizes his experience of "the" human condition across, over, through, and by means of the expendable body-object-woman. Or, as he puts it, "From the world's operating table, the one where his imaginary scalpel opened the strong box women use to hide their illusory one-millionth part dissimilarity."
13. From J. M. Coetzee, *Waiting for the Barbarians* (London: King Penguin, 1982), 43. This novel is an excellent exploration of the relationship between oppressor and oppressed, between the interrogations of the body by torture and the interrogations of the body by desire, between "the lie that Empire tells itself when times are easy" and "the truth that Empire tells when harsh winds blow" (135), that is between what I am calling here soft- and hard-core pornography, soft- and hard-core postmodernism.
14. See chapter 4 in this volume.
15. See chapter 6 in this volume.
16. Arthur Kroker *Body Invaders—Panic Sex in America* (Montreal: New World Perspectives) 16. Kroker's work is exemplary in this respect. It is a symptom of the condition he describes and condones, as if it were new, true, and inevitable: a lament for lost seriousness, perhaps even for the "familism" espoused

by O'Neill, given his nostalgic reference to "the disappearance of reciprocity and love as the basis for human sex" (*Body Invaders*, 14).

17. Literally one's own body. From Maurice Merleau-Ponty, *Phénoménologie de la Perception* (Paris: Editions Gallimard, 1945), English trans. Colin Smith, *Phenomenology of Perception* (London, Routledge and Kegan Paul, 1962). *Le corps propre* designates the lived and living body of experience, the body as subject of both knowledge and action, "le corps sujet" as opposed to the objectified body, the body-object of psychology, science, and traditional dualistic philosophies. Describing this experience of the lived body, of our embodied (inter)subjectivity in the world, is the project of the *Phénoménologie* and all Merleau-Ponty's work. It is impossible to summarize its conclusions here, however, because they emerge progressively and through the practice of a systematic encounter between existential phenomenology and the presuppositions, contradictions, and aporia of dualistic thought for which the body is always a body-object (in both its idealistic and empiricist manifestations). Phenomenologists do not define their terms but engage in an infinite project of their refinement, constantly testing expression against the existence that is its condition of possibility and its end. A few citations from chapter 4 of the English edition of *Phenomenology of Perception* on "The Synthesis of One's Own Body" will, I hope, give some indication of the richness and difference of a philosophy, which does not take the abstract anonymous body as its object of observation and analysis but rather one's own body as subject and ground of our experience of self, world, and others—both as expression and experience.

> To be a body is to be tied to a certain world as we have seen; our body is not primarily *in* space: it is of it (148).
>
> I am not in front of my body, I am in it, or rather I am it (150).
>
> Our body is comparable to a work of art. It is a nexus of living meanings, not the law for a certain number of covariant terms (151).
>
> Our body is not an object for an "I think," it is a grouping of lived-through meanings which moves towards its equilibrium (153).

18. Merleau-Ponty calls the unsituated point of view of objectivist thought "pensée de survol," translated as "high-altitude thinking" by Benita Eisler in Jean-Paul Sartre, *Situations* (New York: Fawcett World Library, 1969), 158 and likewise by Alphonso Lingis in Maurice Merleau-Ponty, *The Visible and the Invisible*, ed. Claude Lefort (Evanston: Northwestern University Press, 1968), 13. It is the thought of those who "taking themselves for small air-planes" forget that "we are grounded from birth"; those who pride themselves "on looking the world in the face," forgetting that "it envelops and produces us" (Sartre paraphrasing Merleau-Ponty, *Situations*, 158). High-altitude thinking is totalizing thought which does not acknowledge its own limits as situated embodied thought: its own foundation and ground in the "corps propre" in relations with others, in the world in which we all inhere (and which inheres in us). It is thought:

> installed in pure vision, in the aerial view of the panorama, [for which] there can be no encounter with another: for the look dominates; it can dominate

> only things, and if it falls upon men it transforms them into puppets which move only by springs. From the heights of Notre-Dame, I cannot, when I like, feel myself to be on equal footing with those who, enclosed within those walls, there minutely pursue incomprehensible tasks. High places attract those who wish to look over the world with an eagle-eye view. Vision ceases to be solipsistic only up close, when the other turns back upon me the luminous rays in which I had caught him, renders precise that corporeal adhesion of which I had a presentiment in the agile movements of his eyes, enlarges beyond measure that blind spot I divined at the center of my sovereign vision, and, invading my field through all its frontiers . . . makes me incapable of solitude (*The Visible and the Invisible*, 77–78).

19. Merleau-Ponty's phenomenology is sometimes described as a philosophy of contingency, that is, a philosophy that takes contingency as both its point of departure and its intentional end—its value. As indicated here and throughout this book, contingency refers to the fundamental *materiality* of every human being and every act of consciousness: the situatedness, the "anchorage," of both being and thought (of both what is and what is known) in concrete, particular, local, and historical conditions in a world that surrounds us and is never still. Jean-Paul Sartre summarizes the implications of this as follows:

> Every historical undertaking has something of an adventure about it, as it is never guaranteed by any *absolutely* rational structure of things. It always involves a utilization of chance, one must always be cunning with things (and with people), since we must bring forth an order inherent in them (Sartre, *Situations*, 163–64).

Taking the standpoint of contingency means giving up high-altitude thinking, its demand for certainty and finality, and the divisions between subjects and objects, self and world, which this entails, in favor of the thought of the "corps propre" (see notes 16 & 17) and the ambiguities of its existence and its knowledge. This puts Merleau-Ponty and the philosophy of contingency four-square in opposition to traditional Western philosophies, whose terms and relevancies continue to set the political and theoretical agenda in our culture, for which necessity, and the certainty of Universals, has always functioned as the privileged term and the objective of its thought and action, that is, the necessary truths of history, nature, reason and fact; the necessary relations between means and ends, cause and effect, idea, and reality, reason and action, essence and existence; and the necessary realities of God and the Laws of Reason and Nature. The political, ethical, and spiritual implications of a philosophy, which takes contingency (le corps propre) and not necessity (la pensée de survol) as its point of departure and end and which acknowledges the materiality and ambiguity of being and thought and the relation between them, are examined in greater detail in Part III of this volume.

20. In Lyotard, *Postmodern Condition*, 63–64:

> By terror I mean the efficiency gained by eliminating, or threatening to eliminate, a player from the language game one shares with him. He is silent or consents, not because he has been refuted, but because his ability to participate has been threatened. . . . The decision makers' arrogance . . . consists in the exercise of terror. It says: "Adapt your aspirations to our ends—or else."

21. See Rose Braidotti, "Envy: Or with My Brains and Your Looks" in Jardine, *Men in Feminism*, 235:

> This sort of "metaphysical cannibalism" which Ti-Grace Atkinson analysed in terms of uterus-envy, positions the woman as the silent groundwork of male subjectivity—the condition of possibility of *his* story.

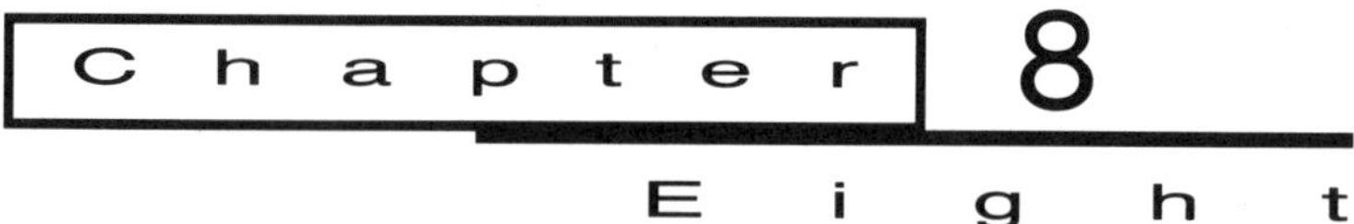

(Why) Are There No Great Women Postmodernists?

"NO BODIES SPEAKING: Subjectivity, Sex, and the Pornography Effect" (chapter 7) was written in response to postmodernism's discourse of "the" body (the undifferentiated, generalized, anonymous, objectified, spectacular, and speechless, and, therefore, pornographic body of no body in particular and every body in general), which continues to privilege the subjectivity and speech of the totalizing (and therefore totalitarian) disembodied eye/I of modernism and to reproduce thereby the familiar discursive and institutional hegemony of its privileged subject, Man, which the discourse of the pornographic eye/I both accomplishes and reveals. This chapter "(Why) Are There No Great Women Postmodernists?" is addressed to another moment in this (re)organization of (white) male hegemony under the guise of a *post*: to postmodernism's (re)constitution of the contemporary intellectual terrain in exclusively masculine terms, that is, in terms of references, relevancies, and realities exclusive to (and, indeed, constitutive of) that same old imperial subject—white (Western) Man. It was originally written for a conference on Cultural Studies and Communication Studies: Convergencies and Divergencies, which was held at Carleton University, Ottawa, in the spring of 1989. A flurry of publications on postmodernism had appeared about that time that included either no women writers at all and/or no feminism,[1] or one of the above, or an apologetic sentence or two in the introduction acknowledging this absence and marking it as a question *for feminism*(!). This essay identifies and names these practices of the (re)constitution of male hegemony in the name of the postmodern and shows how it works in the case of one quite particular and local example. It provides a point-by-point analysis of why this kind of work constitutes bad social theory and an outline of what good critical social theory should be, and is, doing elsewhere.

(Why) Are There No Great Women Postmodernists?[2]

This question, as far as I know, has not yet been asked.[3] I pose it now, not because I share its assumptions (that there are no great women postmodernists, for example) but to point to a process that is producing this question as one of its effects, under our very noses and even as we speak. The process I am referring to is an intellectual one: the process of production of *postmodernism* as a master discourse and discourse of mastery, whose mastery is accomplished through the active and systematic disappearance of women in general and feminism in particular from the framing of its terms and relevances and, correspondingly therefore, from contemporary descriptions and debates of and about culture inasmuch as it is constituted as postmodern.

At its simplest and most transparent, the process consists in the pumping up of the familiar male canon into a new "pantheon of proper names and authoritative texts,"[4] the old pantheon revised to include the new kids on the block: Barthes, Benjamin, Baudrillard, Deleuze, Derrida, Lacan, Lyotard, etc. These are names and texts that function not only as icons of intellect and intelligibility ("ritual objects of academic exegesis and commentary")[5] but also, and more importantly, as the gatekeepers and guardians of the intellectual Holy Grail: legislators and legitimizers of what constitutes "culture" in general and "postmodern" critique in particular.

Identifying the mechanisms and effects of these processes of exclusion, of the containment and mastery of the terrain of the postmodern for men, for Man, is the subject of this paper. My comments fall into four parts: a clarification of the term "postmodern" and what I include under its category; a description and exemplification of the processes whereby both the category and reality of the postmodern are hijacked to and for the old male canon (and thus to and for its continuing and relentless constitution of hegemony, inside and outside academe); a discussion of what is wrong with this from an epistemological as well as political point of view, that is, why it is bad social theory; and a sketch of what good social theory should and could be doing in light of the above.

POSTMODERNISM

I am using the term postmodernism to refer to the after of modernism, that is, to the world modernism has produced which modernist consciousness itself can no longer clarify, continue, or control. The modernism of and after which postmodernists speak cannot be further defined because the *question* of modernity, of its precise content, configuration, and effects, is in fact what constitutes and distinguishes the postmodern. "Modernism" designates not so much a coherent or completed project, period, or praxis but rather a continuum of being and thought that calls itself "modern" within which the problematic and possibility of a *post* modern has emerged as both a question and a demand. Since modernism (the appeal to and practices of the "modern") has taken different forms at different times (in the different contexts of philosophy, science, economics, religion, politics, poetry, art, architecture, music, and dance, for example), so, too, have the appeals to and practices of the postmodern. Nevertheless all appeals to and practices of modernism, to one degree or another, espouse and promote the values and ends of the Enlightenment: of Humanism, History, Progress, Freedom, Reason, Transcendence, and Man. And likewise all appeals to and practices of postmodernism *to one degree or another* (and this question of degree is central to the organizing question of this paper) put those values into question.

This process of questioning the values and ends of the Enlightenment, together with the perception of the inadequacy of the theories and practices of Enlightenment reason—of modernism—to clarify, control, continue or change the world it has produced, has precipitated a series of crises among our intellectuals. These include a crisis of *authority*, for example, specifically the cultural authority vested in Western Europe, its history, culture, and society; a crisis of *control*, specifically the control of nature and society vested in Science, Reason, and Man (in the face of a modern technology that seems to destroy at least as much as it creates and to control us as much as we control it); and a crisis of *faith*, specifically of the humanist faith in the ultimate wisdom, goodness, and salvation of Man. In his technological and rational prowess, for example; in the dream of the global village, which, in its reality, has not so much empowered or united its citizens as homogenized and pacified us, fragmented and totalized us, at one and the same time into both culture and the economy.

In the face of these crises of authority, control, and faith, postmodernists sometimes describe our own era as an Apocalyptic one, as one marked by a series of ends: the end of Man, Reason, History, and Transcendence, for example. Or more precisely as an era marked by the end of the master narratives of Man, Reason, History and Transcendence by which human experience and historical change have for so long in our culture been organized and understood according to a governing and benign teleology or logos (Reason) supposedly immanent within it (within Man, within History itself). In response to these crises and these "ends" of and within modernity, postmodernist thinkers and activists have undertaken a series of radical revisions and initiatives, including the following:

1. A rethinking of the relationship between reality and representation in view of the demise of the self-evidence of the old solidities: History, Reason, Freedom, Progress, Science, and Man, for example.
2. A recognition that reality is socially constructed as are the organizing categories (of history, reason, self, subject, sex, sanity, etc.) by which it is known and reproduced. (This is how I interpret post-structuralist references to the arbitrariness of the sign, the instability

of the referent, the disappearance of the real, the death of the author, the end of philosophy, and so forth.)

3. A reevaluation of the old polarities that modernism has taken for granted as "objective" categories of the real and in terms of which the real has been both organized and reproduced: the familiar, hierarchical oppositions of self/other, subject/object, reason/emotion, mind/body, transcendence/immanence, history/myth, knowledge/opinion, reality/illusion, individual/society, man/woman, culture/nature, identity/difference, order/chaos, sane/insane, etc.
4. A recognition that categories and the relationships between them are always contingent, that is, neither necessary nor essential but socially constructed and imposed as well as regulatory and productive of the realities they purport to merely represent.
5. A revaluation or rejection of those Enlightenment values by which modernism/modernity both animated and authorized its practices: the values of freedom, individualism, and autonomy, for example, taken to be the other side of alienation; of truth as transparency; of knowledge as information; of technology as control; of progress, change, rationality and man as the indisputable and necessary ends of individual and collective life.

The Hijack

How you respond to this crisis of the cultural authority of Western Europe and this rethinking (or rejection) of its old certainties—its "ancient compasses" as one canonized Canadian scholar once expressed it[6]—depends very much, of course, on your position in the Imperium over which it has ruled. And herein lies the origin of the organizing question of this chapter and the exclusionary processes it is intended to address. Those heavily invested in the terms and practices of the culture and institutions of the Western European Cultural Imperium, who believe or once believed in the various rhetorics and strategies of modernism and in the values and ends of Enlightenment Reason, may well find themselves in a panic, faced as they are with what must indeed appear to them to be the apocalypse: the end of the known and signifying universe (of the universe as knowable and *signifiant*), the second death of God. Faced with what they proclaim to be (as they confuse rhetoric with reality and the particular with the universal) the end of History as such: the death of *the* Subject (as if there were only ever One), the loss of *the* social, the disappearance of *the* Real, the absence of *the* Signified, the end of *all* Politics. In this version, which is increasingly the Authorized Version of Postmodernism in some intellectual locations, the collapse of the old certainties (of the modernist myths of Reality, History, Freedom, Reason, and Man) is translated into the collapse of *all* certainties and *all* possibilities of certainty and thence of *all judgment* (all possibility of discrimination, differentiation, and interrogation of and *among* histories, realities, freedoms, and men) into the position of what I have called elsewhere "lyrical nihilism" (see chapter 6): a position that (I argue) *abdicates* ethics and politics and intellectual responsibility in the name of their contemporary impossibility. The following citation from a recent collection of essays *Sojourns in the New World*, edited by Tom Darby, exemplifies this position.[7] Darby was a fellow speaker on the panel on "Critical Theory and Canadian Culture" at the conference Cultural Studies and Communication Studies: Convergences and Divergences for which this chapter was originally prepared. I thought I should read his book before delivering my paper to see to what extent his particular engagement with (post)modernism accorded with or departed from my argument(s). To my combined delight, disappointment, and dismay, I found it demonstrated my case perfectly, and it seemed appropriate to use it as a *local, particular, and concrete working example* (a book written and edited by Canadian scholars and published by a Canadian university press) of the general processes of intellectual canonization, totalization, exclusion, and mastery which are the focus of this chapter. So although Tom Darby's book does not itself figure in the "seminal" debates within and about (post)modernism, and is in fact a self-evidently "modernist" text according to the criteria laid down above, it nevertheless illustrates *precisely* the kind of institutional and discursive hijacking of the contemporary critical intellectual terrain *for men/for Man*—the traditional would-be universal Man of the old world, with which I am concerned. Here is what Darby has to say about "the post-modern man":

> Today, if a person is not a nihilist he can be one of only three things. First, he can simply be ignorant of the New World. . . . Secondly, he can know of it yet . . . misunderstand it. Thirdly, he can know of it and deny it. The first is naive, the second foolish, the third cowardly.[8]

From the standpoint of this subject, this masculine subject as the pronouns make clear, the collapse of the old modernist project leaves only one option: nihilism. Any other attitude or sentiment amounts to naivete, foolishness, or cowardice. Note, however, how the speaker, while purporting to describe the exigencies of the *New* World, the *post* modern world, does so from the standpoint of the traditional subject of the old: from the standpoint of a universal pre-feminist, pre–post-colonial subject for whom all are One and One is always He.

Those of us not so heavily invested in nor so well served by the values and ends of modernism may well find much to celebrate and affirm in the collapse of its authority and control. For it would seem to open up spaces in culture and consciousness where we can speak, hear, and recognize other and heretofore subordinated histories, realities, reasons, subjectivities, knowledges, and values, which have been silenced and suppressed and certainly excluded from the formulations and determinations of the old modernist project. In Canada, for example, where I happen to be living, the postmodern condition (that is, the breakdown of the authority of modernism) consists of, among other things: the emergence of the particular voices and political presence of women, Quebec, aboriginal peoples, gays, lesbians, and blacks; of what English Canadians who live in Ontario call the "regions"; of what white Anglo-Saxon Canadians refer to as "ethnic" groups. That is, the postmodern condition in Canada consists in the emergence of what Linda Hutcheons has called the ex-centric voices of the borders and boundaries of Canada,[9] or as I have come to think of it, the voices of those who do not live in Toronto. Canada thus exemplifies one aspect of the postmodern scene: both constituting and constituted by the disappearance and fragmentation of the unitary Imperial Subject of Western Europe, that universal Man with his singular and monotonous History, Civilization, Reality, and Truth from which many of those who now call themselves Canadian (including myself) once fled.

It is of some concern to me, therefore, that the increasingly hegemonic voice of the Canadian postmodern, the voice that is claiming and controlling the category and thereby the rites of inclusion and exclusion into and from the theories, practices, *and places* it organizes, is not the plural, varied, eccentric, and changing voice(s) of Canada but the familiar voice of Imperium: of a Canada hitched to and thereby disappeared into the Western Imperium itself by way of an already familiar canon of Canadian spokesmen: George Grant, Harold Innis, Marshall McLuhan, Northrop Frye. It is the unsituated (and therefore the decidedly un–postmodern) voice of what Canadian author Margaret Atwood once called the "free floating . . . citizen of the world." It is a totalizing voice that presumes to speak on behalf of and in the name of, (and here the phrases are taken from *The Postmodern Scene: Excremental Culture and Hyper-Aesthetics*, edited by Arthur Kroker & David Cook (Montreal: New World Perspectives, 1986) Western civilization, modern culture, the European mind, the Western Mind, modern experience, Western experience, modern self-consciousness, the citizen of this world, our culture. The same voice speaks less duplicitously perhaps in *Sojourns in the New World* edited by Tom Darby (Ottawa: Carleton University Press, 1986) in the name of the truly modern man, multinational man, the Last man, the masters of the earth, and most apt of all, in the name of the "experience of being a man."[10] Let us listen as one of these voices describes the postmodern condition from *his* point of view, and it is clearly *his*, not hers, as we will see—a condition and a description that is subsequently situated and interpreted within the text in terms of the historic realization of Hegel's Universal and Homogenous State.

> In the practical and everyday manifestation of the New World one can take a taxi down a Los Angeles freeway, catch a plane, and in less than ten hours be in Tokyo. One can stay at the Hilton, ring room service and have a meal of fresh sushi and chilled Rhine wine. When finished one can have a cognac along with Kenyan coffee, puff on a true Havana cigar, and while clad in a pair of genuine American Levis, throw a careless leg over the arm of a crafted piece of Danish furniture. The next day one can take the bullet train to Kyoto and have lunch at McDonald's next to an ancient Buddhist shrine. When this stay is over, one can fly to Toronto, take a taxi home to a California-style modern house between the English Tudor and the French Provincial homes of the neighbours, and relax in one's own hot tub that sits between a big stone and a Mugo pine in the glassed-in Japanese garden.[11]

Well, one can, can one? Who is this "one," this subject of the postmodern, for whom these are the "practical and everyday manifestations of the New World" and who presumes as "one" to speak for us all?

According to Fowler's *Dictionary of Modern English Usage*, "one" stands for "the average person, or the sort of person we happen to be concerned with, or anyone of the class that includes the speaker." The sort of person we happen to be concerned with in this case, the class that includes this particular speaker, though never acknowledged, is actually quite precisely specified in this text. It is people we may not have heard of before, with names like Peter and Michael and Ian and Tom, and other people we are presumed to have heard of before, with names like Strauss, Ellul, Kojève, Heidegger, Kant, Hegel, Plato, Rousseau, Nietzsche, Heraclitus, Deleuze, Guattari, and God. Need I say more?

Let us listen again to another speaker from the same collection of essays edited by Darby. Notice this time the instability of the repeated use of "one" in this passage. It does not always in this case stand for the class that includes the speaker, though it begins this way and the unacknowledged equivocation would have us believe it continues. In this case the use of "one" (and "he") makes for not just bad (plain, old-fashioned modernist) theory but also bad grammar.

> To be modern is to adopt a specific self-understanding or self-interpretation. One sees oneself as autonomous, independent of natural constraints, independent of God, and therefore free to create personal and social meaning. The absence of natural constraints is not, however, absolute. Human beings are not angels; they still have bodies. But for modern self-consciousness, one's body, one's gender, for example, does not constrain the meaning of one's sexuality: gay, straight or kinky, the options of an effectively

> androgynous existence may everywhere be displayed. Likewise the normal or natural consequences of gender differences have effectively been circumvented by the widespread use of contraception and abortion. And finally, what could be more trite than to observe that all this has been described and justified in terms of freedom? Why else would one leave the closet, take the pill, or submit to surgical therapy?[12]

There are no prizes for guessing whether this particular writer is gay, straight, or kinky, has left the closet, taken the pill, or submitted to surgical therapy. As Dorothy Smith might put it, the social relations that organized this particular text are manifest in the text if we have eyes to see it.[13]

Let me clarify what precisely it is that I am objecting to here besides sloppy English usage. I am not criticizing who or what this "one" actually is or does, or who its stands for, or any particular "lifestyle" it may represent (straight, straight, or straight). Though there may well be good reasons for doing so, from an ecological perspective, for example, or from the perspective of political economy or studies in development. What I am objecting to is the presumption, the inscription, the deployment of this "one" as *the* subject of (post)modern consciousness; as the sufficient foundation of a social theory that purports to speak for all of us: for "our culture," "modern self-consciousness," or even, and more specifically, "the experience of being a man" in the New World. This is at one and the same time an epistemological, a logical, and a political objection. I am objecting to the "indifference" of this no one in particular, this everyone in general: a category you can step into and out of as it suits you and that thereby effectively delivers (post)modernism over to the worst excesses of intellectual opportunism. It is an "indifference" that both marks and masks the specific (sexual, racial, and class) difference of the speaker and those with whom he is concerned as the traditional white male (subject) of the imperialist European civilization whose demise postmodernism purports to describe but from whose position of continuing privilege he, the subject, continues to speak. I am objecting to this "indifference" because it simply replicates (confirms and congeals) the rule of the (post)modernist techné it claims to critique, and the strategies of the "global village," the new Imperium, it purports to deplore in its totalizing and totalitarian erasure of the particular histories, experiences, and realities of those over whom that Imperium continues to rule. (The particular histories of those whose labor provides the room service, the sushi, the chilled Rhine wine, the Havana cigar, the genuine American Levis, the crafted piece of Danish furniture, the lunch at McDonald's, etc., which Tom Darby exhibits as the "practical and everyday manifestations of the New World"; the particular experiences of those who leave the closet, take the pill, or submit to surgical therapy, exhibited by Barry Cooper as evidence of his claim that "for modern self-consciousness, one's body, one's gender, for example, does not constrain the meaning of one's sexuality.")

Instead of resisting or disrupting the "desiring machine," the homogenizing régime of modern technological culture, this version of (post)modernism, its increasingly Authorized Version, merely exploits it and reproduces it in its own tendency to become global. You can take this brand of postmodernism anywhere in the world market of ideas (as Tom Darby obviously does), and it will continue to work for you, the "free floating citizen of the world." (It is in this respect that John Rajchman once referred to postmodernism as the "Toyota" of thought: "produced and assembled in several different places and then sold everywhere".)[14] This totalizing tendency of postmodernism replicates the processes and effects of television by disappearing people in particular into the seductive appearances, the simulacra, of every one in general (the one who takes the taxi home to his California-style modern house between the English Tudor and the French Provincial). It constitutes bad social theory (from a logical, epistemological, aesthetic, political, and moral point of view) inasmuch as it continues the modernist practice of *universalizing the particular*—over and over and over again, reinstating under the guise of a "post" the old modernist illusion of the bourgeoisie that takes itself for a universal class. In this sense it is a social theory that has forgotten Marx and therefore scarcely qualifies as *post* modern.

Bad Social Theory

More precisely then I am criticizing a certain tendency in postmodernism because it is not critical enough, if it is critical at all. In its tendency to go global, to universalize the contingencies of its own unexamined particularity and thereby disappear the experiences and realities of the many into the unified consciousness of the one of Western civilization (modern culture, truly modern man), this increasingly authorized and authorizing version of postmodernism fails as *critical* social theory and as *post* modern theory on the following counts:

1. It does not acknowledge the politics of knowledge: its location within a social context organized by and for systematic inequalities of power—of race, class, region, nation, culture, age, sexuality, etc. It does not, for example, acknowledge or examine the politics of its own knowledge claims and interests; nor the politics of the knowledge it chooses to draw upon as the context of its own thought and self-consciousness; nor the politics of that very selectivity itself of why Hegel, Heidegger, Kojève, and Nietzsche are *in*, for example, and Marx, Marcuse, Freud, and Sartre are *out*. It is particularly disturbing that so much of what passes for *post*modernism maintains a characteris-

tically modernist silence on its own relationship to the violence and violations of the Western Imperium whose demise it purports to describe: its relationship to the practices and effects of colonization, for example, which are so clearly one of the conditions of its own possibility.

2. More particularly for the purposes of this chapter, the totalizing tendency of postmodernism does not take gender into account, that is, sexual difference *and the difference it makes*, neither in its use of language nor in its conceptualization of its problematic: the History, Culture, Man, Consciousness, and Civilization that it presumes to be constitutive of the (post)modern world. Where gender is acknowledged, as in Barry Cooper's piece, the difference sexual difference makes is disavowed by way of the typically modernist strategy of division and denial, reduced to more of the Same ("gay, straight or kinky, the options of an effectively androgynous existence may everywhere be displayed. Likewise the normal or natural consequences of gender differences have effectively been circumvented by the widespread use of contraception and abortion"), or more of the Other (gay, straight or kinky, leaving the closet, taking the pill, submitting to surgical therapy). By the exclusivity of its inclusiveness, this globalizing tendency in postmodernism reproduces and reconstructs *women's absence* from history, culture, consciousness, and thought and thereby *women's silence* in its own would-be *post* modern discourse. A discourse which has been precipitated, at least in part, by the emergence of women's voices into history, culture, and consciousness as a political and theoretical force to be reckoned with—as a difference which does, indeed, make a difference.
3. This tendency to go global in postmodern thought thus fails to take into account its own contingency: its own specificity as both a theory and a practice, a description and a way of being, an ideology and a reality that is not always and everywhere the same, nor always and everywhere the necessary and inevitable consequence of modernism. It does not, that is, acknowledge the specificity and limits of what it claims to know and know as real, or the location of its knowledge claims in particular persons, places, uses, and times, in a specific relationship to power and desire, for example, which is constitutive of the presumptive subject of modernity.
4. The political effect of this kind of generalizing postmodernist discourse is not the promotion of difference and change or the disturbance of a "culturally suspicious trouble-making reader"[15] but rather the reproduction and reification of the Same: the same structures of atomization, fragmentation, alienation, homogenization, totalization,

and technological imperialism that constitute its own condition of possibility as well as the content and form of its own praxis. It is, therefore, neither critical nor transformative in its effects but complicit with and reproductive of the political status quo ante. Like all master discourses/discourses of mastery, it stirs up a smoke screen of *achieved universality* behind which lies a very particular (modernist) subjectivity with very particular interests and investments at stake. Speaking for modern experience, our culture, and the truly modern man, this tendency of postmodernism is both reassuring to the established order (of power and privilege, control and influence, prestige and penetration) and easily recuperated by and within it, precisely because it speaks the universal. Hence its hegemonic spread across, between, and within the various academic disciplines, the arts, and culture.

5. Postmodernism of this kind does not open up speaking positions for previously subordinated/silenced subjectivities and knowledges—for women, for example—in either discourse or institutions but ignores them (as in Darby above) or speaks for them (as in Cooper), incorporating them into its own seamless and would-be anonymous voice. It thereby forgets Foucault for whom speaking for others was the greatest indignity[16] and once again disqualifies itself from the *post* of modernism. On the contrary it continues modernism's sclerosis of privileged ideas into religions of meaning and its corresponding organization of political and discursive closure.
6. It is an unreflexive discourse that accepts no responsibility for the position from which it is spoken nor, therefore, for that which is spoken from it. It is in this respect a typically modernist discourse. In Sartre's terms it assumes the perspective of the *false* intellectual because it universalizes the particular, the particular sensibilities and realities of the petit bourgeois academic, the salaried intellectual[17] (his boredom, frenzy, and panic, for example), without confronting the specific contradictions (the suffering and violence) of his very particular situated existence.
7. From my perspective this tendency in postmodern discourse is profoundly ideological; it mystifies reality by presenting particular local and partial truths as if they were the Whole Truth and reifies it by presenting those local and particular truths as if they were the ineluctable, necessary conclusions of History itself. Or, as Althusser might say, the globalizing tendency in postmodernism alludes to reality—the reality of the lives of those who speak it—in an illusory way: representing the imaginary relationships of individuals ("one sees oneself as autonomous, independent of natural constraints, independent of God and therefore free to create personal and social

meaning") to their real conditions of existence (petit bourgeois academics, salaried *male* intellectuals).[18]

8. Inasmuch as it is ideological, postmodernist discourse is not just bad social theory. It is also, I suggest, bad for your mental health in that it actually accomplishes the death of the social it claims to merely diagnose or describe. Like television and pornography it is a discourse in which no body speaks. Like television and pornography it is a discourse that privileges performance over presence: its medium is the message. Its very form (the generality and anonymity of its address, for example) contains, organizes, and constructs its content and its constituency: a collectivity (or series, in Sartre's terms) of anonymous no/bodies (disembodied subjects of the gaze) organized by and around the spectacle of some body else made object: some body else who takes the pill, leaves the closet, submits to surgical therapy, throws a careless leg over the arm of a crafted piece of Danish furniture, and so forth. Like television and pornography the globalizing tendency of postmodernism seduces us by its anonymous and sophisticated appeal away from human presence and the discipline and demands of a reciprocating reality, into the simulacra, the appearances, the imaginary surfaces of its own performance. As such it disarms the already disarmed, passifies the passified, and pre-empts the production of the culturally suspicious troublemaking reader, which would be the minimum requirement of *critical, dissident* social theory.

Two recent Canadian inquiries into the agency and effects of television give substance to this claim that postmodernism, pornography, and television collude in the production of the death of the social, though this collaboration is not the explicit concern of the two texts in question. In *Cambodia: A Book for People Who Find Television too Slow*,[19] Brian Fawcett demonstrates how the implicit telos of North American television and the explicit logos of the Khmer Rouge in Cambodia converge in the politics of what he calls *genocide*, that is, in the obliteration of local memory and imagination (our only resources for struggle, difference, and change) and in the extermination of consciousness and the liquidation of particularity (as Sartre would say) upon which contemporary Imperium depends. Joyce Nelson in *The Perfect Machine: T. V. in the Nuclear Age*[20] develops a similar and supporting argument from a different set of premises. She traces the concrete and specific personal, political, and economic links between the historical production and dissemination of television and the production and dissemination of nuclear weapons to demonstrate how television and nuclear weapons perform, project, and produce the same *intentional* political ends: social death, the disappearance of the body, what she calls the "flesh-free" environment upon which the contemporary North American Imperium of patriarchal capitalism depends. Obviously I cannot do justice to the arguments of these two texts here nor can I substantiate my own suggestion of a collusion between television, pornography, and postmodernism (some versions of) in the active production of the death of the social (but see chapters 4, 5, and 7 for further details). I cite them here as counterexamples to the master discourses of postmodernism referred to above which are the specific focus of this chapter. For in spite of the fact that both of these writers are systematically and self-consciously engaged in a fundamental and radical critique of and disaffection from the authority, control, and faith of Modernism, neither of them invokes the category of postmodernism in their work and neither of them, correspondingly, is included within its canon, in the footnotes and bibliographies of its scholars. And this, I believe, is precisely because they *put the universal into question* from the standpoint and on behalf of the particular. That is, they insist on *embodying* and exploring the globalizing tendency of "Western" discourse (taken for granted and reproduced by the Authorized Version of postmodernism, by Cooper and Darby, for example) to disclose its specific, concrete, and historical roots in particular persons, places, interests, uses, and times and its specific and concrete political logos in Imperium—the continuing organization of power and privilege in the hands of the few who speak as "one." As such both texts exemplify what in my opinion good social theory, which is both radical and responsible (in the very literal meaning of those terms), should be doing and is doing behind the scenes of the mystifying master discourses of the postmodern.

Good Social Theory

In light of the above I would like then to conclude with some positive indications of what good social critique could and should be doing in the face of the collapse of the modernist project:

1. Producing counter-cultural theory and practice focused on *events* (ideology made concrete and practical) rather than texts (ideology made abstract and ideal). Critical social theory develops theory from and for the sake of the political and practical urgencies of the moment—specific, concrete, local and particular theory—and correspondingly struggles to resist the traditional intellectual trajectory of theory for theory's sake: theory for the sake of theoretical mastery, for the sake of the mastery of discourse and the discourse of mastery.
2. Critical social theory is committed to *interrogating the appearances* of the (post)modern world and *not* submitting to or being seduced by them: to interrogating the "practical and everyday manifestation

of the new world" as they reveal themselves to the likes of Tom Darby in the Tokyo Hilton Hotel in the shape of chilled Rhine wine, Kenyan coffee, Havana cigars, Danish furniture, genuine American Levis, or "the options of an effectively androgynous existence . . . everywhere . . . displayed" to Barry Cooper. It means *contesting* dominant ideologies and demystifying ruling representations (of the "everyday" and the "everywhere"), not throwing up our hands in despair ("if a person is not a nihilist"), or complacency in the face of its (false and falsifying) universalizing rhetoric. Fascination with the object, with the objectivity of the object (with chilled Rhine wine, Kenyan Coffee, Havana cigars or "one's own hot tub that sits between a big stone and a Mugo pine in the glassed-in Japanese garden") is not critical social theory (neither critical nor social nor theory) and is certainly no substitute for the concrete and specific *deconstruction* of it: of the object, of the objectivity of the object; and likewise no substitute for the investigation of its social and political conditions of possibility, its social and political (re)productivity, and our own implication in what it is and does. (How precisely, for example, is Tom Darby implicated in his chilled Rhine wine, his genuine American Levis, his Mugo Pine, etc.? How precisely is Barry Cooper implicated in the widespread use of contraception and abortion, coming out of the closet, taking the pill, submitting to surgical therapy?)

3. Deriving social theory from events rather than texts and from the systematic deconstruction of the objectivity of their appearances means revealing the *human presence/praxis* in the making of reality and in the making of its meaning and/or meaninglessness, in the making of the illusion of its universality and/or its end, for example, instead of obscuring the local and historical (racial, sexual, and class) specificities of that presence/praxis beneath the mystifying categories of no-one in particular and everyone in general. In the case in question, for example, it would mean revealing the identities of those whose unacknowledged, unspoken, and *invisible labor and lives* provide our would-be anonymous intellectuals, our free-floating citizens of the world, with their Havana cigars, their room service, their Kenyan coffee, and their taxi rides to and from the Tokyo Hilton Hotel, and with their flattering visions of themselves as having circumvented the "normal or natural consequences of gender differences," to be "autonomous, independent of natural constraints, independent of God and therefore free to create personal and social meaning."
4. Revealing the specific and local human presence/praxis in the making of a reality and in the making of its meanings necessarily entails a perpetual reversal of perspectives—of the world through self and

the self through world. It entails an *interrogation of self* as well as of the world of meaning and sense. In the case in question, it means calling oneself into question as, for example, a jet-setting salaried intellectual of the (post)modern world. Critically contesting contemporary thought and culture means critically contesting ourselves, our tastes, and our knowledge, inasmuch as we have been made both by and for it. It entails, as Sartre once put it, a traversal of the research through the singularity of the researcher, of the universal through the particular.[21] Deconstructing the object, demystifying the objectivity of the object, requires a corresponding deconstruction of the subject: in this case, for example, a demystification of his presumption of universality, knowledge, and truth ("Today, if a person is not a nihilist he can be only three things"; "To be modern is to adopt a specific self-understanding or self-interpretation"). Producing critical counter-cultural theory, interrogating appearance to reveal the specific and local human presence/praxis beneath the veil of achieved universality, requires the researcher to ceaselessly combat the (class, gender, and racially specific) petit-bourgeois ideology embedded in his own social formation, therefore, and his own sentiments and thoughts as these are made manifest in his everyday life: in his taste for fresh sushi, chilled Rhine wine, Havana cigars, and genuine American Levis, for example; in his assumption that his body, his gender, does not constrain the meaning of his sexuality—that "gay, straight, or kinky, the options of an effectively androgynous existence may everywhere be displayed" and that "the normal or natural consequences of gender differences have effectively been circumvented by the widespread use of contraception and abortion." *Whose* widespread use of contraception and abortion? The natural consequences of *whose* gender differences? Interrogating oneself as part of the process of critical interrogation of the reality and appearances of one's culture means being prepared to give something up in the interest of social and political change. It means modifying one's own sensibilities and thoughts as well as those of "culture" and "society" such as one's taste for sushi, Havana cigars, and taxi rides, as well as one's cheerful embrace of nihilism and the unthinking presuppositions of the sensibilities of a white, urban petit-bourgeois heterosexual male intellectual who thinks his experience entitles him to speak for all.

5. Producing counter-cultural critical theory also means resisting in our practice as intellectuals what Naomi Goldenberg has called the Apocalypse in Everyday Life,[22] referring to the progressive and systematic disappearance of people from each other in the routine practices of

daily life in the (post)modern world. Particular persons, histories, and lives are disappeared into texts, screens, and machines, for example, into bureaucratic forms and functions, and then again into the hermetic patois of abstract universals of those who would make sense of it all. Producing theory that resists this disappearing tendency of the (post)modern world means *revealing ourselves* in our work: owning the knowledge and experience we attribute to the (post)modern condition, and *taking responsibility* for it, our part and our investment in its production and reproduction. It means saying "I" and renouncing the use of the anonymous "he," "one," or "man" which only and always obfuscates the reality in question by concealing the local, concrete, and specific determinations of local, concrete, and specific thought beneath a blanket of impersonal generalization. Being a concrete, specific, and particular and thereby response-able intellectual means not simply reading the appearances and ideas (the simulacra) of (post)modernity against the appearances and ideas of earlier times immortalized in texts but investigating the origins and effects of those appearances in and on particular persons and populations. In the case in question, the case of the Authorized Versions of postmodernism as exemplified here by Darby and Cooper, this would entail some reflection upon the relationship of white male privilege and domination to the postmodern condition under review, together with some acknowledgment of the specific contradictions, violences, and pain particular to this particular privilege; contradictions, violences, and pain which must surely underlie that tendency to nihilism which characterizes so much of this kind of global theorizing.

Revealing oneself in one's intellectual work means acknowledging the politics of the work itself and taking a side, a position, in that politics. It means passing judgments and taking risks, both personal and intellectual. While assuming the (false) position of the universal global intellectual, the free-floating citizen of the world, allows you to avoid that and thereby to support the ruling order (if only implicitly) by reproducing its *ex cathedra* discourse of singular Truth(s).

6. Finally critical social theory, which aims to trouble the status quo and resist its reification of reality and politics, should strive to create space within theoretical discourse for the voices, knowledges, and realities of previously subordinated and silenced subjects, instead of continuing to speak for them as Barry Cooper does where he hijacks (appropriates) the experiences of Man's Others, of women and gays, for example (those who come out of the closet, take the pill, or submit to surgical therapy), for his own particular version of

what it means to be (post)modern. Critical social theory would, on the contrary, systematically avoid closure to maintain *the openness* of the world and its possible truths by speaking always from the contingencies, borders, and boundaries of its master discourses, its discourses of mastery, instead of from the necessities of its dead (fixed, still, enclosed) center.

Conclusion

Why, then, are there no great women postmodernists? What I have tried to show here is the process that produces the conditions for posing questions like this: the active process of *disappearing people* from the collective consciousness which interprets and shapes our culture and what counts as knowledge of it or even resistance to it. It is a process that disappears not only women, of course, though that has been the focus of this particular essay. It also disappears Canada as you may have noticed,[23] and the particularity of a Canadian experience of the (post)modern. And as indicated earlier, it disappears the labor and lives of those who produce the reality of the postmodern condition for its spokesmen and their illusion of its universality and/or end.

Dorothy Smith addresses these discursive processes of exclusion and their relationship to the ruling apparatus in her work which she calls "institutional ethnography." Ten years ago she described these processes as they operate in sociology. I would like to end therefore with a quotation from that essay, modified very slightly to highlight its relevance to the contemporary discourse(s) of postmodernism. Notice as you read how you can replace "men" here with a reference to any ruling élite, and "women" with any subordinated group and the description will work for the discursive organization of every and any hierarchy, hegemony or institutionalized order of dominance.

> Women do not appear to men as men do to one another, as persons who might share in the common construction of a social reality where that is essentially an ideological construction. There is, we discovered a circle effect—men attend to and treat as significant what men say and have said. The circle of men whose writing and talk has been significant to one another extends back in time as far as our records reach. What men were doing has been relevant to men, was written by men about men for men. Men listened and listen to what one another say. A tradition is formed, traditions form, in a discourse with the past within the present. The themes, problematics, assumptions, metaphors, and images form as the circle of those present draws upon the work of those speaking from the past and builds it up to project it into the future. From the circle women have been almost entirely excluded. When admitted, it has been only by special li-

> cence, and as individuals, never as representatives of their sex. They could share in this circle only by receiving its terms and relevances. These have been and still are to a large extent the terms and relevances of a discourse among men.[24]

For those of you who are still wondering whether there are any (great) women postmodernists, I have attached a bibliography to help you decide.[25] It consists entirely of women's names and women's writing and is a partial (and now rather dated) list of what is available, the likes of which has provided the context (not the canon) of my own reflections over the last twenty years. I suggest you read *all* of these titles and only books by women until you are through. In the meantime do all your research and writing entirely in the terms and relevancies of this discourse among women (not all of whom are dead or European). I predict that before long you will see more to being human, or even to being a man, than the options currently on offer from the Orthodox Versions of Postmodernism: the lyrical nihilism of those who bespeak the end of modernity (History, Freedom, and Man), exemplified here, perhaps, by Tom Darby, or the nostalgic rationalism of those who would revive its dead and dying social body, exemplified perhaps by Barry Cooper. Well, why not? You obviously have nothing to lose. Or do you? That is the question I would like you to think about as you consider this discourse of (post)modernism among women.

BIBLIOGRAPHY

For the reasons discussed in the Introduction, I have included in this bibliography only works signed or cosigned as written by women. Since it combines entries about feminism, theories of reading, and post-modernism, it is for practical reasons mostly limited to works I have drawn on in some way for the essays in this book. Essays published in anthologies are not listed separately under their authors' names.

From *The Pirate's Fiancée, Feminism Reading Postmodernism* Meaghan Morris, (London: Verso, 1988).

Abel, Elizabeth, ed. *Writing and Sexual Difference*. Brighton, 1982.

Allen, Judith, and Elizabeth Grosz ed. *Feminism and the Body. Australian Feminist Studies* 5 (1987).

Allen, Judith, and Paul Patton, eds. *Beyond Marxism? Interventions After Marx*. Sydney, 1983.

Atkinson, Ti-Grace. *Amazon Odyssey*. New York, 1974.

Bell, Diane. *Daughters of the Dreaming*. Melbourne, 1983.

Bergstrom, Janet. "Enunciation and Sexual Difference (Part 1)." *Camera Obscura* 3–4 (1979).

Bergstrom, Janet. "Violence and Enunciation." *Camera Obscura* 8/9/10 (1982).

Bergstrom, Janet. "Androids and Androgyny." *Camera Obscura* 15 (1986).

Bernstein, Cheryl. "Performance as News: Notes on an Intermedia Guerilla Art Group." In *Performance in Postmodern Culture*, edited by Michel Benamou and Charles Caramello. Milwaukee, 1977.

Braidotti, Rosi. *Feminisme et philosophie: La philosophie contemporaine comme critique du pouvoir par rapport à la pensée féministe*. Université de Paris-1, 1981.

Brooke-Rose, Christine. *A Rhetoric of the Unreal*. Cambridge, 1981.

Brown, Denise Scott; Steven Izenour; and Robert Venturi. *Learning from Las Vegas: The Forgotten Symbolism of Architectural Form*. Cambridge, Mass., and London, 1977.

Bruno, Giuliana. "Postmodernism and *Blade Runner*." *October* 41 (1987).

Bruss, Elizabeth W. *Beautiful Theories: The Spectacle of Discourse in Contemporary Criticism*. Baltimore and London, 1982.

Burchill, Louise. "Either/Or: Peripeteia of an Alternative in Jean Baudrillard's *De la séduction*." In *Seduced and Abandoned: The Baudrillard Scene*, edited by André Frankovits. Sydney, 1984.

Cameron, Deborah. *Feminism and Linguistic Theory*. London, 1985.

Chow, Rey. "Rereading Mandarin Ducks and Butterflies: A Response to the 'Postmodern' Condition." *Cultural Critique* 5 (1986–87).

Cixous, Hélène, et al. *La Venue à l'écriture*. Paris, 1977.

Clément, Catherine, and Hélène Cixous. *La Jeune Née*. Paris, 1975.

Clément, Catherine. *Miroirs du sujet*. Paris, 1975.

Clément, Catherine. *Les Fils de Freud sont fatigués*. Paris, 1978; *The Weary Sons of Freud*. London, 1987.

Clément, Catherine. *Vies et légendes de Jacques Lacan*. Paris, 1981; *The Lives and Legends of Jacques Lacan*. New York, 1983.

Collins, Felicity. "A (Sad) Song of the Body," *Screen* 28, no. 1 (1987).

Cornillon, Susan Koppelman. *Images of Women in Fiction: Feminist Perspectives*. Ohio, 1972.

Coventry, Virginia. *The Critical Distance: Work with Photography/Politics/Writing*. Sydney, 1986.

Coward, Rosalind. *Female Desire*. London, 1984.

Coward, Rosalind, and John Ellis. *Language and Materialism: Developments in Semiology and the Theory of the Subject*. London, 1977.

Creed, Barbara. "From Here to Modernity—Feminism and Postmodernism." *Screen* 28, no. 2 (1987).

Daly, Mary. *Beyond God the Father; Towards a Philosophy of Women's Liberation*. Boston, 1973.

Daly Mary. *Gyn/Ecology: The Metaethics of Radical Feminism*. Boston, 1978.

Davidson, Robyn. *Tracks*. London, 1980.

Delphy, Christine. *The Main Enemy: A Materialist Analysis of Women's Oppression*. London, 1977.

Doane, Mary Ann. "Woman's Stake: Filming the Female Body." *October* 17 (1981).

Doane, Mary Ann. "Film and the Masquerade: Theorizing the Female Spectator." *Screen* 23, no. 24 (1982).

Doane, Mary Ann. "When the Direction of the Force Acting on the Body Is Changed: The Moving Image." *Wide Angle* 7, nos. 1–2 (1985).

Doane, Mary Ann. *The Desire to Desire: The Woman's Film of the 1940s*. Indiana, 1987.

Dubreuil-Blondin, Nicole. "Feminism and Modernism: Paradoxes." In *Modernism*

and Modernity, edited by Benjamin Buchloh, et al. Nova Scotia, 1983.
Duras, Marguerite, and Xavière Gauthier. *Les Parleuses*. Paris, 1974.
Ecker, Gisela, ed. *Feminist Aesthetics*. London, 1985.
Eisenstein, Hester, and Alice Jardine, eds. *The Future of Difference*. Boston, 1980.
Ellmann, Mary. *Thinking about Women*. London, 1985.
Ewen, Elizabeth, and Stuart Ewen. *Channels of Desire: Mass Images and the Shaping of American Consciousness*. New York, 1972.
Felman, Shoshana. *La Folie et la chose littéraire*. Paris, 1978; *Writing and Madness*. Ithaca, 1986.
Felman, Shoshana, ed. "Literature and Psychoanalysis, the Question of Reading: Otherwise." *Yale French Studies* 55–6, 1977.
Felman, Shoshana. *Le Scandale du corps parlant: Don Juan avec Austin ou la séduction en deux langues*. Paris, 1980.
Ferguson, Frances. "The Nuclear Sublime." *Diacritics* 14, no. 2 (1984).
Fraser, Nancy. "The French Derrideans: Politicizing Deconstruction or Deconstructing Politics." *New German Critique* 33 (1984).
Fraser, Nancy. "What's Critical about Critical Theory? The Case of Habermas and Gender." *New German Critique* 35 (1985).
Freadman, Anne. "On Being Here and Still Doing It." In *The Foreign Bodies Papers*, edited by P. Botsman, C. Burns, and P. Hutchings. Sydney, 1981.
Freadman, Anne. "Sandpaper." *Southern Review* 16, no. 1 (1983).
Freadman, Anne. "Riffaterra Cognita: A Late Contribution to the 'Formalism' Debate." *SubStance* 42 (1984).
Freadman, Anne. "Reading the Visual." *Framework* 30–31 (1986).
Gaines, Jane. "White Privilege and Looking Relations: Race and Gender in Feminist Film Theory." *Cultural Critique* 4 (1986).
Gallop, Jane. *Intersections: A Reading of Sade with Bataille, Blanchot, and Klossowski*. Nebraska, 1981.
Gallop, Jane. *Feminism and Psychoanalysis: The Daughter's Seduction*. London, 1982.
Gallop, Jane. *Reading Lacan*. Ithaca and London, 1985,
Gaudin, Colette, et al. "Feminist Readings: French Texts/American Contexts." *Yale French Studies* 62 (1981).
Gould, Carol C., and Marx W. Wartofsky, eds. *Women and Philosophy: Toward a Theory of Liberation*. New York, 1976.
Gross, Elizabeth. "Derrida, Irigaray and Deconstruction." *Leftwright, Intervention*, 20 (1986).
Gross, Elizabeth. "Irigaray and the Divine." Local Consumption Occasional Paper 9. Sydney, 1986.
Grosz, Elizabeth. "Every Picture Tells a Story: Art and Theory Re-examined." In *Sighting References*, edited by Gary Sangster. Sydney, 1987.
Grosz, Elizabeth. "The 'People of the Book': Representation and Alterity in Emmanuel Levinas." *Art & Text* 26 (1987).
Grosz, Elizabeth, et al., eds. *Futur Fall: Excursions into Post-Modernity*. Sydney, 1986.
Gunew, Sneja. "Feminist Criticism: Positions and Questions." *Southern Review* 16, no. 1 (1983).
Gunew, Sneja, and Ian Reid. *Not the Whole Story*. Sydney, 1984.
Gusevich, Miriam. "Purity and Transgression: Reflections on the Architectural Avantgarde's Rejection of Kitsch." Working Paper, Center for Twentieth Century Studies, University of Wisconsin-Milwaukee, 1986.

Haraway, Donna. "A Manifesto for Cyborgs: Science, Technology and Socialist Feminism in the 1980s." *Socialist Review*, 80 (1985).
Hartsock, Nancy C. M. *Money, Sex, and Power: Toward a Feminist Historical Materialism*. Boston, 1985.
Hermann, Claudine. *Les Voleuses de langue*. Paris, 1976.
Hill, Ernestine. *The Great Australian Loneliness*. Melbourne, 1940.
Hutcheon, Linda. *Narcissistic Narrative: The Metafictional Paradox*. Ontario, 1980.
Hutcheon, Linda. "A Poetics of Postmodernism." *Diacritics* 13, no. 4 (1983).
Hutcheon, Linda. *A Theory of Parody: The Teachings of Twentieth Century Art Forms*. New York and London, 1985.
Hutcheon, Linda. "Beginning to Theorize Postmodernism." *Textual Practice* 1, no. 1, (1987).
Irigaray, Luce. *Speculum de l'autre femme*. Paris, 1974; *Speculum of the Other Woman*. Ithaca, 1985.
Irigaray, Luce. *Ce sexe qui n'en est pas un*. Paris 1977; *This Sex Which Is Not One*. Ithaca, 1985.
Jacobus, Mary, ed. *Women Writing and Writing about Women*. London, 1979.
Jardine, Alice. *Gynesis: Configurations of Woman and Modernity*. Ithaca and London, 1985.
Jardine, Alice, and Paul Smith. *Men in Feminism*. New York and London, 1987.
Jayamanne, Laleen, and Anna Rodrigo. "To Render the Body Ecstatic." *Fade to Black*, Sydney College of the Arts Occasional Publication, 1985.
Jayamanne, Laleen; Geeta Kapur; and Yvonne Rainer. "Discussing Modernity, 'Third World,' and *The Man Who Envied Women*." *Art & Text* 23/4 (1987).
Jennings, Kate. *Come to Me My Melancholy Baby*. Melbourne, 1975.
Johnson, Barbara. *The Critical Difference: Essays in the Contemporary Rhetoric of Reading*. Baltimore and London, 1980.
Johnson, Barbara. "Thresholds of Difference: Structures of Address in Zora Neale Hurston." In *"Race," Writing, and Difference, Critical Inquiry*, edited by Henry Louis L. Gates. Vol. 12, no. 1, Chicago, 1985.
Johnston, Jill. *Gullibles Travels*. New York and London, 1974.
Jones Lyndal. "Prediction Piece #9." *Art & Text* 9 (1983).
Kaplan, Cora. *Sea Changes: Culture and Feminism*. London, 1986.
Kelly, Mary. "Re-viewing Modernist Criticism." *Screen* 22, no. 3 (1981).
Kofman, Sarah. *Nietzsche et la métaphore*. Paris, 1972.
Kofman, Sarah. *Comment s'en sortir?* Paris, 1983.
Kofman, Sarah. *Un métier impossible*. Paris, 1983.
Kofman, Sarah. *L'Enigme de la femme*. Paris, 1980; *The Enigma of Woman*, Ithaca, 1985.
Kramarae, Cheris, and Paula A. Treichler. *A Feminist Dictionary*. Boston, London and Henley, 1985.
Krauss, Rosalind E. *The Originality of the Avant-Garde and Other Modernist Myths*. Cambridge, Mass., and London, 1985.
Kristeva, Julia. *Desire in Language: A Semiotic Approach to Literature and Art*. Oxford, 1980.
Kristeva, Julia. *The Kristeva Reader*, edited by Toril Moi. Oxford, 1986.
de Lauretis, Teresa. *Alice Doesn't: Feminism, Semiotics, Cinema*. Indiana, 1984.
de Lauretis, Teresa, ed. *Feminist Studies/Critical Studies*. Indiana, 1986.
de Lauretis, Teresa. *Technologies of Gender: Essays on Theory, Film and Fiction*. Indiana, 1987.

Lawson, Sylvia. *The Archibald Paradox: A Strange Case of Authorship*. London and Sydney, 1983.
Le Doeuff, Michèle. "Women and Philosophy." *Radical Philosophy* 17 (1977).
Le Doeuff, Michèle. "Operative Philosophy: Simone de Beauvoir and Existentialism." *Governing the Present, I&C* 6 (1979).
Le Doeuff, Michèle. *L'Imaginaire philosophique*. Paris, 1980.
Le Doeuff, Michèle. "Pierre Roussel's Chiasmas." *Life, Labour and Insecurity, I&C* 9 (1981/2).
Lewitt, Vivienne Shark. "Why Egyptian Mods Didn't Bother to Bleach Their Hair or More Notes about Parkas and Combs." *Art & Text* 3 (1981).
Lewitt, Vivienne Shark. "The End of Civilisation Part 2: Love among the Ruins." *Art & Text* 10 (1983).
Lippard, Lucy. *Changing: Essays in Art Criticism*. New York, 1971.
Lloyd, Genevieve. *The Man of Reason: "Male" and "Female" in Western Philosophy*. London, 1984.
Long, Elizabeth. "Reading Groups and the Postmodern Crisis of Cultural Authority." *Cultural Studies* 1, no. 3 (1987).
Marini, Marcelle. *Territoires du féminin avec Marguerite Duras*. Paris, 1977.
Marks, Elaine, and Isabelle de Courtivron, eds. *New French Feminisms*. Amherst, 1980.
McRobbie, Angela. "Settling Accounts with Subcultures." *Screen Education* 34 (1980).
McRobbie, Angela. "The Politics of Feminist Research: Between Talk, Text and Action." *Feminist Review* 12 (1982).
McRobbie, Angela. "Strategies of Vigilance, an Interview with Gayatri Chakravorty Spivak." *Block* 10 (1985).
McRobbie, Angela. "Postmodernism and Popular Culture." *Postmodernism*, ICA Documents 4. London, 1986.
McRobbie, Angela, and Mica Nava, eds. *Gender and Generation*. London, 1984.
Mellencamp, Patricia. "Film History and Sexual Economics." *Enclitic* 7, no. 2 (1983).
Mellencamp, Patricia. "Postmodern TV: Wegman and Smith." *Afterimage* 13, no. 5 (1985).
Mellencamp, Patricia. "Situation and Simulation." *Screen* 26, no. 2 (1985).
Mellencamp, Patricia. "Uncanny Feminism: The Exquisite Corpses of Cecilia Condit." *Framework* 32/3, (1986).
Mellencamp, Patricia. "Images of Language and Indiscreet Dialogue—'The Man Who Envied Women.'" *Screen* 28, no. 2 (1987).
Mellencamp, Patricia. "Last Seen in the Streets of Modernism." Hawaiian Film Festival, publication forthcoming.
Miller, Nancy K., ed. *The Poetics of Gender*. New York, 1986.
Millett, Kate. *Sexual Politics*. London, 1970.
Minh-ha, Trinh T. "The Plural Void: Barthes and Asia." *SubStance* 36 (1982).
Minh-ha, Trinh T., ed. "The Inappropriate/d Other." *Discourse* 8 (1986/7).
Mitchell, Juliet. *Woman's Estate*. London, 1971.
Mitchell, Juliet. *Psychoanalysis and Feminism*. London, 1974.
Mitchell, Juliet, and Anne Oakley, eds. *The Rights and Wrongs of Women*. Harmondsworth, 1976.
Modleski, Tania. *Loving with a Vengeance: Mass-Produced Fantasies for Women*. New York and London, 1982.
Modleski, Tania. "Femininity as Mas(s)querade: A Feminist Approach to Mass Culture." In *High Theory/Low Culture*, edited by Colin MacCabe. Manchester, 1986.

Modleski, Tania, ed. *Studies in Entertainment: Critical Approaches to Mass Culture*. Indiana, 1986.
Moi, Toril. *Sexual/Textual Politics: Feminist Literary Theory*. London and New York, 1985.
Montrelay, Michèle. *L'Ombre et le nom, sur la femininité*. Paris, 1977.
Moore, Catriona, and Stephen Muecke "Racism and the Representation of Aborigines in Film." *Australian Cultural Studies*, 2, no. 1 (1984).
Morgan, Robin, ed. *Sisterhood Is Powerful*. New York, 1970.
Morgan, Robin. *Monster*. Private printing, 1972.
Mouffe, Chantal. "Radical Democracy: Modern or Postmodern." In *Universal Abandon? The Politics of Postmodernism*, edited by Andrew Ross. Minneapolis, 1988.
Mouffe, Chantal, and Ernesto Laclau. *Hegemony and Socialist Strategy: Towards a Radical Democratic Politics*. London, 1985.
Mulvey, Laura. "Visual Pleasure and Narrative Cinema." *Screen* 16, no. 3 (1975).
Pateman, Carole. *The Problem of Political Obligation*. Cambridge, 1985.
Pateman, Carole, and Elizabeth Gross, eds. *Feminist Challenges: Social and Political Theory*. Sydney, London, and Boston, 1986.
Penley, Constance. "The Avant-Garde and Its Imaginary." *Camera Obscura* 2 (1977).
Penley, Constance. "Time Travel, Primal Scene, and the Critical Dystopia." *Camera Obscura* 15 (1986).
Petro, Patrice. "Mass Culture and the Feminine: The 'Place' of Television in Film Studies." *Cinema Journal* 25, no. 3 (1986).
Petro, Patrice. "Modernity and Mass Culture in Weimar: Contours of a Discourse on Sexuality in Early Theories of Perception and Representation." *New German Critique* 40 (1987).
Petro, Patrice, *Joyless Streets: Women and Melodramatic Representation in Weimar Germany*. Princeton, 1988.
Pratt, Mary Louise. "Interpretive Strategies/Strategic Interpretations: On Anglo-American Reader-Response Criticism." In *Post-modernism and Politics*, edited by Jonathan Arac. Manchester, 1986.
Probyn, Elizabeth. "Bodies and Anti-Bodies: Feminism and the Postmodern." *Cultural Studies* 1, no. 3 (1987).
Rich, Adrienne. *Of Woman Born: Motherhood as Experience and Institution*. London, 1977.
Rich, Adrienne. *On Lies, Secrets and Silence, Selected Prose 1966–1978*. London, 1980.
Richard, Nelly. "Body without Soul: On the Mechanism of Quotation in the Pictorial Materialism of Juan Davila." *Art & Text* 12–13 (1984).
Richard, Nelly. "Notes Towards a (Critical) Re-evaluation of the Critique of the Avant-Garde." *Art & Text* 16 (1984).
Richard, Nelly. "Love in Quotes: On the Painting of Juan Davila." In *Hysterical Tears: Juan Davila*, edited by Paul Taylor. Melbourne, 1985.
Richard, Nelly. "Margins and Institutions: Art in Chile since 1973." *Art & Text* 21 (1986).
Rose, Jacqueline. *Sexuality in the Field of Vision*. London, 1986.
van Rossum-Guyon, Françoise, ed. *Ecriture, féminité, féminisme, Revue des sciences humaines* 168 (1977)—4.
Rowbotham, Sheila. *Hidden from History*. London, 1974.
Russ, Joanna. *How to Suppress Women's Writing*. Austin, 1983.
Schor, Naomi. *Breaking the Chain: Women, Theory and French Realist Fiction*. Columbia, 1985.

Schor, Naomi. *Reading in Detail: Aesthetics and the Feminine*. New York and London, 1987.

Schor, Naomi, and Henry F. Majewski, eds. *Flaubert and Postmodernism*. Nebraska, 1984.

Showalter, Elaine. *A Literature of Their Own; British Women Novelists from Bronte to Lessing*. Princeton, 1977.

Showalter, Elaine, ed. *The New Feminist Criticism: Essays on Women, Literature, Theory*. New York, 1985.

Silverman, Kaja. *The Subject of Semiotics*. New York and Oxford, 1983.

Smock, Anne. "Learn to Read, She Said." *October* 41 (1987).

Solanas, Valerie. *The Scum Manifesto*. London, 1983.

Sontag, Susan. *Against Interpretation*. New York, 1966.

Sontag, Susan. *On Photography*. London, 1977.

Sontag, Susan. *I, etcetera*. London, 1979.

Sontag, Susan. *Under the Sign of Saturn*. New York, 1981.

Spivak, Gayatri Chakravorty. "Displacement and the Discourse of Woman." In *Displacement: Derrida and After*, edited by Mark Krupnick. Indiana, 1983.

Spivak, Gayatri Chakravorty. *In Other Worlds: Essays in Cultural Politics*. New York and London, 1987.

Stanton, Domna C., ed. *The Female Autograph*. New York, 1984.

Stein, Gertrude. *How Writing Is Written*. Los Angeles, 1974.

Stein, Gertrude. *How to Write*. Toronto and London, 1975.

Stern, Lesley. "The Body as Evidence." *Screen* 23, no. 5 (1982).

Suleiman, Susan Rubin. *Authoritarian Fictions: The Ideological Novel as a Literary Genre*, New York, 1983.

Suleiman, Susan Rubin, ed. *The Female Body in Western Culture*. Cambridge, Mass and London, 1986.

Whiteside, Anna, and Michael Issacharoff, eds. *On Referring in Literature*. Indiana, 1987.

Williamson, Judith. *Consuming Passions: The Dynamics of Popular Culture*. London and New York, 1986.

Wilson, Elizabeth. *Adorned in Dreams: Fashion and Modernity*. London, 1985.

Wolff, Janet. "The Invisible Flaneuse: Women and the Literature of Modernity." *The Fate of Modernity, Theory Culture and Society* 2, no. 3 (1985).

NOTES

1. Absolutely exemplary in this respect is Douglas Kellner, ed., *Postmodernism. Jameson. Critique* (Washington: Maissoneuve Press, 1989).
2. First published in Valda Blundell, John Shepherd, and Ian Taylor, eds., *Relocating Cultural Studies. Developments in Theory and Research* (London: Routledge, 1993) 123–52.
3. The question is anticipated, however, by Meaghan Morris in *The Pirate's Fiancée: Feminism Reading Postmodernism* (London: Verso, 1988), in her discussion of the absence of women's name and women's voices from postmodern texts written and referenced by contemporary male critics who, as is customary, cite each other and not the work of women, even as they lament our absence.
4. Ibid., 12.

5. Ibid.
6. "Our present is like being lost in the wilderness, where every pine and rock and bay appears to us as both known and unknown, and therefore as uncertain pointers on the way back to human habitation. The sun is hidden by the clouds and the usefulness of our ancient compasses has been put into question. Even what is beautiful . . . has been made equivocal for us both in detail and in definition." George Grant, *Time as History* (Toronto: Canadian Broadcasting Corporation, 1969), 52.
7. Tom Darby, ed., *Sojourns in the New World* (Ottawa: Carleton University Press, 1986).
8. Ibid., 4.
9. Linda Hutcheons, *The Canadian Postmodern: A Study of Contemporary English-Canadian Fiction* (Oxford: Oxford University Press, 1988).
10. Tom Darby, *Soujourns*, 134.
11. Ibid., v.
12. Barry Cooper, "Hegelian Imperialism," in *Sojourns in the New World*, ed., Tom Darby (Ottawa: Carleton University Press, 1986), 35.
13. Dorothy Smith, *The Everyday World as Problematic: A Feminist Sociology* (Toronto: University of Toronto Press, 1987).
14. John Rajchman, "Postmodernism in a Nominalist Frame," *Flash Art* 137 (November/December 1987): 51.
15. Tony Bennett, presentation at Carleton University, March 1989.
16. Michel Foucault, *Power/Knowledge*, ed. Colin Gordon (New York: Pantheon Books, 1980).
17. Jean-Paul Sartre, "A Plea for Intellectuals" in *Between Existentialism and Marxism*, trans. J. Matthews (London: New Left Books, 1974), 252–54.
18. Louis Althusser, "Ideology and Ideological State Apparatuses," in *Lenin and Philosophy and Other Essays* (London and New York: Monthly Review Press, 1971), pp. 127–86.
19. Brian Fawcett, *Cambodia, A Book of People Who Find Television too Slow* (Vancouver: Talon Books, 1986).
20. Joyce Nelson, *The Perfect Machine: T.V. in the Nuclear Age* (Toronto: Between the Lines, 1987).
21. Jean-Paul Sartre, "A Plea for Intellectuals" in *Between Existentialism and Marxism*, 249.
22. Naomi Goldenberg, *Returning Words to Flesh: Feminism, Psychoanalysis and the Resurrection of the Body* (Boston: Beacon Press, 1990).
23. This paper was originally presented at a conference of Cultural Studies and Communication Studies: Convergencies and Divergencies, Carleton University, Ottawa, in Spring 1989. It was prepared for a session on Critical Theory and Canadian Culture. The speakers were myself originally from England, Tom Darby originally from the United States, and Bela Egyed originally from Hungary—all of us speaking with the appropriate accents.
24. Dorothy Smith, "A Sociology for Women," in *The Prism of Sex: Essays in the Sociology of Knowledge*, eds., J. Sherman and E. T. Beck (Madison: University of Wisconsin Press, 1979), 135–87.
25. Taken (with permission) from Meaghan Morris, *Pirate's Fiancée*, 17–23.

Chapter 9 Nine

The Politics of Postmodernism: Postmodernism as Ideology and Effect

THIS CHAPTER IS BASED on a paper I presented on "The Politics of Postmodernism. A Feminist Perspective" at the annual conference of the Canadian Society for Hermeneutics and Postmodern Thought at the University of Laval in May 1989. It continues the reflection on the politics of postmodernism initiated in chapter 6 and developed in chapters 7 and 8. But where those essays focused on the political intentionalities and ends of postmodernism, this one raises the question of its *political origins*: the question of its material and intellectual conditions of possibility. To get at those conditions I propose a symptomatic reading of postmodernism that is a reading of postmodernism as ideology and effect—as discourse which (following Althusser's description of ideology) alludes to reality, albeit in illusory ways, representing "the imaginary relationship of individuals to their real conditions of existence."[1] In this chapter I try to get at those real conditions of postmodern existence by reading through and beyond their imaginary representation as the universal condition of nobody and nowhere in particular, everybody and everywhere in general.

The arguments of chapters 6, 7, and 8 on the political tendencies of postmodernism are the point of departure for this inquiry into its conditions of possibility inasmuch as they define the specificity of its object. Since I could not assume a familiarity with those arguments on the part of the audience for whom this essay was originally prepared, they were summarized or repeated in the original text. Most of these repetitions have been excised from the chapter as it appears here, but some have been retained for emphasis and clarification and to maintain the coherence and momentum of my argument.

The Politics of Postmodernism: Postmodernism as Ideology and Effect

I have written three papers over the last year (1988–89) exploring different aspects of the politics of postmodernism from a feminist perspective. The first (chapter 6) identified two political tendencies within postmodernism toward what I call "lyrical nihilism" on the one hand (characteristic of but not exclusive to the "French") and "nostalgic rationalism" on the other (characteristic of but not exclusive to the "German"). Tendencies which, I argue, converge in a traditional and thus decidedly pre–postmodern politics of totalization and what Brian Fawcett describes as "genocide," referring to the obliteration of particularity, of local memory and imagination.[2] The second paper (chapter 7) addressed the political implications of postmodernism's discourse of "the" body, arguing that postmodernism colludes with pornography to produce the same pornographic effects—the silencing of women and the continuing hegemony of disembodied male speech—by putting "the" body into discursive play precisely as a pornographic body of pleasure and desire, jouissance and death: anonymous, silent, seductive, and Other. The third paper (chapter 8) focused on the way postmodernism functions as a category and practice of exclusion, disappearing women in general and feminism in particular from the framing of its debates and thereby from the "postmodern condition" itself and the institutions, discourses, and sites it organizes and controls.

What I want to do here is turn my attention away from the political tendencies of postmodernism and the implicit and explicit intentionalities of its discourse and ends to examine the *political conditions of its possibility*, that is, to situate postmodern discourse within the context of power relations in general (between populations, nations, races, classes, markets, economies, languages, ideologies, and religions, for example) and recent shifts in those relations and in the relations between men and women in the context of those shifts.

The postmodernism whose conditions of possibility I am considering is the postmodernism which circulates with most ease and authority in academic and cultural discourse. It is a postmodernism which presents itself as a discourse *of and among men*, taking its bearings exclusively from the authority of men: Barthes, Battaille, Baudrillard, Benjamin, Deleuze, Derrida, Foucault, Gadamer, Guattari, Habermas, Jameson, Lacan, Lyotard, Nietzsche, etc. In this discourse among men, postmodernism refers to both a theory and a practice: that is to both a way of life (a condition of existence, the "postmodern condition") and a thought about that life (an interpretation of its meaning and value). At its most general, postmodernism refers to the world modernism has produced and at the same time to the recognition of the inadequacy of modernist consciousness for understanding, negotiating, or transforming that world. The modernism against which postmodernism defines itself and upon which it therefore relies for the specificity of its project likewise refers to a theory and a practice of and among men. At its most general, it designates the practices, intentionalities, values, and ends of the Enlightenment: of Humanism, Rationality, Science, History, Progress, Freedom, Reason, and Man. Practices, intentionalities, values, and ends articulated, organized, and accomplished exclusively and explicitly by and for white European men in particular, and in the name of that particular Man's accomplishments, potential, and power.

The postmodern condition emerges first and foremost then as *a condition of men*, and more precisely as a condition of Western (white, European born, educated, or identified) men. The closer your life is to the life of such men, that is, the more your experience of daily life coincides with or parallels that of an urban, educated, white, Western male, the more comfortable and *competent* are you likely to be with the various debates around postmodernism that are articulated in his name, by his constituency, and from the standpoint of his particular condition. Correspondingly the more your experience differs from that of an urban educated, white, Western man, the less comfortable you will be with its self-representation as postmodern and the less articulate, therefore, in its discourse, and so the more excluded from the terms and relevancies that organize its debates and the privileges and powers that accrue to it as the increasingly hegemonic discourse of culture and academe.

This then is my first political point: that postmodernism designates not so much a condition, crisis, or end of the History of Western Civilization in general as its rhetoric often suggests, but first and foremost a condition, crisis, or end in the history, authority, privilege, expectation, and experience of its *clerisy*. A condition of existence not of Everyman (and certainly not of Everywoman) in a postmodern world, which is always and everywhere the same, but of those very particular men who aspire to be the spokes men of the West and the legislators, legitimizers, apologists, and ideologues of its consciousness and culture. What then are those conditions of existence, the conditions of existence of Western intellectuals, which the totalizing rhetoric of postmodernism clearly speaks *from* but never directly to or of, and to which it must therefore allude, albeit in imaginary and illusory ways? What particular realities/relations of intellectual production does postmodernism at once reveal and conceal in its mystifying discourse of no-body in particular and every-one in general?

What I have to offer in response to these questions are a number of proposals—points of departure for further discussion rather than conclusions of an already accomplished inquiry. They point to recent changes in the conditions of intellectual production in the West and their effects on its product, that is, on thought; *as these appear to me* in my quite particular location (an Anglophone woman living and working in Quebec) and from my quite particular perspective (postwar British born and educated, white, originally working class, Ph.D. in European Philosophy, unable to secure a university position, etc.).[3] Each point I make calls for much more precise specification and is presented here as a provocation to thought and enquiry and not as the conclusion of an already achieved research.

1. It seems to me that postmodernism's apocalyptic discourse of ends (the end of History, the death of the Subject, the loss of the Social, the disappearance of the Real) and of the arbitrariness and impossibility of values (political, ethical, or aesthetic) has to be seen in the context of the relatively recent displacement of learned white men and the tradition of scholarship with which they identify from their formerly uncontested position of social and political centrality (as the authorized and authoritative knowers of the Real and the Right, interpreters of History and Truth, arbiters of Consciousness, Culture, and Society) by and for the always transitional and provisional instrumentalities and expertise of *Science* on the one hand, and the ephemera (the increasingly instant technologies and relatively disposable personalities) of the mass *media* on the other. In recent years and to varying degrees in different locations, learned white men and the tradition of Western scholarship they represent have lost control of the *public* space of authoritative speech and thereby access to the practical effectivity and social and cultural capital that accrues to it and that they once commanded.
2. At the same time, control of the university, the traditional *private* and cloistered space of Western intellectuals once dominated, defined, and determined entirely and exclusively in terms of the society, subjectivity, identity, history, intentionality, knowledge, values, and ends of learned men—has also been usurped from them (and from the terms and relevancies that directed traditional intellectual work); by and for the interests of governments, economies, and states, whose intentionalities and ends are in the last analysis determined by the unpredictable and always shifting contingencies of international markets and the exigencies of a capitalism that has gone global.

   The traditional clerisy of the West has lost, that is, both the public and private space that once authorized, legitimized, and enabled its traditional and specific praxis and thus the material and ideological conditions that *made sense* of its words/works, that is, that gave meaning and direction (*sens* in French) to their learning and lives; that made their abstractions *matter*—turned them into matter by materializing their ideas in and as the real. In the face of this loss of both the public and private space of their particular *sens* and their particular *raison d'être* (of the concrete and collective ground of their abstract signifying practice), we should not be surprised to find that so many of our learned men are now experiencing themselves as *de trop*: as decentered fragmented subjects whose History, Politics and Society, Meaning, Value, and Truth have come to an end.

3. This general condition of Western intellectuals is surely exacerbated by the fact that, while humanities departments are routinely and systematically underfunded and/or displaced within the universities, they are at the same time increasingly overwhelmed by large populations of relatively uninformed, uninterested, and undirected students for whom humanities courses are either prerequisites for other programs, a last resort, or a place to be because there are no jobs. Professors of humanities, who were nurtured in the pre–postmodern university with pre–postmodern expectations, values, and ends, may well feel that the History, Politics, Truth, and Future of Man have disappeared (for they and their students have no history, politics, truth, or future in common); and that, likewise, the Culture(s) they represent to and for each other are arbitrary, ephemeral, and unreal: mere simulacra of a reality that has disappeared forever, imploded into a plurality of floating signifiers, into the shifting fluidities of a thousand plateaus.
4. At the same time the halls of academia have been invaded by women who make up the majority of students in humanities programs. This means that learned men can no longer entertain one of their favorite illusions, that they are disembodied, sexless, universal knowers distinguished and distinguishable from women (and mere matter: mere matter as woman, woman as mere matter) by virtue of their superior intellect and uniquely transcendent subjectivity. On the contrary the specificities of sexual difference, the particularities of personal embodiment, the realities of gendered power relations, and the complicity of these with Western history, knowledge, culture, and authority can no longer be ignored by men in universities, nor obfuscated beneath the rhetoric of universals—of Man, History, Truth. Not in the face of so much female flesh that insists on talking back and with the authority of an ever-increasing body of alternative feminist and postcolonial knowledge.

This profound transformation of the sexual/textual politics of the university classroom, a historically determining and determinate condition of possibility of intellectual life, has obviously thrown our (mostly white male) academics into a panic as it threatens the legitimacy, authority, and practice of (their) knowledge (their Consciousness and their Truth) on the one hand and the material and ideological practices which have constituted their *masculinity* on the other: the masculinity inscribed in the History, Culture, and Consciousness of Western Man. The overwhelming presence of women in humanities classrooms has, for example, completely disrupted the traditional pederastic relationship of knowledge/power/love between master and student upon which learned men have heretofore relied for the reproduction and continuity of their privilege and power, so that contemporary scholars who once assumed the position of "eromenos" to "erastes" in their own pre–postmodern student days no longer get to play master to the next generation.[4] Deprived of this inheritance they may indeed feel bereft of the purpose, power, identity, subjectivity, society, civilization, and future they once assumed to be their destiny as scholars.

The presence of women in the intellectual arena also disrupts the taken-for-granted organization of academe into and by the traditional categories of binary thought: the oppositional categories of public and private, reason and emotion, mind and body, self and other, subject and object, for example. Categories that have always been articulated—metaphysically and metaphorically, in theory and in practice—to the hierarchy of the masculine/feminine difference which can no longer be sustained in innocence or as "nature." The collapse of these categories of opposition and difference has clearly left those who once genuflected before them feeling bereft of *all* categories of differentiation and thus of *all* standards (of weights and measures).[5] And so, it seems, bereft of History, Civilization, and Meaning itself. Postmodernism's apocalyptic vision of ends (end of History, death of the Subject, disappearance of the Real), and its corresponding (re)construction of yet another *grand récit* to support that vision (consisting of the recitation of the same old names: Plato, Aristotle, Augustine, Sponoza, Kant, Hegel, Nietzsche—they are all coming back into vogue) and the restitution thereby of the same old canon of white Western male authorities, can be seen as both a symptom of and response to this recent disablement/disinheritance/dislocation of learned men by learned women in the Western academy i.e. as an effort to reconstitute the traditional intellectual and cultural hegemony of Man, and so undercut the emerging authority, knowledge, and power of women that so profoundly discredits and disturbs it.

5. At the same time shifts in the international order of power—among populations, languages, locations, economies, races, religions, and nations—have displaced and/or transformed the material and ideological conditions of Western imperialism upon which the traditional authority of Western intellectuals depended for its plausibility and effects. And once again we can see why our learned men—defrocked and dethroned from their former position of Reason and Right—might experience themselves as *de trop*: as decentered, fragmented, or even *dead* subjects, and the conditions of their existence as a

series of *dead* ends. The relationship between the cultural authority of Western Man and the brutality of his Empire has become both increasingly visible and increasingly untenable in Western universities, leaving intellectuals nurtured in and for that tradition with a profound sense of both futility and loss—of having nowhere to go (no common sense/*sens*) and nothing to say or do about it.

6. One of the consequences of these shifts in the national and international organization of power is a radical transformation in the real conditions of existence—and consequently in the culture and consciousness—of the *students* and graduates of contemporary universities. And I think the emergence of postmodernism as an authoritative category of both the theory and practice of Western culture is linked to these changes in student experience as well. Western universities are now full of *displaced* students uprooted from their past—the past of their parents and grandparents (as I am, for example), with no place in the present or the future other than that which they can forge for themselves from the shards and tatters that come their way. These students have no obvious loyalties to the Western tradition, that is, to the canon and curricula of their university courses, and no shared history other than the fact of their displacement from elsewhere. They are, therefore, ripe for new and transitory/transitional discourses like postmodernism with which to define the specificity and difference of their knowledge and experience, their learning and lives, and fashion their always precarious and provisional community.

   Most of these students are in university to get jobs. (This is not a critical or cynical remark: serving the economy has become the governing telos of the university—its organization, ideology, substance, and structure.) And if they are smart, they approach ideas as they would any other product of (their) labor: as a marketable commodity whose (truth) value is as fleeting, as arbitrary, as its fungibility in the ruthless, volatile, unpredictable, and increasingly global economy in which they must compete. And this is as true for those with intellectual ambition and ability as it is for those without. For they, too, are obliged to hock their wares in a marketplace that has gone global and to tailor their ideas to fit those ends: for nowhere and nobody in particular, for everywhere and everyone in general. With no jobs, no status, and no voice, that is, with no institutionalized place from which to utter authoritative and authorized speech; with no ideology and no illusions of a rightful—national or international—cultural heritage or entitlement; these new scholars, who do not always look or speak or dress like their (white European male) elders from whose modernism they measure their distance, are indeed decentered, fragmented, nomadic subjects with no common sense (*sens commun*) other than the non-sense (the arbitrary *sens*) of their present and the indeterminacy and undecidability of the future.

7. Finally traditional (modernist) categories of political critique and the forms of resistance corresponding to them have little purchase on the political realities of the postmodern condition outlined above and certainly no appeal to the specific intellectuals of that condition who define the specificity of their politics precisely by the measure of its distance from their ancestors. To those who cannot see through or beyond the reality and politics of modernity (Habermas and Baudrillard, for example), postmodernism's repudiation of modernist politics—of its categories, values, intentionalities, praxes, and ends—may look like the abdication of politics *tout court* and thus the end of History, Reason, Freedom, Man, Meaning, Civilization itself. While what is really at stake here is a very particular practice of politics; a very particular interpretation of history, civilization, reason, freedom, meaning, and man, and a very particular expertise and authority in these arenas. Particularities that are obfuscated and thus mystified in debates about postmodernism which assume the totalizing categories of modernity as the terms of their own critique.

Instead of these various mystifications (representations of the *imaginary* relations) of the postmodern condition, I would like the spokesmen of postmodernism to address directly the *real* conditions of their labor and lives as intellectuals inside or outside academe. I would like them to speak *personally*, that is, reflexively and reflectively, concretely, systematically, and critically, about their particular experiences of the postmodern condition and to reveal themselves in their talk. Instead of disappearing those realities and themselves into the totalizing rhetoric—the ideology—of *the* postmodern: of *the* Western Mind, Western Civilization, History, Reason; *the* Body, *the* Subject, etc., I would like them to acknowledge the local, historical, political, and personal specificities of the position from which they speak *as postmodern*, as well as their *responsibility* for it: to acknowledge, that is their own investment in and collusion with the condition they describe and that which is spoken from it. I would like them to renounce the impersonal voice of Western Man, Modern Consciousness, etc., which obfuscates and mystifies the real (concrete and particular) conditions of (their) knowledge and experience, and to *own (up to) the (specific) experience(s)* of which they speak: The death of which particular subject? The end of whose history? The disappearance of which reality? Whose body is in ruins? Whose particular panic, frenzy, futility, boredom, and jouissance define the experience of the postmodern condition?

The spokesmen of postmodernism describe a profoundly unhappy consciousness and conditions of existence that are clearly intolerable since, apparently, they can only be ex-sisted as as series of (dead) ends. Yet the attitude with which they assume those ends—of nostalgic rationalism on the one hand, and lyrical nihilism on the other[6]—betrays an ambivalence in their experience and a corresponding duplicity in their descriptions. I am therefore asking the spokesmen of postmodernism to own (up to) the unhappiness of their particular consciousness/*conscience* if it is indeed theirs (or to confess the duplicity of their description if it is not) and the specificities of the conditions of its existence. Instead of obscuring and exacerbating them, and their agency and effects, by displacing them onto a universal (consciousness, condition, Man), which relieves everybody of the responsibility of paying attention to the particular realities that confront them and the possibility thereby of making a difference.

Twenty-five years ago Jean-Paul Sartre described intellectuals as men-in-contradiction—the monstrous products of a monstrous society.

> He has been a "humanist" from his earliest childhood—which means he was taught to believe that all men are equal. Yet, if he considers himself, he becomes aware that he is living proof that all men are *not* equal. He possesses a measure of social *power* by virtue of his knowledge become skill. This knowledge came to him, the son of a civil servant or manager or member of the liberal professions, as a *heritage*: culture resided in his family even before he was born into it. Thus to be born into his family and to be born into culture were one and the same thing for him. And if he happens to be one of the few who have risen from the ranks of the working class, he will have succeeded only by traversing a complex and *invariably unjust* system of selection which has eliminated most of his comrades. He is thus always the possessor of an unjustified privilege even, and in a certain sense above all, if he has brilliantly passed all the tests. This privilege, or monopoly of knowledge, is in radical contradiction with the tenets of humanist egalitarianism. In other words he ought to renounce it. But since he *is* this privilege, he can only renounce it by abolishing himself, a course which would contradict the instinct for life that is so deeply rooted in most men.[7]

I am suggesting that the spokesmen of postmodernism are speaking from and of a similar condition of contradiction, alienation, and solitude, albeit in an illusory and thereby falsifying way.

> Let us say that the intellectual is characterized as having a mandate from no one, and receiving his statute from no authority. He is, as such, not the product of a particular decision—as are doctors, teachers, etc., in as much as they are agents of authority—but the monstrous product of a monstrous society. He is claimed by no one and recognized by no one

> (neither the State, nor the power-elite, nor the lobbies, nor the organizations of the exploited classes, nor the masses). We can be sensible of what he *says* but not of his existence . . . if an intellectual's arguments take effect and are widely accepted they will be presented in *themselves*, without any reference to he who first developed them. They will become an *anonymous* outlook, the common property of all. The intellectual is suppressed by the very manner in which his products are used.
>
> Thus no one concedes him any rights or status. In fact, his existence cannot be admitted, since it cannot even admit itself.[8]

I am asking our intellectuals to acknowledge, examine, and assume responsibility for the specificity of the conditions of their existence as intellectuals, instead of obscuring it in the name and for the sake of a false universal—the postmodern condition—which caters to the needs of the ruling order and secures everything safely to and for the status quo ante. I am asking them to engage *politically and critically* with and against the experiences and categories of postmodernism, which entails not just a revealing of self in the description of the condition as argued above but a *calling of oneself into question along with it*: what Sartre described in the same essay as a traversal of research through the singularity of the researcher.

> The mistake of the *philosophes* was to believe that they could directly apply a universal (an analytic) method to the society in which they existed, when precisely *they lived within it*: for in fact it conditioned them historically in such a way that its ideological presuppositions infiltrated their positive research and even their negative will to combat them. The reason for their error is obvious: they were *organic intellectuals* working for the very class that had produced them, and their universality was simply the false universality of the bourgeoisie, which took itself to be a universal class. Thus when they sought man, they got no further than the bourgeois. True intellectual investigation, if it is to free truth from the myths which obscure it, implies a traversal of research through the singularity of the researcher. The latter needs to situate *himself* in the social universe in order to be able to grasp and destroy within and without himself the limits that ideology imposes on knowledge. It is at the level of the *situation* that the dialectic of interiorization and exteriorization is operative; the intellectual's thought must ceaselessly turn back on itself in order always to apprehend itself as a *singular universal*—a thought secretly singularized by the class prejudices inculcated in him since childhood, even while it believed itself to be free of them and to have attained the universal.[9]

Without this reflexive and critical moment, this *concern with oneself and the return of the unbearable reality*,[10] the spokesmen of postmodernism simply collude in and (re)produce *as universal* the conditions of alienation, anomie, death, despair, panic, frenzy, futility, fascination, boredom, etc., they purport to merely document or sometimes even oppose. They become what Nizan called watch-dogs of the dominant class, "defending its particularist ideology by arguments which claim to be rigorous products of exact reasoning,"[11] and what Sartre calls false intellectuals.

> They wear the appearance of intellectuals and also start by contesting the ideology of the dominant class—but their's [sic] is a pseudo-contestation, whose rapid exhaustion merely serves to demonstrate that the dominant ideology is resistant to all contestation. In other words, the false intellectual, unlike the true, does not say *no*, but rather cultivates the "no, but . . ." or the "I know, but still . . ." attitude.[12]

Speaking reflexively and critically from the local and historical specificities of one's own position makes that collusion with the ideology and politics of one's own situation both visible and available for contestation and change. It is not only less conducive to global thinking than is speaking the universal, it is actually a form of resistance to it and its insistent politics of final solutions: of liquidating particularity by obliterating local memory and imagination. Thought that is self-reflexive and situated in the specificities of a particular experience is *embodied* reversible thought (thought both seeing and seen, speaking and spoken[13]) and therefore less amenable to the bifurcations of mind and body, self and other, subject and object, freedom and necessity, etc., upon which the totalizing discourse of ends and final solutions depends and from which it draws both its legitimacy and power.

Finally *speaking personally*, that is, theorizing culture and consciousness from one's own practical position, from the position of oneself as body as event/advent in the world (which is different from speaking as or from postmodernism's *discursive* body—of nobody in particular and everybody in general which I discuss in chapter 7) and interrogating culture, politics and ideology through an interrogation of oneself who has been formed by it means never losing sight of the politics, provisionality, and partiality of what you know and see and of the fact that you can't see everything nor everything you do see clearly. It maintains the openness of the world (of the discourse of the world) and thus of the future (of the possibility of a future, that is, of difference and change) that the authorized and authoritative discourse of postmodernism—the ideology of postmodernism—so systematically obscures (obfuscates and denies) by (beneath and within) its totalizing rhetoric of ends: of nobody and nowhere in particular, everyone and everywhere in general.

I have tried to reveal the specific and motivating conditions of intellectual existence to which this universalizing discourse of postmodernism alludes (in an illusory way) in this chapter, to make them available for investigation, analysis, contestation, and change. And to set the stage for the chapters that follow, which take the particularity and contingency of knowledge and experience as their point of departure, as both the measure and means of an alternative engagement with the relationship between discourse and violence and its implications for an *ethical* intellectual/political praxis that can offer us more than more of the Same.

NOTES

1. From Louis Althusser, "Ideology and Ideological State Apparatuses" in *Lenin and Philosophy and Other Essays*, trans. Ben Brewster (London and New York: Monthly Review Press, 1971) 162.
2. In Brian Fawcett, *Cambodia. A Book for People Who Find Television too Slow* (Vancouver: Talonbooks, 1986).
3. This changed in 1990 when I assumed my present position as associate professor of cultural studies at Carleton University in Canada.
4. On the relationship between eromenos and erastes in classical Greece see K. J. Dover, *Greek Homosexuality* (Cambridge: Harvard University Press, 1978) and Michel Foucault, *The Use of Pleasure*, Vol. 2 of *The History of Sexuality*, trans. Robert Hurley (New York: Pantheon Books, 1985), 2: 196–97.
5. Standard, from the French *estandard*: standard or ensign; flag. *Ensign* from Latin in, upon; signum, a mark; that is, "with a mark on it" (from *A Concise Etymological Dictionary of the English Language* by the Rev. Walter Skeat (1882, reprint, New York: Perigree Books, 1980). Hence standard implies mark: A phallic mark? The mark of political correctness?
6. See chapter 6 in this volume.
7. Jean-Paul Sartre, "A Plea for Intellectuals" in *Jean-Paul Sartre. Between Existentialism and Marxism*, trans. John Matthews (London: New Left Books, 1974), 239–40.
8. Ibid., 246–47.
9. Ibid., 248–49.
10. I am citing Roland Barthes from memory here. I have been unable to locate the precise quotation.
11. Sartre, "A Plea," 252.
12. Ibid.
13. The reversibility of the flesh is introduced in Maurice Merleau-Ponty, *The Visible and the Invisible*, trans. Alphonso Lingis (Evanston: Northwestern University Press, 1968). Its political implications are explored in the following and subsequent chapters. For clarification of the flesh, see in particular chapter 10. n. 9.

Part 3 Three

ON THE FUTURE

Chapter 10 Ten

THE POLITICS OF CONTINGENCY. THE CONTINGENCY OF POLITICS

ALL OF THE PRECEDING essays following "Why Althusser Killed His Wife," which supplies not just the title but the point of departure and the problematic of this book, were written in response to specific requests for clarification of the ideas advanced in that polemic concerning the relationship between (intellectual/academic) discourse and (personal/political) violence. Each essay offers a symptomatic reading of selected aspects of modernist and postmodernist discourse (the discourses of Science and Sex, for example) to reveal the politics at stake in their various debates and the suppositions and effects of power—and violence—they institute and assume.

These essays were originally written for oral presentation, and most of them have been presented more than once. In the discussions that followed their presentation, I found myself increasingly called upon to provide an "alternative" to the practices and politics I critize (an alternative Science or Sexuality, for example), and/or to explicate the *possibility of alternatives* implicit in my critique, and the political and discursive position from which my critique is spoken. Chapters 8 and 9 begin to do this with respect to postmodernism, outlining a critical, political, intellectual practice that eschews the temptations of totalization—of what I call final solutions—which, I argue, characterize modernism and postmodernism alike, while maintaining a commitment to the possibility and necessity of political change and of challenging the status quo.

The chapters in the final section of this book respond to this call for "alternatives" more directly. They (re)present the affirmative moment of my critical practice, which takes its substance and inspiration from the phenomenological tradition in general and the work of Maurice Merleau-Ponty and Emmanuel Levinas in particular. These chapters were not written in response to the requests of others seeking clarification of what I had already said but in response to my own desire to say something new: to think beyond the categories of (post)modernism and to articulate a politics and an ethics that do not reproduce the aporia of the past but, on the contrary, acknowledge, inhabit, and assume response-ability for the openness of the future and the possibility of difference/différance and change.

"The Politics of Contingency. The Contingency of Politics" was originally prepared for the Annual Meeting of the Merleau-Ponty Circle at Canisius College in September 1989. It explores the political implications of Merleau-Ponty's ontology of the flesh and its relevance to contemporary struggles against racism and sexism in particular—two forms of oppression that are quite literally articulated to and inscribed upon the flesh, that is, upon the entirely arbitrary but nevertheless entirely real and in sexist and racist societies determining contingencies of skin and genitalia, "The Politics of Contingency" takes the standpoint of this flesh (the standpoint of the oppressed) as both its point of departure and its intentional end, giving rise to a politics that is quite distinct in its discourse and its practice from the traditional politics of necessity, which is assumed by both modernism and postmodernism (see chapter 6) and which I argue repudiates the flesh of particular and situated existence for the standpoint of privilege and power: of a disembodied spectator consciousness, of "pensée de survol," of what I call here "the Prince."

"The Politics of Contingency" returns us to the question of violence and its relationship to discourse, privilege, and power; linking violence once again with the politics of necessity—of final solutions—and the assumption of an identity and/or place *of one's own* (which one owns) from which others can be, indeed must be, rightfully "othered" and likewise rightfully expelled. Unlike a traditional politics of necessity, the politics of contingency offers no safe place for the politically correct, no guarantees of security or success, and thus no a priori rationalizations of the violence done in its name. It offers no relief, that is, from the *ethical responsibility* each one of us bears for *choosing* our relationship to others—regardless of their or our political status. The question of ethics and its relationship to violence, politics, discourse, and power is taken up and developed in subsequent chapters with reference to spirituality in chapter 11 and as the explicit focus of inquiry and with reference to identity politics in particular in chapter 12.

"The Politics of Contingency. The Contingency of Politics"[1]

What does this talk of flesh and chiasms amount to politically?
—Kerry Whiteside, *Merleau-Ponty and the Foundation of an Existential Politics*

The argument of this chapter is that Merleau-Ponty's ontology of flesh and chiasms moves us well beyond the terms and relevancies of traditional politics which I described in chapter 6 as a "politics of final solutions,"[2] which is the politics of Hegel and Marx and Habermas as much as it is the politics of Hitler and the Ayatollah, toward a radically new and yet to be articulated *politics of contingency*. By this I mean a politics theorized and practiced from the standpoint of *contingency* rather than necessity, of *ambiguity* rather than apodicticity, of the intertwinings of the *flesh* rather than the separations and negations of a would-be autonomous subject(ivity) or individual consciousness.[3] It is, in this sense, a politics of and for the "people" rather than the Prince: a politics of and for those whose experience of contingency, ambiguity, and the flesh cannot be easily disavowed (denied, distorted, or dissimulated from themselves) or mystified by the various rhetorics of transcendence, universality, and necessity that maintain the power of Princes by masking the ambiguities of the particular flesh that is the specific and contingent condition of their privilege. It is a politics that renders traditional political discourse redundant, therefore, to the extent that it is spoken from the privileged position (the position of historical necessity and final solutions, the position of the Prince) and to the extent that it relies on the traditional ontological assumptions of high-altitude thinking, thinking forgetful of its contingent roots in particular persons, places, and times.[4]

Commentators on the political implications of Merleau-Ponty's philosophy of ambiguity have, I think, consistently underestimated the distance of his thought from the ontological assumptions that inform traditional politics (of necessity), and likewise the inadequacy of traditional political concepts and categories for articulating the very different politics it implies. Writers like Barry Cooper, Sonia Kruks, and Kerry Whiteside, for example,[5] have measured Merleau-Ponty's politics against the yardstick of traditional political theory—against Marx and Hegel and contemporary "liberals" like Michael Walzer and Richard Rorty—and, not surprisingly, found him lacking. But this is surely to miss the point of Merleau-Ponty's retreat from and challenge to conventional politics, the very rationality of which is thrown into question by his ontology of chiasms and flesh: its roots in the ancient metaphysics of necessity—of consciousness and apodicticity, of affirmation and negation, of freedom and determinism, self and other, subject and object, etc., as well as its implicit telos toward some form or other of "final solution"—of achievement and completion of a human project presumed to be immanent in history.[6]

It is the argument of this chapter that Merleau-Ponty's ontology of flesh and chiasms calls for a complete rethinking of politics: of how much of life (and history) is contained within its category; of its ground in human being and consciousness, and of what in its light, therefore, constitutes the limits, scope, and "end" of political action. I suggest specific ways in which the politics of contingency is both broader and narrower in its scope than the traditional politics of necessity that frames Merleau-Ponty's own (explicitly) political essays of the forties and fifties and that continues to determine and delimit contemporary political debate in general, as well as the thinking of Merleau-Ponty's commentators in particular. My objective is twofold: to defend Merleau-Ponty from the common criticism that he exchanged politics for philosophy in his later years and thereby to challenge both the notion of politics implicit in that claim as well as the presumption of a disjuncture between political and philosophical engagement, and to consider the incidence as well as the rationalizations of political violence in the contemporary world (including the kind of account offered by Merleau-Ponty in *Humanism and Terror*) from the perspective of a politics of contingency rather than necessity and from the standpoint of its traditional victims (the "people") rather than those who are or would be its agents and apologists (the Prince). The historical and continuing resistance of women to their particular "occupation" by men and the historical and continuing resistance of blacks to their historical and continuing "occupation" by whites supply the concrete contexts for these reflections on contemporary political violence and its relationship to the politics of contingency and necessity.

Beyond Traditional Politics

Merleau-Ponty did not wake up to the facts of power and the reality of politics as a necessary contingency of his own life until World War II and the occupation of France forced him up against it and made it impossible for him to any longer not-see and not-choose for or against a power in which he was implicated.[7] The relatively simple politics of the Resistance, however, where differences between one's political allies and opponents (between us and them, good and evil, freedom and domination, masters and slaves) were easy to recognize, at least in their larger configurations (of Nazi and Jew, occupier and liberator, dictator and democrat), gave way after the war to the increasingly complex, ambivalent, and, for Merleau-Ponty, abstract and distant politics of the Cold War that ultimately led him to abandon political speech altogether in favor of philosophical reflection.[8]

In the light of that reflection and the political aporias that preceded (and possibly precipitated) it, I see Merleau-Ponty's withdrawal from political speech not so much as an abandonment of politics *tout court*—of the problematics of power, responsibility, and resistance—as a deepening of his engagement with it. Faced as he was with the inadequacy of traditional political categories (inherited from Machiavelli, Hegel, Marx and Weber, for example) to make practical sense of the political situation he found himself in, Merleau-Ponty went back to the drawing board so to speak, to renew his efforts to think beyond them: to think beyond the political divisions and philosophical aporias of Cartesian dualism and Hegelian dialectics that supplied traditional politics with its ontological and ethical reasons. I see this not as a retreat from politics but as a very particular retreat from a very particular politics—that of the Prince—a dominant politics that is also a politics of domination both theorized and practiced by and on behalf of those who rule; those who have (or believe themselves entitled to have) political power (over others); those who claim to have necessity, history, freedom, reason, and right (all the grand universals) on their side. Merleau-Ponty abandoned this particular politics and its particular philosophical presuppositions for a very different philosophical project, an ontology of chiasms and flesh theorized from the standpoint of a "fold in being," the political implications of which have scarcely been considered.[9]

Merleau-Ponty made few explicitly political claims in his later work and certainly offers no platform or program for a "politics of the flesh"—requirements of politics in the abandoned traditional sense. But it is not difficult to identify the kind of politics his phenomenology of the flesh would exclude: all politics that rely on dualistic ontologies of subjects and objects, freedom and necessity, self and other (perhaps even master and slave); all politics that assume a universal telos or essence to human being(s): some generalized human project or destiny the realization of which is taken to be the particular task of politics as well as the transcendent meaning of History. The ontology of the flesh rules out, that is, all politics of what I have been calling necessity and/or final solutions: politics that postulate ideal ends which leave no remainder and which negate the present inasmuch as it is merely the means to a future that is forever deferred. It rules out all traditional politics inasmuch as they aim for closure (completion, fulfilment, ends) and seek thereby to suture all contingencies (differences, divergencies, disagreements, conflicts, confusions, possibilities, peoples, and pains) into the seamless linear narrative of historical necessity, of some "grand récit"; a politics that leave no openings for an other, for a future that can (must) be different, unknown for life, for the world, for the flesh—for the "reversibility that defines the flesh,"[10] which is "always imminent and never realized in fact."[11]

Thus Merleau-Ponty's talk of flesh and chiasms puts out of play modernist and postmodernist politics alike to the extent that they both rely on the terms and relevancies and implicit metaphysics of traditional politics: of the Hegelian dialectic of Subjects and Objects (Man and History, Culture and Nature, Freedom and Necessity) and its ultimate realization one way or another in some "Universal and Homogeneous State." Modernist politics (liberal, marxist, nationalist, for example) continue to affirm and pursue traditional abstract political ends like Freedom, Sovereignty, Subjectivity, and Man as if they were absolutes—categorical, necessary, immanent. While post-modernism's (would-be) abdication of *all* political "sens" merely confirms the absoluteness of modernism's ends in its inability to think beyond them: to imagine a politics that is different from traditional politics that is for and of the other(s) not the Same, for and of the people not the Prince, for and of contingency (the flesh) not Necessity (consciousness). For both modernism and postmodernism alike, politics remains a question of all or nothing, of sink or swim, of necessity, of "final solutions," and all the practicalities this entails:[12] what Sartre called "the liquidation of particularity" with reference to Stalinism,[13] and Brian Fawcett, more recently and closer to home, has called "genocide" with reference to the shared intentionalities (telos) of American television (slow) on the one hand and Cambodia's Khmer Rouge (fast) on the other.[14] For both modernist and postmodernist politics tend in the same direction—away from the particularities and contingencies of the flesh and the future, which would have to be the point of departure for any politics consistent with Merleau-Ponty's ontology—and toward the universality, necessity, and finality of Imperium; toward, that is, a politics whose totalizing praxis renders individual memory and imagination superfluous, "creating in its stead a single focus on the monodic truth,"[15] toward what Lyotard has rightly called terror.[16]

Toward a Politics of Contingency

I have been arguing that traditional politics is at once a politics of necessity and final solutions and a politics articulated from and on behalf of the position of the Prince: a politics that assumes the standpoint of privilege and power (of autonomy, freedom, reason, universality, necessity, history, consciousness, Man, etc.) even when it puts itself at the service of the people. A politics of contingency, by contrast, would take its point of departure from the side of the Other of traditional politics, the side of Necessity's other, the Prince's other. Not to confirm its Otherness nor the Oneness of the Prince (of the Enlightenment ideal of the opposite and privileged pole) but to resist and subvert the already political polarization itself and the obliteration of particularity and difference that speaking (and organizing) the Universal from the side of the Prince, of the Subject, and the privileged pole (of Reason, Freedom, History, God, etc.) always entails. Thinking (and acting) politically from the standpoint of those who have been the objects, the material, the instruments, and the excluded of traditional politics will transform the very meaning and "sens" of politics itself. As when the figure becomes ground and the ground the figure when we change the focus and intentionality of our perception of an ambiguous image. What emerges from the standpoint of contingency as "political"—political experience, knowledge, vision, change, struggle, resistance, and power, for example—will be phenomenologically distinct from what emerges as "political" from the standpoint of necessity, offering a politics that is both broader and narrower in its scope than the politics of the tradition.

One of the ways in which politics as disclosed from the standpoint of the flesh (of chiasms and reversibility) is broader in its scope than traditional politics is that it cannot be reduced—without destroying the phenomena of experience itself—to the relatively simple question of taking sides in a conflict of opposites in a system of polarized differences of self and other, us and them, subject and object, reason and violence, etc. This is because the experience of the flesh, of our being as a fold in being, *including our experience of political power itself*, is always ambiguous and reversible and cannot, therefore, support a politics that requires us to identify others as Others, as the Enemy *once and for all*. The politics of racism and sexism, for example, is quite literally a *politics of the flesh*: a hierarchy of power, privilege, and control built on the absolutely arbitrary and contingent, but nevertheless real, differences of skin color and genitalia. Racist and sexist power is thus inscribed on our very bodies and inseparable from who we are and the flesh of "our" world(s). As far as sexist and racist power is concerned, it is we who are occupied by "enemy" powers, not "our" country.[17] Our struggle against that occupation is always, therefore, a struggle against ourselves *and those we love*—mothers, fathers, lovers, brothers, sisters, friends, children, neighbors: a sustained internecine struggle against the "enemy" within and not an easy confrontation of opposites—us/them, right/wrong, self/other, good/evil, friend/foe, and so forth.

Resistance to the politics of the flesh is therefore always as ambiguous and as reversible as the flesh it organizes, as personal as it is political (personal because political, political because personal), as private as it is public, because it is grounded in as well as directed toward the very flesh of our own political being-in-the-world. It rarely takes so simple a form, therefore, as directing a gun at the "other" or the "enemy," for the other and the enemy are within us as well as those we have grown to love, admire, and rely on, and those whose lives we aspire to. Resistance in these circumstances takes forms unrecognized by and often invisible to traditional revolutionary strategists[18] who continue to theorize politics from the standpoint of the Prince—of necessity, of "pensée de survol."[19] It is, for example, embedded in, intertwined with, the very minutiae of daily life: in how we wear our hair, our clothes, our face and in how and where and when we walk, talk, smile, listen, look, and pass someone on the street. Nor are such resistances exclusive of "collaboration" and "collusion," for the politics of contingency cannot sustain the rigid boundaries implicit in such exclusions. Performing "woman" or "native" well, for example, can be both subversive and submissive, rebellious and acquiescent, in racist and sexist societies, at different times or even at one and the same time. Push-up bras, painted nails, lipstick and fuck-me shoes, for instance, can be used to rebel *against* the hierarchical divisions of man/woman, good/bad, white/black, labor/leisure, public/private, virgin/whore, and the system of oppressions they organize, as well as to sustain it. Similarly having or not-having a baby, an abortion, a husband, an education, a job, or going or not-going to church, to work, to vote, to the beach, or to the bar, can be revolutionary choices (choices from which the revolution will be created) depending on the specificities of circumstance and context. As can "loving" the "enemy."

This means that politics experienced and practiced from the standpoint of contingency is broader in its scope than the politics of necessity in that it is also a politics that has no place, no place proper to it. It cannot be restricted to the polis, for example, to sites of government and business, to the targeting of "public" institutions, as the only proper objects of political agency and change. On the contrary from the standpoint of contingency (of chiasms, of the flesh, of subordination), politics encompasses the whole of one's life, including its most personal and seemingly private moments, as suggested above. For we do not slough off our skins or our genitals (or our class, our nationality, our language, our education, our wealth, or even our good looks) on the doorstep of our "homes" when we leave the "public" sphere, nor do we drop their social and political meanings on the doormat with the mud from our shoes. The skin, the genitals, the class, the language, the nationality, the education, the wealth, the good looks and their social and political meanings remain with us wherever we are and whatever we are doing, feeling, or thinking. They *are* who we are, and our struggles against the political hierarchies built upon them, against racism and sexism, for example, is one that is waged within and against ourselves and our own "subjectivity" and experience, as much as within and against the "objectivity" of the institutions that govern us and the "subjectivity" of those who rule. This makes the politics of contingency a profoundly radical politics in that it reaches to the very roots of our being. It is a relentless politics of everyday life and consciousness, a guerilla politics of everywhere in general and nowhere in particular.

This truth of politics and power—its lack of proper place—is often invisible to and unrecognized by those whose privilege protects them from it, that is, the traditional spokesmen of traditional politics. As Nadine Gordimer has observed of the different place of politics in the antiapartheid struggles of whites and blacks in South Africa:

> We whites have still to thrust the spade under the roots of our lives: for most of us, including myself, struggle is still something that has a place. But for blacks it is every where or nowhere.[20]

In the same paragraph she cites the example of an overhead remark of a young black woman: "I break the law because I am alive." And in an earlier essay written from Johannesburg in 1976, two months after the Soweto killings, she cites the words of a black intellectual "whose commitment to liberation no one would question, although he risks the violent disapproval of blacks by still having contact with whites":

> When I go home tonight, I don't know which to be more afraid of—the police getting me when they shoot at anything that moves, or my own people getting me when I walk across the yard to the lavatory.[21]

This truth about the different place of politics in the lives of blacks and whites in racist society is true of the politics of all social hierarchies: of the experience and place of sexual politics in the lives of women and men, for example. Women in sexist society, like blacks in racist society, occupy Man's World on his terms and at his discretion—like guests whose invitation can be withdrawn at any time and for any reason. We run exactly the same risks when we go home as the black (male) intellectual cited above: not knowing which to be more afraid of—the men in the street who feel free to harrass us when we are not escorted ("legitimized") by another man or "our own people," the men in "our home" whose violence we are, as a matter of fact, most commonly subjected to. (Whose streets are they really, then? Whose people? Whose home?) Women do not, as men, have a "private" sphere into which we can retreat from the "public" world of politics and power. The politics of our subordination and oppression is centered in our homes—in men's private sphere—where we are most likely to experience violence: to be beaten, raped, and killed, in the bedroom and the kitchen (i.e., where we belong) by "our own people" that is, our male kin, on Sundays—their day of rest.[22]

It seems to me that this specific difference of political experience between men and women—that for women, it has no place, no polis—conditions the nature and direction and probably the incidence of violence in political struggles, coinciding as it must with a particular and specific consciousness of oppression and its place, of what of oneself and one's community is at stake in resistance to it, and the price one is prepared for what is understood to be "liberation." Women do not characteristically resort to the same kind of violence as men in either their liberation struggles and their struggles for justice or in their various daily practices of conflict resolution—as mothers, for example, or as mainstays of the service industries. I think this is because women—as the Other of Man in sexist society—have no place from which to articulate a politics of necessity, of means and ends, of necessary destiny. They have no proper place, that is, no place proper to them, which is their own, which they *can* own (they take their father's or their husband's name, not their mother's), which defines who they are (some man's property), and with which they can I-dentify: no place to which they can retreat from the contingency, chaos, and confusion of the flesh—from which they can organize "attacks" on the same contingencies and over which they can imagine themselves to be in some sense sovereign, Prince (not even their own bodies). Women, unlike men, have no place from which to assume the political standpoint of the Prince—no place that is exclusively their own, which *is* themselves and from which others can and must, therefore, be dis-placed, ex-cluded, dis-tanced and ob-jectified as Other. Having such a place—or at least, feeling entitled to claim such a place—seems to me to be a condition of political violence which always flows one way: from and between would-be Princes, would-be Sovereignties, against whatever stands in the way of its (illusory) achievement. Political violence is always, in some sense, top-down, male and tribal: organized and articulated from the standpoint of the Prince (of necessity and historical destiny) against others who are clearly Other (the Enemies of the One) for the sake of an "I"—an Identity—which is clear and distinct, and a place which that I-dentity claims as exclusively his own.[23]

Patriarchal social relations make this standpoint available—even necessary—to men inasmuch as masculinity is defined in its terms: in terms of necessity, identity, and difference and not to women, who *as women* are confined to contingency and the ambiguity and reversibility of chiasms and flesh. This is not to suggest that women are not as capable as men of "violence"—political or otherwise—but that there are significant differences and discontinuities between "violences": between those perpetrated by and in the name of patriarchal tribes, for example, and those perpetrated by and in the name of specific individuals: between necklacing and dropping bombs, for instance, and having an abortion or beating a child.[24] These are differences that philosophers, philosophizing from the standpoint of the Prince, have consistently obscured, and thereby the political relations that I have been suggesting constitute and coincide with them. Theorizing violence from the standpoint of contingency makes these relations and these discontinuities—these *specificities* of violence—visible and brings them into focus for further reflection on the political possibilities "inherent" in the "human condition."

Just as from the standpoint of contingency politics has no proper place, so also has it no proper time, that is, no time proper to it apart from the local, particular, and immanent, and therefore constantly shifting, temporalities of specific political actions and people. In other words the politics of contingency is broader in its scope than traditional politics in that, just as it cannot be reduced to the taking of sides, so it cannot be reduced to the planning and pursuit of parties, platforms, and programs that postulate definitive and transcendent (usually universal and historically necessary) ends to which present and past meanings ("sens")—and people—are subordinated as means, as contingent and particular instrumentalities. Instead of a politics of propaganda and programs, of means and ends, and transcendent teleologies, the ontology of flesh and chiasms calls for a creative politics of "bricolage" and original/originating speech (parole originaire)[25] grounded in the local and historical specificities of particular people, places, and times for originating action that will disrupt the sedimented meanings/sens of the past, of history, power, and necessity, and thus give birth to new norms and to futures that can be different. It calls, that is, for a "politique originaire" (to use the words of Eleanor Godway),[26] which when successful—and there is no guarantee of this—will invent what in the future will appear to have been required at the time.

Keeping alive local memory and imagination as a reservoir of meanings, truths, and possibilities for a different future is thus absolutely central to a politics of contingency.[27] This means refusing all totalizations of destiny, universality, necessity, and Reason, wherever they appear. In our own case this means resisting not only television as Fawcett argues,[28] but also the lure of traditional political formations (both of which tend toward the liquidation of particular memory and local imagination) with ordinary (not now so ordinary) everyday speech. It means eschewing the old abstractions of universality, destiny, and necessity by being present to each other (face to face) in all the ambiguities and reversibilities of the flesh in conversation and speech. It means, that is, resisting the old modernist and would-be *post* modernist tendency to go global—with either one's projections or one's rationalization of realities.[29] The best documented example I am familiar with of the strength, power, possibilities, and in some sense success of this kind of local political resistance is that of Black Americans and South Africans, as evidenced in their music, for example; but especially as it is practiced in the poetry and fiction of Black American women.[30] I think the same kind of politics (of contingency) made possible the changes in Eastern Europe we witnessed in 1989, which took so many political commentators (of necessity) by surprise, and that the possibility of its continuing—as a politics of contingency—in the different locations (Romania, Poland, Germany, Czechoslovakia) will determine the direction and "success" of these changes in the future.[31]

This aspect of the politics of contingency, that it has no place or time proper to it other than that of the specific and local practicalities within which it is realized, means that it can offer no necessities and no guarantees to its participants who must, therefore, assume responsibility for what they choose to do in its name. This means that there is an inescapable *ethical* dimension to the politics of contingency that can neither be abstracted from nor reduced to it, to politics itself, as is so often the case in a traditional politics of necessity. There, personal decisions, responsibilities, and accountability are consistently denied, dissolved, disavowed, and displaced from individual actors onto political abstractions like History, Reason, Nature, Society, the State, the Struggle, and the various necessities of Liberation. By contrast a politics of contingency offers no safe place for the "politically correct", thus no way of protecting oneself from the exigencies of moral choice and "political" responsibility within both the personal *and* the public sphere. Nadine Gordimer has observed that for whites in South Africa this means:

> It is not simply a matter of follow-the-leader behind the blacks; it's taking on, as blacks do, choices to be made out of confusion, empirically, pragmatically, ideologically or idealistically about the practical moralities of the struggle.[32]

It means, that is, taking on choices and their consequences from the standpoint of contingency, of those who know they do not know, the standpoint of the "unredeemed," the oppressed, as opposed to the standpoint of power, of the "chosen race," of those who think they know which is the standpoint of necessity, of the Prince. It means giving up the illusion of political purity or control and always running the risk of being in the wrong, and assuming responsibility for this.

This aspect of the politics of contingency is also relevant to the problem of violence in both its incidence and its various rationalizations. For from the standpoint of necessity, wherein ends justify means and good (Reason, History, Freedom, Man) conquers all, and the present merely realizes the past and the future the present, political violence can be done, has been done, and is done "innocently": in both confidence and good faith as the necessary means to necessary ends, the necessary negation of the negation, for the sake of an ultimate affirmation presumed to be immanent in it.

It is in this precise sense that the politics of contingency is *narrower* in its scope than traditional politics in that it does not reduce politics to ontology. It does not, that is, mask the concrete and contingent specificities of *political* violence, which is always local and particular, beneath the mystifying veil of an abstracted Universality and Necessity supposedly immanent in History (Man, Freedom, Reason). As does Merleau-Ponty himself, and the commentators who follow his example, in his defense of violence in *Humanism and Terror* where he assimilates political violence into the ontological necessities of an "intersubjectivity" described, not in terms of chiasms and reversibility as in his later work, but in terms of "encroachment" and "intrusion."[33] Both Merleau-Ponty and his commentators conflate political rationality within which alone political violence makes "sens" with the falsely posited (and later repudiated) but familiar existential rationality of the subject-object dichotomy and dialectic:[34]

> Political problems come from the fact that we are all subjects and yet we look upon other people and treat them as objects.[35]

My point is not that Merleau-Ponty was wrong to defend the necessity of political violence in the contingent (political) conditions within which he was himself embedded and to which he felt himself obliged to respond—I am not espousing an antiviolence position here—but that he was wrong to do so on ontological grounds rather than political ones: on the grounds, for example, that "inasmuch as we are incarnate beings, violence is our lot."[36] I am objecting to the tendency in traditional politics, exemplified by Merleau-Ponty in *Humanism and Terror*, to collapse all human conflict, suffering, force, constraint, sacrifice, loss, pain, hurt, destruction, and "sin" into the general undifferentiated category of a "violence" presumed to be intrinsic to and ineradicable from the facts of corporeality itself, to a "sort of evil in collective life."[37] I am objecting to this tendency because it obfuscates the politics of particular acts of violence and the specific political and personal stakes of its agents, objects, interests, and intentionalities. It thus obscures the very phenomena of violence itself, pre-empting an interrogative phenomenology of violence in relation to politics by subordinating the question of the contingent conditions of possibility of particular "violences" to the postulate of the necessities of an "elemental," "ineradicable" violence inherent in the human condition. The practical-political-ethical problems posed by acts of real violence are thus forever forestalled by the abstracted philosophical problem posed to a "conscience" of choosing between necessary violences: the necessary violence of the State, for example, or the equally necessary violences of those who would resist it? Our violence or theirs? The ethical standpoint of contingency, of personal responsibility, accountability, and judgment is thereby forsaken for the frankly Machiavellian standpoint of the Prince, of necessity, premised not on the lived ambiguities and reversibilities of the flesh but on the posited divisions and contradictions of subjects and objects, individual praxis and collective life.[38]

It has been the argument of this chapter that Merleau-Ponty's ontology of the flesh moves us well beyond the hypostasis of these old oppositions and aporia and the various political rationalities (of History, Freedom, Reason, and Man) they have been called upon to support toward a politics of contingency, which takes both its point of departure and its always provisional "ends" from the local and historical specificities of particular political experience. I have argued that the ontology of the flesh both requires and enables us to think politics anew and have suggested precise and significant ways in which this politics is both broader and narrower in its scope than the traditional political thinking that informed Merleau-Ponty's earlier work and continues to determine the interpretations of his principal political commentators. I have argued that the politics of contingency implicit in the ontology of chiasms and flesh is more radical than a traditional politics of necessity in that it extends to the very roots of our being—as men and women, blacks and whites, in racist and sexist society, for example—and leaves us with "no safe place" for transcending our political status or the *ethical implications* of how we choose to live it out. Unlike traditional politics the politics of contingency offers not only no safe place but also no final solutions, no guarantees, no consolations, and no crowning glories—no principles, programs, or plans. Instead it offers us a future and a world to be made, the resources for doing it, and the challenge of what Eleanor Godway calls a "politique originaire"[39] in place of the "politique secondaire" of that which is already known. Could this be the *post* modern politics we have been looking for?

NOTES

1. First published in Thomas Busch and Shaun, Gallagher, eds., *Merleau-Ponty, Hermeneutics and Postmodernism* (Albany: SUNY Press, 1992), 171–87.
2. Chapter 6 in this volume.
3. For clarification of "contingency," see chapter 7, n. 18. For "chiasm" and "flesh," see n. 9 this chapter.
4. For "high-altitude thinking" (pensée de survol), see chapter 7, n. 7.
5. Barry Cooper, *Merleau-Ponty and Marxism: From Terror to Reform* (Toronto: University of Toronto Press, 1979); Sonia Kruks, *The Political Philosophy of Merleau-Ponty* (Sussex: Harvester Press, 1981); and Kerry Whiteside, *Merleau-Ponty and the Foundation of an Existential Politics* (Princeton, N.J.: Princeton University Press, 1988).
6. See chapter 6 in this volume.
7. "We knew that concentration camps existed, that the Jews were being persecuted, but these certainties belonged to the world of thought. We were not as yet living face to face with cruelty and death: we had not as yet been given the choice of submitting to them or confronting them." Maurice Merleau-Ponty, *Sense and Non-Sense*, trans. H. L. Dreyfus and P. A. Dreyfus (Evanston: Northwestern University Press, 1964), 139.
8. "Unity had been easy during the Resistance, because relationships were almost always man-to-man. . . . And in this sense it must be said that the Resistance experience . . . fostered our illusions of 1939 and masked the truth of the incredible power of history which the Occupation taught us in another connection. We have returned to the time of the *institutions*. The distance between the laws and those to whom they apply is once more apparent; once again one legislated for X; and once again the good will of some resumes its class features which make it unrecognizable to others." Merleau-Ponty, *Sense and Non-Sense*, 151.
9. Merleau-Ponty introduces the concepts of "flesh" and the "chiasm" in *The Visible and the Invisible*, trans. Alphonso Lingis (Evanston: Northwestern University Press, 1968), the unfinished manuscript he was working on when he died. "Flesh"

displaces "consciousness" and the "body" in this work as the locus of sensibility, experience, and expression, of our point of view on the world in which we inhere and which in turn inheres in us.

> The thickness of flesh between seer and the thing is constitutive for the thing of its visibility as for the seer of his corporeity; it is not an obstacle between them, it is their means of communication. (135)

"Flesh" here refers to the flesh of the world (not the flesh of an individual human body), which constitutes the reciprocal visibility of the seer and the seen, and the reversibility, the intertwining, the "chiasm" of each with the other: "the coiling over of the visible upon the seeing body, of the tangible upon the touching body" (146).

> The world seen is not "in" my body, and my body is not "in" the visible world ultimately: as flesh applied to a flesh, the world neither surrounds it nor is surrounded by it. A participation in and kinship with the visible, the vision neither envelops it nor is enveloped by it definitively. (138)

> The flesh is not matter, is not mind, is not substance. To designate it, we should need the old term "element," in the sense it was used to speak of water, air, earth, and fire, that is, in the sense of a *general thing*, midway between the spatio-temporal individual and the idea, a sort of incarnate principle that brings a style of being wherever there is a fragment of being. The flesh is in this sense an "element" of Being. (139)

> We must not think the flesh starting from substances, from body and spirit—for then it would be the union of contradictories—but we must think it, as we said, as an element, as the concrete emblem of a general manner of being. (147)

10. Merleau-Ponty, *The Visible and the Invisible*, 144.
11. Ibid., 147.
12. See chapter 6 of this volume.
13. Jean-Paul Sartre, *Critique of Dialectical Reason*, trans. Alan Sheridan-Smith (London: New Left Books, 1976).
14. Brian Fawcett, *Cambodia. A Book for People Who Find Television too Slow* (Vancouver: Talonbooks, 1986).
15. Ibid., 63.
16. Jean-François Lyotard, *The Postmodern Condition: A Report on Knowledge* (Minneapolis: University of Minnesota Press, 1984), 63–64.
17. To put it another way:

> "Our country" . . . throughout the greater part of its history has treated me as a slave; it has denied me education or any share in its possessions . . . in fact, as a woman, I have no country. As a woman I want no country. As a woman my country is the whole world. Virginia Woolf, *Three Guineas* (London: Hogarth Press, 1938), 125.

18. I am paraphrasing Nadine Gordimer here, but I have been unable to locate the precise citation I have in mind.
19. See note 4 above.
20. Nadine Gordimer, *The Essential Gesture. Writing, Politics and Places*, ed. Stephen Clingman (New York: Alfred Knopf, 1988), 271.
21. Ibid., 131.
22. For further exploration of the different relationship of men and women to the incidence and rationalizations of violence, see Geraldine Finn, "Taking Gender into Account in the 'Theatre of Terror': Violence, Media and the Maintenance of Male Dominance," *Canadian Journal of Women and the Law* 3, no. 2 (1989–1990) 375–94 and chapter 2 in this volume.
23. There is clearly a connection between what I am suggesting here about the masculinity and tribalism of political violence and Nancy Jay's analysis of rituals of blood sacrifice, including the Christian Eucharist, as evidence of and at the same time means of constituting lines of patrilineal descent. See Nancy Jay, "Sacrifice as Remedy for Having Been Born of Woman," in *Immaculate and Powerful*, eds. Clarissa Atkinson, Constance Buchanan, and Margaret Miles (Boston: Beacon Press, 1985) 283–309 and *Throughout Your Generations Forever: Sacrifice, Religion and Paternity* (Chicago: University of Chicago Press, 1992). According to Jay, blood sacrifice only occurs in societies that trace their kinship relations through the fathers' and not the mothers' line. And only men sacrifice in these societies. William Beers argues that men are saying "No to the mother" when they sacrifice in *Women & Sacrifice: Male Narcissism and the Psychology of Religion* (Detroit: Wayne State University Press, 1992). According to Eli Sagan, men are both making and marking their transition from kinship to kingship: from an-archical matrilineal society to hierarchies of patrilineal status society. See Eli Sagan, *At the Dawn of Tyranny: The Origins of Individuality, Political Oppression and the State* (New York: Alfred Knopf, 1985). Ritual sacrifice is thus both the means and the expression of male bonding *over and against women*. It is a way of distinguishing men from women, masculinity from femininity, culture from nature, and at the same time of establishing a hierarchy of one over the other. It is always accompanied by the culturally prescribed fear and abjection of women (i.e., by misogyny) and of their capacity to give birth as the occasions of moral impurity and "human" degradation. It is in the light of these analyses of ritual sacrifice that I am beginning to understand the more familiar incidences of ritual blood shedding by men in our own society: in wars and terrorism, mass murders, medical interventions, horror movies, and so forth.
24. Acts of violence perpetrated by women are characteristically less "senseless," "random," "impersonal," bloody, ritualized, collective, and "rationalized" than male-stream violence. They are most often directed by individual women at individual abusive men who are known to them, to save their own lives, or to particular children, sometimes to save theirs, through some tragic distortion of maternal care. See, for example, Fay Weldon's *Praxis* (New York: Pocketbooks, 1978), and Toni Morrison's *Beloved* (New York: Plume Books, New American Library, 1988) for two powerful, fictional explorations of this theme.
25. That is speech that institutes new meanings, as distinct from "parole parlée," which merely reproduces the familiar and sedimented meanings of the already said.
26. Eleanor Godway, "Towards a Phenomenology of Politics: Expression and Praxis,"

in *Merleau-Ponty: Hermeneutics and Postmodernism,* eds. Thomas Busch and Shaun Gallagher, (New York: SUNY Press, 1964), 210. See also note 39 below.

27. Women's "gossip" can thus be seen as a form of political resistance to men's "reasoning," keeping alive the local and particular memory and knowledge of women, in the face of men's totalizing histories which always leave them out. For an interesting discussion of men's "reasoning" in the context of Rastafarianism, see Carole Yawney, "To Grow a Daughter: Cultural Liberation and the Dynamics of Oppression in Jamaica" in *Feminism. From Pressure to Politics,* eds. Angela Miles and Geraldine Finn (Montreal: Black Rose Books, 1989), 177–202.
28. Fawcett, *Cambodia.*
29. See chapters 6, 8, and 9, in this volume.
30. See, for example, the work of Audre Lorde, Alice Walker, and Toni Morrison.
31. The plays of Vaclav Havel are perhaps the most obvious example of the kind of political resistance I am referring to here, keeping alive local memory and imagination in the face of the totalizing rhetorics of repressive knowledges and institutions.
32. Gordimer, *Essential Gesture*, 268.
33. Maurice Merleau-Ponty, *Humanism and Terror*, trans. John O'Neill (Boston: Beacon Press, 1969) 109.
34. Monika Langer, for example, draws on a few key passages from *The Phenomenology of Perception* and *Humanism and Terror* to argue the following:

    It has emerged that there is a kind of violence inherent in the human condition as such. This elemental violence permeates all forms of human coexistence, from the simplest level of human perception to the most complex modes of human interaction. . . . Given the ontological origin of violence, it becomes "a law of human action" and "a fact of political life" that human beings encroach, or intrude, upon one another. . . . *No politics will ever be able to get rid of that violence which has to do with humanity's fundamental way of being in the world.* (Langer, "Merleau-Ponty: The Ontological Limitations of Politics" in *Domination* edited by Alkis Kontos (Toronto: Toronto University Press, 1975) 102–14. Original emphases.)

35. Merleau-Ponty, *Humanism and Terror*, 110.
36. Ibid., 109.
37. Ibid., xxxviii.
38. The relationship between ethical and political praxis (realities, truths, judgments, experiences) is explored in greater detail in chapters 11 and 12 in this volume.
39. To participate in history in this way is to be drawn into a gesture which allows a meaning to be born, creates possibilities, and, by making the present a turning point, opens a future and changes the meaning of the past.

    Politique originaire is embodied in the acceptance of this responsibility, which commits itself to a future with others. *Politique secondaire*, like *parole parlée*, takes over what is already in place, and has no intimation of a future. In reaffirming only what has already been said—what therefore, is now said by no-one—it is, says Merleau-Ponty, a way of staying silent. (Eleanor Godway, "Phenomenology of Politics," 165, 168.)

Chapter 11
Eleven

The Politics of Spirituality. The Spirituality of Politics

THE LAST CHAPTER WAS written in the summer and presented in the fall of 1989, just before the fall of the Berlin Wall and the breakup of the Soviet Union that followed. These events—*this advent* of a new political dispensation, a *politique originaire*[1]—provided a timely illustration of the *politics of contingency* at work, and, not surprisingly, confounded the commentators who, inured to the politics of necessity, were (at first) unable to make sense (*sens*) of what they were witnessing in its terms. Unfortunately, for the future and for the fecund and transformative possibilities of *politique originaire*, there were no other terms available in the political forum at the time. And the events of fall 1989 were quickly recuperated by, for, and into traditional political discourse and its traditional political stakes (which may be won or lost; posts to which persons were tied to be burned to death)[2] of competing freedoms, identities, territories, and ends. By, for, and into a politics of final solutions, that is, which the brutalities now raging in the former Yugoslavia only confirm.

In the absence of political terms adequate to the specificity and originality of this moment (the moment of the end of the USSR), responsible commentators, that is commentators who were response-able to the originality of the moment (to its specific difference from a simplistic embrace of "the West," for example, or of an equally simplistic politics of either/or: either us or them, East or West, capitalism or communism) fell back on the language of spirituality as the only available alternative to politics for making sense (*sens*) of events of such import. Following the example of Vaclav Havel himself, whose political writings had always focused on the specifically *spiritual degradation* and impoverishment of the communist regime:

> It needs little imagination to see that such a situation can lead towards the gradual erosion of all moral standards, the breakdown of all criteria of decency, and the widespread destruction of confidence in the meaning of any such values as truth, adherence to principles, sincerity, altruism, dignity and honour. Life must needs sink to a biological, vegetable level

> amidst a demoralization in "in depth," stemming from the loss of hope and the loss of belief that life has meaning. It can but confront us once more with that tragic aspect of man's status in modern technological civilization marked by a declining awareness of the absolute, and which I propose to call a *crisis of human identity*. . . .
>
> Order has been established. At the price of a paralysis of the spirit, a deadening of the heart, and devastation of life.
>
> Surface "consolidation" has been achieved. At the price of a *spiritual and moral crisis in society*.[3]

This essay on "The Politics of Spirituality. The Spirituality of Politics" was inspired by the events of 1989 that marked the end of the USSR, and the poverty of the spiritual and political discourse that ultimately organized their *sens* away from the *politique originaire* they inaugurated and accomplished to the familiar discourse and ends of the politics of the Prince; a *politique secondaire* which "like parole parlée takes over what is already in place, and has no intimation of a future."[4] It takes issue with the presupposition of a disjuncture between political meanings and ends and spiritual meanings and ends, which the discourses of both politics and spirituality take for granted, and with the relegation/elevation of morality from the sphere of politics (and materiality) to the sphere of spirituality (and meaning) that coincides with it (and which is exemplified in the citation from Havel quoted above).

Although its point of departure is the events of 1989, the argument of this essay was developed as a response to, an intervention in, and an implicit critique of the following: postmodernism's abdication of all meanings, moralities, politics, and *sens*, in the name of contingency and the death of God (of the Subject, History, Truth, etc.) on the one hand, and feminism's quest for alternatives, that is, for a feminist ethics and/or a women's spirituality, on the other—with its presupposition of identity as a value and end, and/or of experience that is out-of-this-world. The essay tries to hold onto the values informing postmodernism's repudiation of value and feminism's insistence on alternatives, by reworking/rewording them in terms of a politics of contingency that offers more than more of the Same. It draws on the work of Emmanuel Levinas to argue for the possibility and necessity of the ethical encounter with the Other in the *space-between experience and expression* (between category and reality, language and life) as both the product and premise of politics, and the material reality of 'spiritual' life: reclaiming the experiences, values, and ends of the 'spirit' for the concrete and complex reality of the flesh of the material world. The relationship between ethics and politics articulated here to the space-between language and life is explored in more detail in chapter 12 with reference to the quest for a feminist ethics in particular, and the politics of identity it most often assumes.

The Politics of Spirituality. The Spirituality of Politics[5]

> Happiness occurs when people can give the whole of themselves to the moment being lived, when being and becoming are the same thing.

These are the words of John Berger. They are from an essay he wrote on the political changes in eastern Europe that was published in *The Guardian* newspaper in March 1990.[6] The essay was accompanied by a large tinted photograph of the faces of people at a mass demonstration in eastern Europe, of the kind we got used to seeing on our TV screens and in our newspapers in the fall of 1989. This picture, Berger tells us, was taken in Prague, but it could just as well have been Warsaw, Leipzig, Budapest, or Sofia. The people were standing shoulder to shoulder, in winter clothes, looking up and over each other in the direction of the camera. Their faces are grave and attentive, expectant and concerned, tense and eager, yet calm and self-contained. They seem to be energized for collective action yet-to-be-determined and united in a shared experience yet-to-be-articulated—one that is neither fear nor joy, triumph nor despair. Nobody is talking or gesticulating, and there is scarcely a hint of a smile on any of the approximately three hundred fifty faces in the picture. This is clearly not a football crowd, nor even a demonstration for peace.

I like this picture a lot. I find it moving and compelling and inspiring in its singularity, particularity, and detail. In its otherness. In its opaqueness to easy or familiar interpretation, in its resistance to common sense—to *sens commun*. I like it because it both affirms and performs what is shows, and because what it shows nourishes me: the truth of the ethical encounter with the other (to use Levinas's terms),[7] of the movement when "being and becoming are the same thing" (to use Berger's). What this photograph shows, affirms, and performs is the relationship with others as a responsibility that does not refer to (my) freedom (to my "will" or my political status), that is, the relationship with others as an alliance, a "neighbouring" that was not chosen. It shows, affirms, and performs the encounter with the *face* of the other in particular as a singularity: as a "trace" outside all categories, which puts me into question as well as the relationship, the world, and the "common sense" we share. It shows and affirms the face of the other as a "signification beyond all intentionalities": all phenomenological constitutions and sociopolitical constructions; the face of the other as a visitation, a "transcendence," an epiphany, an imperative that demands and commands me. It reveals the other as an exteriority that cannot be integrated into the (old Imperialisms of the) Same, which is and must therefore be the starting point of philosophy in the best sense, that is, of *parole originaire* and, as I hope eventually to demonstrate, *politique originaire*.[8] This is the imperative—the demand, the command, the responsibility, and the promise of the picture and the event(s) it commemorates: to think and be anew, to risk being "otherwise than being" what we have already known and become.[9]

This is not an encounter I expect to have when I read the newspaper, watch TV, do the groceries, or even engage in political or philosophical debate(s). Though I have come to expect it from the likes of John Berger, and it is one I constantly seek and seek to produce in my relations with others and in my own intellectual work as a reader, writer, and teacher. I used to think of this desire of mine for what I now (following the letter, though perhaps not the spirit, of Levinas) am calling the *ethical* encounter with others (with otherness), this seeking for being-otherwise-than-being simply a member, a re-presentative of a category or class (man, woman, child; Catholic, Protestant, Jew; bourgeois, aristocrat, prole) as a form of *intellectual* snobbery. Since it led me away from not only the everyday taken-for-granted discourse, practices, and alliances of my colleagues and peers but also away from the more sophisticated but still formulaic and predicative posturings of the church and state and the equally predicative clichés of the spiritual and political movements that would oppose them—into the arcane and increasingly esoteric and always shifting, unresolved and disputatious worlds of literature, philosophy, and art.

Eventually it became clear to me however that what I had been identifying as "intellectual" desires, preferences, commitments, pleasures, and pains (and chastising myself for) were really *political* desires, preferences, commitments, pleasures, and pains (of which I could be proud). That what I was really seeking in both my work and my personal life was the possibility of a being-in-the-world-with-others, which was not always already pre-dicated, pre-determined, and pre-scribed—and thereby foreclosed—by language and the various institutionalized political relations that organize its meanings and *sens*, and thereby the meanings and *sens* of both our consciousness and our lives. I was seeking to inhabit the space of becoming, to use Berger's terms, the *space between* experience and expression, reality and representation, existence and essence: the concrete fertile pre-thematic and an-archic space *where we actually live*, the space of sensibility and affect, of undecidability and chance, of being-otherwise-than-being a man, a woman, a Christian, a Jew, a mother, daughter, father, son, etc. I was seeking, that is, to establish relationships with others in "excess" of (beyond and between) the categories that render us knowable and/or already known (as re-presentations of the Same, the familiar); relationships beyond and between the categorical imperatives predicated upon our being-as a man, a woman, a Christian, a Jew; relationships beyond and between the classifications and identities that preempt the specifically *ethical* encounter with others *as other:* as otherwise-than-being man, woman, Christian, Jew, etc.

This space between representation and reality, text and context, expression and experience, language and being is the necessary and indispensable space of judgment and critique, creativity and value, resistance and change. It is the ground of the critical intentions and originating experiences that enable us to call the political status quo into question and challenge the already-known universe and its organization into and by the predicative and prescriptive categories of "practical reason." As such it is the ethical space—the space of the specifically ethical relation with others—and the only place from which the conventionality, the contingency (the "arbitrariness") of reality (of political positivities and identities) can be seen and challenged. Managing this silent but nevertheless signifying/*signifiant* space between the pre-thematic, an-archical-ethical, and the categorical hierarchical-political encounter with others, this space of the otherwise-than-being a re-presentative of a category or class is absolutely central therefore to the exercise of political power and to the organization of our subjection to it. It is absolutely central, that is, to our "subjectivity": to our being as subjects of experiences and actions which "count," of sentences which make sense in the *polis*. (Which should give us pause in claiming our "subjectivity" as "woman," "black" or "gay," for example—as anything other than an always strategic political identity deployed provisionally for and against particular political ends.)

Categorical schemas and institutionalized discourses (the discourses of politics, philosophy, science, sex, literature, and art, for example) work toward this end of managing—and in our own society, suturing, though this need not be the case—this vital space between representation and reality, language and being. They channel the affective, anarchical-ethical experience of "wild being" (Merleau-Ponty), of being-as-becoming (Berger), of being-otherwise-than-being (Levinas) into articulated, hierarchical, predicative meanings, intentionalities, and desires compatible with and amenable to the controlling interests of prevailing political powers. The task, however, is never accomplished. For the contingent and changing concrete world always exceeds the ideal categories of thought within which we attempt to express and contain it. And the same is true of people. We are always both more and less than the categories that name and divide us. More and less that is than a woman, a man, a Christian, a Jew, a lesbian, a mother, a wife. More and less than what we stand for in the *polis* and what stands for us. More and less than anything that can be said about us. Our lives leave remainders (they say more than they mean) just as our categories leave residues (they mean more than they say). Lives and categories precipitate, that is, an-archical *sens/signifiance* that exists beyond and between given categorical frameworks, beyond and between the knowable and the already known, as an always available (re)source of difference, resistance, and change, of being-otherwise-than-being.

Politics speaks directly to this an-archic "precipitate" of being and thought, this (re)source of *différance* and change, this space-between being and being-as: this fertile, disruptive, unpredictable space of the relation with an otherness, which ex-ceeds established categories of predication and control. Conservative politics speak to this space in order to contain, deny, or negate its excesses: to recuperate its deviations and *différance* into and for the hegemonic categories and relations that constitute the status quo. Radical, progressive, and/or revolutionary politics speak to and from the same "precipitate" (the same space between category and experience, representation and reality) to *affirm* it: to inhabit and expand it, and to organize it for political resistance and change. At least radical politics must *begin* there as any critical moment must, in the *space between* category and reality, language and experience: in the space of excess and disjuncture, deviation, and *différance*; the space from which the "arbitrariness" of political divisions and classifications and the incommensurability of being and thought (of my being and my being a woman, a lesbian, a black, a Jew, etc.) are both visible and lived, visible because lived. Radical politics must originate this way, in the as-yet-untamed "precipitate" (the residues and remainders) of languages and lives, and take its inspiration and direction from the an-archical *ethical* relation with others/otherness that occurs there, between and beyond the categorical imperatives of regulated institutionalized thought. But it seldom recognizes or acknowledges that fact or the place of its origin (not surprisingly, since we are systematically bereft of an adequate language with which to do so) nor therefore the implications of that space of its own origination for its own would-be "alternative" political praxis. As a consequence radical politics tend toward the same kind of political positivities and "final solutions" as the "conservative" régimes they purport to resist, transform, subvert, or replace, with their categorical assertions of competing imperatives, identities, and ends (the identities and ends of "women," "blacks," "minorities," or "gays," for example). Would-be radical politics thereby collude with the powers that be and bind us all the more securely to our assigned identities and political destinies (as woman, black, or gay) by obscuring once again that experience of excess—of the space between reality and representation, being and being-as—from which they can be deconstructed and resisted.

I once thought of this tendency in the theories and practices of would-be radical politics (of the politics of feminism and postmodernism, most recently, for example) as an abdication of *politics:* as an abdication of the space of political judgment and critique, of political self-consciousness and reflection, of having to take a stand and acknowledge responsibility for it—for the place from which you have chosen to speak (as a woman, a man, a black, a lesbian) and for what, therefore, is spoken from it. But I have recently come to see it as an *abdication of ethics for politics*; as a flight into the relatively safe categorical (familiar, known, and predetermined) space of the *polis*—of the political relation with others—away from the risky, uncertain, creative, accountable, and responsible space-between of the an-archic *ethical* relation.

Which brings me back to the Prague photograph, John Berger's essay on it, and the relationship between *spirituality and politics* that is the focus of this paper. For Berger takes the same flight path from the ethical to the political but *by way of the spiritual* in this article: away from the place of the in-between, of excess, contingency, undecidability, and chance, of *parole* and *politique originaire,* back to the familiar and safe place of the *polis,* of necessity and identity and more of the Same, and all in the name of systematic and fundamental change! The language of spirituality mediates this flight from ethics to politics while at the same time obscuring it and thereby its own relationship to politics and to the ethical encounter with others/otherness which, I have been arguing, politics both organizes and obscures—organizes to obscure. This deployment of "spirituality" against "ethics" in the service of "politics" is, I believe, inherent in the discourses and practices of "spirituality" itself in our culture and not some deviation and aberration from it, or from some purer version of it, on John Berger's part—as the analysis that follows is intended to show.

Berger argues that the picture from Prague bespeaks a (re)turn to spirituality in eastern Europe following the demise of communism and what he refers to as the "materialist" philosophy that fueled it. And he sees the (re)emergence of religious and nationalist movements as harbingers of this (re)turn to spirituality. This is how he makes the connections:

> Independence movements all make economic and territorial demands, but their first claim is of a spiritual order . . . all of them want to be free of distant, foreign centres which, through long, bitter experience, they have come to know as soulless. . . .
>
> The spiritual, marginalized, driven into the corners, is beginning to reclaim its lost terrain. . . . The old reasoning, the old common sense, even old forms of courage have been abandoned, unfamiliar recognitions and hopes, long banished to the peripheries are returning to claim their own. This is where the happiness behind the faces in the photo starts. . . .
>
> Nothing is finally determined. The soul and the operator have come out of hiding together. All are back in the human condition.

Well, yes and no. It all depends on what he means by soul and spirit, the human condition and, elsewhere in the article, "transcendent vision" and "enclaves of the beyond" of "materialist explanations." These are abstract and contentious categories, mere slogans as long as their meanings are not made clear and concrete—slogans which, like democracy, freedom, and progress, have been used to support a lot of rather nasty political practices in their time. And when they are linked both historically and conceptually—and indisciminately—as they are here, to the affirmation and promotion of religious and nationalist movements (the Catholic Church in Latin America, Islam in the Middle East, the Irish, the Basques, the Kurds, the Kasovans, the Azerbaijanis, the Puerto Ricans, the Latvians) because of their commitment to bringing "social justice" to the poor, the landless, the exiled, and those "treated as historical trash" (does this extend to women, do you think?), well! I begin to feel not only nervous, but disappointed, cheated and angry. I feel nervous about what is being promoted in the name of "spirituality" and the return to the "human condition." I feel cheated of the promise of difference and change, of the possibility of *parole* and *politique originaire*, of the truth of the anarchical-ethical relation that the Prague photo testifies to. And I feel angry at the obfuscation, the mystification, the falsification, the recuperation, the pre-emptive and pre-mature reduction of that promise yet again by one of our would-be oppositional and (I would argue not coincidentally) white male intellectuals, into the ancient and familiar *political* categories and ends of good old patriarchal praxis: nationalism and religion—paraded in this case under the purportedly nonmaterialist flagship of "spirituality," "soul," and the "human condition."

I am not of course opposed a priori to the various liberation movements that are organized by and in the name of religion and nationality (or any other "identity": to women's, gay, or black liberation, for example) but rather to that in the name of which and ultimately, therefore, for the sake of which they are organized and made practical and concrete: "identity" itself. In this case it is the tribal identities of particular patriarchal religions, particular patriarchal nation-states. I am objecting, that is, to the particular political ends (though not all political ends) to which the originally non-aligned, anarchic-*ethical* experience of and desire for being-otherwise-than-being a representative or member of a class, that is, for being beyond political determinations, are repeatedly subordinated. And to the language of *spirituality* in particular, which in this case, as I fear in most in our culture, colludes in that process of subordination of the ethical to the political: recuperating the aspiration to being-beyond to being-as, parole originaire to parole parlée, politique originaire to politique secondaire.[10]

I have always been uncomfortable with the language of spirituality and its tendency to "other-worldliness" in particular; that is, with its presumption of and aspiration to a being-otherwise-than-being *in and of the material world*—to a being beyond "materialist interpretations" as Berger puts it in this article. This tendency to "other-worldliness" sets up an opposition, a separation, a hiatus between "spiritual" and "material" being, between "spirit" and "flesh" and "soul" and "body" from which depend a whole series of autogenous binary oppositions by means of which relations of ruling are rationalized and reproduced (personal/political, self/other, mind/body, particular/universal, etc.). The differentiation of "spirit" from "matter," for example, both mystifies and falsifies the complex reality of material being by splitting off from it its most creative and potentially subversive possibilities and effects and syphoning them off into and for some "transcendent" space of other-worldliness, of the *immaterial*: of God, the soul, and/or the human spirit. This postulate of an immaterial and "transcendent" soul, spirituality, or "Otherness" secures the "quiddity" of the material world as it is and at the same time the safety of the political status quo that organizes it. It thus abandons us to politics—and politics to politicians—by appropriating the mundane ethical experience of and motivation toward otherness, to being-otherwise-than-being the realization of a pre-existing category or class, for a "spirituality" that is "out of this world."

The experiences, knowledges, values, aspirations, and desires characteristically claimed for a transcendent "spirituality" do not, I believe, require nor are they well served by "other-worldly" and/or would-be "non-materialist" interpretations: I mean experiences of the "beyond" and the "ineffable," for example, of "transcendence," "oneness," the "absolute," and "God," and of the humility, grace, fear, love, sin, or guilt that living in "God's presence" can entail. All of these can, I think, be understood in terms of the particular and specific contingencies, complexities, and neccessary mysteries of our existence as particular and specific, contingent and complex material beings: beings who can think and speak, but always only from a spatio-temporally particular and partial point of view; beings who live in a particular and specific contingent and complex material world that thinks and speaks through us. The experience of so-called "spiritual" transcendent and necessary realities like "God," for example, can be understood as and in terms of the experience of the necessary excess of being over thought (and vice versa): as and in terms of experiences of the necessary and inevitable incommensurability of thought and that of which it is the thought, for thinking beings and beings thought (*that think in us*) that are neither dead nor complete—if complete, then dead.[11]

This experience of both the mystery and necessity of the incommensurability of being and thought, this apprehension of both reality and experience as *more than* what appears, more than what we know or can ever know, as that which exceeds any cognitive or practical grasp we have of it—this experience of "being-beyond-being," if you like—has been claimed for "God" by traditional religions and institutionalized discourses of spirituality, that is, it has been claimed for a spirituality that transcends the material world. I want to claim it back for our material experience of the material world, which in its contingency and temporality always exceeds any and every consciousness we have of it and any and every organizing structure we impose upon it. Just as we exceed every and any particular category which names us, and our categories exceed any and every particular application of them. The language of "transcendence" (of a "spirituality" that "transcends" the material world) misrepresents (mystifies and falsifies, obscures and obfuscates) this vital, dynamic, and always ambiguous negotiated and negotiable relationship of excess (of the necessary and constant movement of convergence and divergence between being and otherwise-than-being) with its implicit or explicit hypostasis of a division in human being, in Being itself, which is absolute, constitutive, and irremediable. On the contrary so-called "spiritual" experiences, aspirations, and values do not refer to a reality (or Being) beyond the material world but to a reality (or being) beyond its categorical frameworks and any particular apprehension or *sens/signifiance* we may have of it. They refer, that is, to what I have been calling the *space-between* category and reality, text and context, language and being, the space that is also the condition of possibility (and necessity) of both our ethical and political relations with others (with otherness). I said earlier that managing, and in our own case suturing, this space-between is absolutely central to any and every political system and that categorical schemes and institutionalized knowledges work toward this end by organizing and interpreting our experience into meanings and activities that preserve and reproduce the interests and intrumentalities of the powers that be. Institutionalized religions and discourses of spirituality are part of this management process, part of the apparatus of ruling. They pick up the "slack" of the secular categorical schemas, the residues and remainders of languages and lives that are potential resources for *parole* and *politique originaire*, for disaffection and resistance, and work them up into supplementary systems of authorized meanings, which reconcile us to the status quo while offering us the illusion of negotiating ourselves a better deal within it. The consumer economy and the discourse of commodities and needs that fuels it does the same thing. It, too, speaks to the excess of being over being-as, to our experience of this excess and to our desire to have this experienced excess, this *space-between* category and reality, acknowledged, valued, and inhabited. But the consumer economy and the discourse of commodities do so by re-covering and recuperating this excess all the more securely into the old systems of meanings for more of the Same: the same old identities, meanings, loyalties, relations, realities, and values of family, sexuality, self, freedom, modernity, masculinity, femininity, identity, progress, etc.

It saddens me to see contemporary would-be critical theorists of the modern and/or postmodern condition (like Berger here) doing the same thing: speaking to and from the *space-between* which is the condition of possibility of their critical speech as it is of all (radical/ethical) judgment and critique, only to obfuscate that space of *parole* and *politique originaire* under familiar political categories of traditional identities, nationalities and religions (here masquerading as an immaterial "spirituality") and thereby denying the significance of the ethical relation, of the space-between, as a (political) reality, experience, or value worth fighting for. This is precisely how would-be radical progressive and/or revolutionary political movements lose their radical, progressive, and/or revolutionary edge and end up reproducing the systems they set out to critique and/or offer alternatives to. Contemporary struggles within and about feminism and postmodernism, for example, tend to assume the terms and relevancies of the politics they purport to reject—the ancient and familiar categories of subjects and objects, self and other, identity and difference, man and woman, freedom and necessity, for example—as if these categories of thought were commensurate with the contingent and concrete realities they organize and describe, and as if the categories, the realities, and especially the *relationship between* them were unambivalent and transparent. It is as if we are afraid to "come out" from the categories that—uncomfortable and contradictory as the lives they afford us may be—at least supply us with a place in the *polis*, that is with the appropriate mask of "objective" authoritative knowledge and a voice that will be heard as, and because, it is "re-presentative" of an identifiable category or class: as the voice of Québec, or Canada, or black women, or gay men, or whatever. Organizing under and identifying with the category that organizes our position in and exclusions from the *polis* (with the category of woman, lesbian, Jew, black, or native, for example) may be necessary for winning for ourselves (as women, lesbians, Jews, blacks, or natives) more and better space within it. But if this is as far as the political gesture goes, if it stops with the institutionalized categories themselves, then it is not really subversive of the politics with which it is engaged. Our lives exceed the categories that organize our relationship to power and to each other. Claiming that excess against the category that names and contains us broadens the political scope of the category and thus the political scope of our lives. But it leaves the category and the "class" system it articulates intact and available for recuperation and control by and for the ruling apparatus if this is all it does. If it does not at the same time challenge the politics and practices of representation itself, that is the organization of experience and affect into discrete and exclusive categories of being (identities) through which our encounter with the world and others is mediated as always-already predicative the prescriptive, and thereby irresponsible to the otherness of others and the possibilities of fundamental difference and change, of *parole* and *politique originaire*. If politics is "merely" politics, that is, if political struggle fails to acknowledge or inhabit the space-between of the *ethical* relation with others, then no matter how radical or subversive its claims and selfconscious ends, it will always reproduce the instrumentalities and ends of its "point du départ," of the regimes it purports to oppose. As I have argued elsewhere, the politics of postmodernism in its most visible and increasingly hegemonic (and productive) manifestations does this.[12] It takes modernist representations of reality at face value and proceeds to reject or reform them, all the time speaking not from the *space-between* reality and representation, context, and text, which permits the critique in the first place, but from the places prescribed by modernism itself, from the spaces of the modernist text.[13] It thus binds us all the more securely and narrowly to and within the sedimented meanings, instrumentalities, and ends of the modernist status quo: to and within, that is, the increasingly atomized, volatilized, fragmented, and impoverished categories of subjective/subjected being upon which the contemporary version of the "modernist project" depends.

Meanwhile business is booming in the "psyche" departments and the doctors of the "soul" and "spirit" (gurus, therapists, healers, homeopaths, etc.) have never had it so good. And business will continue to boom in the "psyche" department (and we will get even more "sick" and "fed-up") as long as we confuse ourselves and our world with our categories. As long, that is, as we insist, in theory and in practice, on *coinciding* with our social and political identities—with our names—on the one hand and *pathologizing* our experiences of excess, disjuncture, difference, ambiguity, undecidability, contingency, chaos, and chance on the other. As long as we insist, that is, on pathologizing and abjecting our experience of the *ethical* relation with others, which is our nourishment and our hope: our experience of being-otherwise-than-being a re-presentative of the category or class that names and contains us and separates us from each other; of being more and less than a man, a woman, a black, a mother, a lesbian, a Jew, etc. As I have argued, these experiences of excess are not only ineradicable for material beings in a material world, they are the necessary and indispensable conditions of ecstasy, creativity, change, and critique—and of *parole* and *politique originaire*.

The Prague photograph, and the political events it commemorates, speaks to me of and to these experiences of excess—of being beyond and between being-as. It bespeaks, that is, not a (re)turn to "spiritual" values supposedly antithetical to and repudiated and abandoned by "materialist" philosophies but the truth, promise, and openness of the *space-between* identities, national and religious. It affirms, inhabits, and performs the space of the specifically ethical relation with others and the possibility, therefore, of a future that could (always) be otherwise: otherwise-than-being more of the same.[14]

NOTES

1. Eleanor Godway introduces the concept of *politique originaire* in "Towards a Phenomenology of Politics: Expression and Praxis" *Merleau-Ponty, Hermeneutics and Post-modernism*, eds. in Thomas Busch and Shaun Gallagher (New York: SUNY Press, 1992) 161–70. See chapter 10 *passim,* and especially note 39.
2. Under "stake" in the *Penguin English Dictionary* (Harmondsworth, Middlesex, England: Penguin Books, 1965), 667.
3. Vaclav Havel, "Letter to Dr. Gustav Husak," in *Living in Truth*, ed. Jan Vladislav, trans. A. G. Brain (London: Faber and Faber, 1987), 15; original emphases.
4. Godway, "Phenomenology of Politics," 168.
5. First published in Philippa Berry and Andrew Wernick, eds. *Shadow of Spirit. Postmodernism and Religion* (London: Routledge, 1992), 111–22; and in *Listening. Journal of Religion and Culture* 27, no. 2 (Spring 1992): 119–32.
6. *The Guardian,* Thursday, 22 March 1990, 23 & 25.
7. All subsequent references and citations are to and from Emmanuel Levinas, *Collected Philosophical Papers*, trans. by Alphonso Lingis (The Hague: Martinus Nijhoff, 1987).
8. Godway, "Phenomonology of Politics." 168.
9. This paragraph juxtaposes, paraphrases, and condenses a number of Levinas's ideas and observations from a number of different essays and contexts. Some precise citations are given below but for further clarification of Levinas's precise uses of these terms (which is not reflected here), see *Collected Philosophical Papers*,

   "A relationship with the absolute other . . . opens the very dimensions of infinity, of what puts a stop to the irresistible imperialism of the same and the 'I'." (55).

   "The ethical relationship is not grafted on to an antecedent relationship of cognition; it is a foundation and not a superstructure" (56).

   "The other appears to me . . . as what measures me" (57).

   "The face of the other would be the very starting point of philosophy" (59).

   "The relationship with the infinite is not a cognition but an approach, a neighbouring with what signifies itself without revealing itself" (73).

   "The relationship with the other puts me into question. . . . I did not know I was so rich, but I no longer have the right to keep anything for myself" (94).

   "Consciousness is called into question by a face. . . . A face confounds the intentionality that aims at it. . . . The I before the other is infinitely responsible" (97).

   "The beyond from which a face comes signifies as a trace" (103).

   "A trace is a presence of that which properly speaking has never been there, of what is always past" (105).

   "Proximity, beyond intentionality, is the relationship with the neighbour in the moral sense of the term" (119).

   "What is ineffable or incommunicable in inwardness and cannot adhere in the said is a responsibility, prior to freedom" (133).

   "We can have responsibilities for which we cannot consent to death. It is despite myself that the other concerns me" (138).

   "Ethics is not a moment of being; it is otherwise and better than being, the very possibility of the beyond" (165)
10. A similar slippage between the language of politics, ethics, and spirituality

occurs in the writing of Vaclav Havel. Like Berger, Havel presumes a hiatus and an opposition between "material" and "spiritual" being and locates the possibility of both "morality" and human "identity" in the latter: in the sphere of spirituality, and what he calls "transcendence." And like Berger he, too, describes the "spiritual and moral crisis" in eastern Europe as the effect of "a system that drives each man into a foxhole of purely material existence" and in terms of a lost "identity" that is essentially phallic: in terms of impotence, castration, and emasculation. See, for example, Havel, "Letter to Dr. Gustav Husak," 3–35. Nevertheless both Havel and Berger elsewhere in their work espouse an ethics and a politics consistent with and supportive of the "space-between" proposed here. My point is that the traditional discourses and institutions of politics, ethics, and spirituality do not serve their vision well and do not do justice to the "space-between," in fact, obscure and obfuscate it under categories that ultimately reproduce more of the Same.

11. To be sure, the ego knows itself as reflected by all the objective reality it has constituted, or in which it has collaborated; it thus knows itself on the basis of a conceptual reality. But if this conceptual reality exhausted his being, a living man would not be different from a dead man. Generalization is death; it inserts the ego into, and dissolves, it in, the generality of its work. The irreplaceable singularity of the ego is due to its life. (Levinas, *Collected Philosophical Papers*, 36.)
12. See chapters 6, 7, 8, and 9 in this volume.
13. This is particularly and disturbingly true of postmodern debates around sexuality and the body. See chapter 7.
14. The possibility and promise of *politique originaire* inaugurated by the events of 1989, which the Prague photograph bears witness to and which John Berger celebrates in *The Guardian* article, were all too quickly recuperated by, for, and into a familiar politics of final solutions: a *politique secondaire* realized most vividly and tragically in the "ethnic cleansing" of the former Yugoslavia, which is going on even as I write.

Chapter 12
Twelve

The Space-Between Ethics and Politics. Or, More of the Same?

THIS CHAPTER WAS ORIGINALLY written as a keynote presentation for the Annual Meeting of the Canadian Society for the Study of Practical Ethics, which was held at Queen's University in Kingston Ontario in May 1991. The subject of the conference was "Feminist Approaches to Practical Ethics," and I was asked to address this question in my opening remarks. I used the occasion to develop the reflection on the relationship between ethics and politics introduced in "The Politics of Contingency" (chapter 10) and elaborated in more detail in the essay on sprituality that followed (chapter 11). Although the question of *feminist* ethics provided the occasion for these reflections, and a concrete and immediate example of the issues involved, the problematic they address extends beyond feminism (or any other particular politics) to the *question of ethics* itself—the question that *is* ethics, as I argue below—and its relationship to the political exigencies of our language(s) and lives.

I argue here that ethics (ethical experience, knowledge, value, truth, reality) is precisely that which puts politics into question from the standpoint of the space-between: the space between category and reality, the space of the ethical encounter with the other as other and not more of the Same. That an ethics which relies on the (political) categories of established thought and/or seeks to solidify or cement them into institutionalized rights and freedoms, rules and regulations, and principles of practice—as feminist ethics often does—is not so much an ethics, therefore, *as an abidcation of ethics for politics* under another description. As it exchanges the undecidability, the an-archy, the response-ability of the space-between of the ethical encounter with others for the security, the hier-archy, of the pre-scribed and pre-scriptive places of the categories. Ethical praxis cannot *renounce* politics because it is actually constituted by it, in the space between experience and the (political) categories that organize its *sens*. But it cannot simply identify with politics either for then it would lose its specificity as ethical—as that which brings the political into view *as politics,* that is, as an effect and strategy of the organization of power rather than nature or choice—and as an appropriate object therefore for judgment, contestation, intervention, and change.

This book began as a study of the relationship between discourse and violence. Chapters 1 through 9 show how relations of dominance (division and denial) are both assumed and reproduced, and obfuscated and obscured, in and by the taken-for-granted categories of modernist and postmodernist discourse alike: their presupposition of (white) Western Man as the measure of History, Reason, Meaning, Freedom, and Truth, for example, and the rhetoric of nobody in particular and everyone in general that coincides with it. These chapters explore the power effects/the effects of power of the taken-for-granted categories of (post)modern discourse(s) (the discourses of science and sex, politics, subjectivity, and freedom, for example) and the various liquidations of particularity they accomplish: their silencing—their disappearing—of particular bodies, peoples, realities, histories, experiences, knowledges, values, and truths.

Brian Fawcett calls this liquidation of particularity—this obliteration of local memory and imagination—genocide.[1] Jean-Paul Sartre and Jean-François Lyotard call it Terror.[2] And I call it, in chapter 6 for example, the politics of final solutions.

> The method is identical with Terror in its inflexible refusal to differentiate; its goal is total assimilation at the least possible effort. The aim is not to integrate what is different as such, while preserving for it a relative autonomy, but rather to suppress it. Thus the perpetual movement toward identification reflects the bureaucrats' practice of unifying everything.[3]

Speaking as and on behalf of nobody in particular and everyone in general, this "bureaucrats' practice of unifying everything" suppresses not just difference(s) but the contingency, temporality, materiality, and originality of the flesh of human being/of being human itself and thus the very *possibility of difference*: of political difference—of a different politics—of things being otherwise than they have already been.

In chapter 10 I described this politics of final solutions as a politics of the Prince—a politics of privilege and power, of *parole parlée*, of *pensée de survol*—and outlined the possibility of a different politics, a politics of *différance*,[4] which takes its point of departure and its end(s) not from the (abstract) principals and proprieties of the Prince (the Sovereign Subject of History, Reason, Freedom, and Truth) but from the (concrete) particularities and ambiguities—the contingencies—of the flesh. The question of ethics—of the ethical encounter with the other as other and not more of the Same—came into view from this standpoint of contingency, beyond and between the categories that otherwise obscure it and obfuscate its possibilities. Hence the violence—the effects of violence—of authorized/authoritative discourse(s). For in its insistence on totality, on unifying everything, in both its modern and postmodern manifestations, authorized/authoritative discourse leaves no place for the other: for the encounter with the face/the flesh of the other that "breaks up the system"[5] (exceeds the calculus of the already known) and provokes the ethical response, that is, the infinite responsibility of the I before the other whose gaze "forbids me my conquest,"[6] which is "a foundation and not a superstructure"[7] (a command and not a choice) and of which the logos is "You shall not kill."[8]

Thus a book that began as a study of discourse and violence ends with a discussion of ethics and its relationship to politics and philosophy, a relationship that could not emerge as a question or a responsibility from the standpoint of politics and/or the established philosophies that support it. For it comes into view as a possibility and reality only in the space between categories in the an-archic experience of being they organize and contain. Although they appear at the end of this book, the ideas expounded here on the relationship between ethics and politics should not be regarded as conclusive. On the contrary they represent just the beginning of an inquiry that is ongoing and that will be presented in greater detail in a future work.

The Space-Between Ethics and Politics. Or, More of the Same?[9]

For the past several years I have been trying to understand the relationship between ethics and politics: between ethical realities, convictions, experiences, principles, purposes, and ends and political realities, convictions, experiences, principles, purposes, and ends. And I am happy to report that I have come to some conclusions.

My point of departure in this reflection has been that ethics and politics are *not* the same and that attempts to reduce one to the other, while tempting and comforting and in some sense enabling, whichever way the reduction operates: ethics to politics or vice versa, never do justice to the complexity and particularity of the concrete issues involved. I now think that these reductive moves, to collapse ethics and politics into each other, also sabotage the ethical and/or political motivations and ends they are usually intended to serve. Nevertheless it seems to me that this is in fact the direction most efforts to think and practice ethics and politics *together* take: resolving into some form or other of either a classical 'idealist' position, which privileges ethics and posits politics as merely ethics writ large (characteristic of but not exclusive to the political Right), or the alternative 'materialist' position, which privileges politics and posits ethics as merely politics writ small (characteristic of but not exclusive to the political Left). What I have been trying to develop is an understanding and practice of ethics and politics *together* that preserves the specificity of each while honoring their inherent and inevitable connectedness.

I believe everyone has an ethics, just as everyone has a politics; whether or not they articulate, acknowledge, or deny it. What I mean by this is that our choices and actions are always and to some extent grounded in and motivated by our experiences and assumptions about the nature, value, and meaning of human existence in general and our own lives in particular. And this is what I mean by "having an ethics." Likewise our choices and actions are always in some sense and to some extent grounded in and motivated by our experiences and assumptions about the nature, value, and meaning of power in general and our own relationship to it in particular. And this is what I mean by "having a politics."

These two sets of experiences—knowledges and realities, the ethical and the political—are obviously connected. Ethical experience (knowledge and reality) always and only occurs within the context of power, that is, within a social situation already organized and interpreted by and for specific political interests, agents, and ends. While politics, the social organization and institutionalization of power, only and always occurs within the context of an ethics that can enable and excuse it. The subtleties and specifics of this relationship between ethical and political realities (experiences, knowledges, values, and ends) and the implications of this for feminist praxis are the subject of this chapter.

Since ethical praxis always occurs within a particular political context, it will (either by default or design) *confirm* the values, goals, and ends of the political situation within which it is situated and thereby the hierarchies of power and control that they enable and sustain, or it will *contest* them. Ethical praxis will, that is, either *endorse* a particular society's vision of the "good life," the life worth living and dying for, which is discursively and concretely embodied in its landscape, architecture, and institutions as much as it is in its actual ideologies, or it will call that vision and those institutions into question. I espouse the kind of ethical praxis that puts the values, principles, and practices of the political status quo and the vision of the "good life" which animates and is animated by it, into question. In fact I go further than this to define ethical praxis in these terms: in terms of the question that *is* ethics, an ethics that must always pose the question of ethics and put the political status quo into question.

Ethical praxis which merely rearticulates the values and goals of the status quo to realities identified as problematic, for it seem to me to be not so much *ethical* interventions directed toward fundamental issues of right and wrong and the constitution of the good life as *technical* and for that reason *political* interventions directed toward the fine tuning of the norms and procedures already in place to accommodate new realities within the system that might otherwise disturb its hierarchies of power and control or its appearance of Reason and Right. Much of what passes for "ethical" in the theories and practices of professional, practical, and applied ethics is not really ethical at all therefore from this point of view but rather technical-political in the given sense. For they do not actually raise or address *ethical* questions about the implicit or explicit values animating and directing the arguments, institutions, and practices under their scrutiny and the society that has produced them but rather technical, pragmatic, logistical, *political* questions about professional etiquette, accountability, and control, and the policing of the boundaries of competing individual and institutional jurisdictions.

Calls for the construction of an alternative feminist ethics,[10] or for a code of ethics for feminist praxis—in business, medicine, or research, for example—tend to fall under this description: raising not so much *ethical* questions about the fundamental norms and values animating Western society and its institutionalized practices and priorities; nor even *ethical* questions about the values animating feminism in general or its own feminist agenda in particular, but *technical-political* questions about extending or modifying the norms and values already in place to accommodate women and/or feminist criticisms of practices that have been done in their name. They are, that is, more about regulation, accountability, and control than ethics.

This tendency to pre-empt the ethical question(s) by and for technical-political ones characterizes most feminist praxis, including that which explicity calls itself ethical. This includes feminist interventions in sexuality and reproduction (around issues of abortion, pornography, sexual preference, custody, new reproductive technologies, etc.), in economics (on issues of affirmative action, equal pay for work of equal value, pensions, housework, welfare, and so on), in the areas of physical and mental health (around questions of consent and the medicalization of women's bodies), and in the various movements for peace and protection of the environment. Feminist interventions in these and other areas—both practical and theoretical—tend not to *challenge* the *ethical* premises of the institutions and practices that are the focus of their concern but rather to *use* them to criticize the *political* praxis that is done in their name. They do not pose the ethical question (the question which *is* ethics, the question *of* ethics) but, on the contrary, assume the ethical premises of the system as adequate to and for their own struggles against it.

Feminist praxis tends, that is, to pre-empt ethical enquiry and thus the possibility of forging the conditions for real change—for the fulfilment of its own radical ends—by articulating its criticisms and objectives in terms of the categories and values already endorsed by and institutionalized in the political realities we are struggling to change: the values of autonomy, control, freedom, equality, identity, ownership, choice, utility, agency, reason, responsibility, and rights. These are the authorized and regulatory categories of moral debate in our society. So much so that if you do not express yourself in their terms you will not be heard as having an ethics worthy of the name nor, therefore, an argument or cause worthy of discussion, respect, or public debate. Claims to moral goods, which are not or cannot be articulated within these authorized categories of Western thought, are ruled out of court: out of the discursive domains of both ethics and politics as irrelevant, idiosyncratic, arbitrary, atavistic, subjective, sentimental, naive, or merely "relative"; as gratuitous personal or culturally specific whims beyond rational accountability or therefore collective intervention or control; as matters of aesthetics—of taste and "lifestyle"—rather than ethics, and as matters for individual and personal and not collective and political agency, responsibility, or change.

It is entirely understandable that feminists should make their claims against the system in terms the system recognizes as reasonable, rational, and possibly right. Indeed it is more than understandable, it is absolutely indispensable to feminist praxis, as it is to any and all politics. But it is not enough, and it certainly is not *ethical* in the sense proposed here, if this is *all* we do. If we do not at the same time question the values we are obliged to invoke in making our claims against the status quo, the values of freedom, identity, equality, choice, and control—for example; the values of liberal individualism upon which the contemporary *polis* relies for its legitimation, reproduction, and control. We may have to articulate our claims against that *polis* in its terms, but we do not have to *believe* in them. Indeed we must not believe in them, for they actually betray the truth of our political praxis: its ethical motivation and its condition of possibility in the *space-between* the categories of political thought. This I will now explain.

There would not be dissent, disaffection, resistance, or change (or social or individual pathology, for that matter) if the articulated and authoritative categories, norms, and values of society were adequate to experience. If, that is, language were commensurate with life, or representation with reality. But this is not the case. The contingent and changing concrete world always exceeds the ideal categories of thought within which we attempt to express and contain it. And the same is true of people. We are always both more and less than the categories that name and divide us—more and less, that is, than a woman, a man, a Christian, a Jew, a mother, a worker, a wife. More and less than *what we stand for in the polis and what stands for us*. Our lives leave remainders (they say more than they mean) just as our categories leave residues (they mean more than they say). Lives and categories are incommensurable. They exceed each other, leaving in their wake a fertile precipitate of an-archical *sens* or *signifiance*[11] which ex-sists beyond and between given categorical frameworks—beyond and between the knowable and the already known—as an always available (re)source of difference, resistance, and change: of being-otherwise-than-being a *re*-presentation of an already instituted (and therefore *pre*-scribed, *pre*-dicated, and *pre*-determined) category or class: man, woman, child, Christian, Muslim, Jew.

This space between category and experience, representation and reality, language and life, is, I believe, the necessary and indispensable space of judgment: of creativity and value, resistance and change. It is the ground of the critical intentions and originating experiences that enable us to call the status quo into question and challenge the already known universe and its organization into the predicative and prescriptive categories of practical reason. It constitutes the space and the experience within which the conventionality, the contingency, the arbitrariness of the familiar realities of the natural attitude—of its categorical positivities and identities—can be seen and challenged.

In another context I identified this space as the space and ground of "spirituality" and "desire,"[12] that is, of our experience of and aspiration to "transcendence": not of the *flesh* of the material world itself but of the categories that frame and contain it and the possibilities of our own being within it. It is as such *the* ethical space, the space of the specifically *ethical* encounter with others (with otherness) as *other* and not more of the same: as otherwise-than-being simply a re-presentation of a pre-conceived, pre-scribed, predetermined and thus pre-dicative category and class—a re-presentation that relieves us of the ethical responsibility of attending to the particularity of the other and inventing our relationship with it (him or her). By contrast the space-between reality and representation presents me with, puts me in the presence of, that which has never been there before: the other in all its singularity as a visitation, an epiphany (to use Levinas's terms),[13] an absolute exteriority that cannot, without violence, be integrated into the Same. It is a presenting, a presence, that puts *me* into question as well as the relationship, the world, and the common sense (*sens commun*) we may or may not share. It is an encounter that demands/commands me to think and be anew: to risk being-otherwise-than-being what I have already become.

Managing this silent but nevertheless signifying (*signifiant*) space between the pre-thematic an-archical/ethical and the categorical/hier-archical encounter with others—this space of the otherwise-than-being a re-presentation of a pre-existing category or class—is absolutely central to the exercise of political power and to the organization of our subjection to it. Absolutely central that is to our "subjectivity": our being as subjects of experiences and actions that "count" (or don't count as the case may be), of sentences that make sense (*sens*) in the polis; central that is to our access to language and thus to our social status and survival. (Which should give us pause, therefore, when claiming our "identities" as women, blacks, or gays, for example, as anything other than a provisional strategic political claim for provisional, strategic political ends. I will be coming back to this later.) Categorical schemas and institutionalized discourses (the discourses of politics, ethics, philosophy, science, religion, spirituality, sport, sex, literature, art, etc.) work toward this end of managing and in our own society suturing—though this need not be the case—this vital ethical space between representation and reality, language and life.[14] They channel the affective anarchical ethical residues and remainders of experience (of being-otherwise-than-being) into authorized categorical hierarchical meanings, intentionalities and desires compatible with and amenable to the controlling interests of prevailing political powers.

All political praxis speaks to and from this space, this irrepressible precipitate of being and thought, this constant (re)source of différance,[15] disruption, and change. *Conservative* politics speaks to it to contain, deny, or negate its excesses: to recuperate its deviations and différance into and for the hegemonic categories and relations that constitute and sustain the status quo. Radical or revolutionary politics, like feminism, speak to and from the same precipitate (the same space between representation and reality) to *affirm* it: to inhabit and extend it and to organize it against the status quo for political resistance and change. At least radical politics must begin here, as any critical moment must, in the *experience of disjuncture*, of the incommensurability between language and life, between authorized categories of experience and experience itself. Radical politics must originate here in the as yet untamed excesses and precipitates (residues and remainders) of language and lives, and take its inspiration and direction—at least in the beginning—from the anarchical, ethical relation with others that occurs there between and beyond the categorical imperatives of regulated institutionalized thought. But it cannot remain here if it is to become practical in politics, for to do that it must subordinate its original/originating *ethical* motivations and ends to the strategic necessities of political action within and against the *polis* on its terms—the only terms it will recognize as rational and real.

What concerns me is not that this *subordination of ethics to politics* takes place. On the contrary I recognize it to be an indispensable and inevitable moment of political practice, of engaging in politics for the purpose of producing change.[16] What concerns me is that this truth of the ethical encounter with others/with otherness and its strategic subordination to the exigencies of politics is obfuscated by politics itself: neither recognized nor acknowledged, nor therefore managed or mourned by or within the theories and practices of the would-be radical and resisting politics it actually inspires. And this means that the ethical motivations of politics, in the space between and beyond the categories of the political itself, are lost to its own self-consciousness and, more seriously, abandoned in its praxis. Just as they have been lost and abandoned in the theories and practices of the conservative politics to which they are opposed. And this is what concerns me.

We see this lapse, this collapse, of ethics into politics—this abandonment of liberation for regulation and repression—repeatedly in the trajectories of political movements that begin as movements of resistance or reform. I do not think we need to despair or become cynical about this, as conservative political theorists might suggest—attributing it to the inexorable logic of power, for example, or an inherent failure of human nature. We should rather seek to situate it within the exigencies and antinomies of politics itself and the complexities of the relationship between ethical and political truth. For this disappearance of the ethical into the political in politics which begin as movements of liberation grounded in the ethical encounter with others/with otherness, while alarming, is not surprising. We live in a society that systematically deprives us of a language and a context within which this experience of the space between category and reality can be acknowledged, inhabited, or even named—except as pathological:[17] something to be fixed up or abandoned; a society that actually obfuscates, (denies, distorts, and mystifies) the possibilities and realities of ethical experience, of the ethical encounter with others as other (and not more of the same)—the only encounter that makes a difference and demands a response-ability from me that is not already *pre*-scribed. I do not believe that this is an accidental effect of the discursive and institutional organization of power in Western society, but, on the contrary, a systematic strategy that keeps us tied to our political identities, our tribes (as man, woman, child, black, white, Christian, Jew, etc.). Tied that is to categories that divide and contain us and organize our respective places in the *polis*; that individualize us as appropriate, accessible, and amenable surfaces/subjects for the applications and manipulations of power; and that supply us thereby with our particular interests and *stakes* in the status quo.

It saddens me nevertheless to see the same abandonment of ethics to politics in the theories and practices of contemporary politics of resistance and change, like feminism; in their tendency to assume the terms and relevancies of the politics they purport to reject in the articulation of their own values and ends: the categories of self and other, identity and difference, man and woman, freedom and necessity, for example. As if these categories of thought were commensurate with the contingent and concrete realities they organize and describe, and as if the categories, the realities, and the relationship between them were unambivalent and transparent. As I suggested in the previous chapter, it is as if we are afraid to "come out" from the categories that, uncomfortable and contradictory as the lives they afford us may be, at least supply us with a place in the *polis* and with the mask of re-presentation and authority; with a voice that can be heard *as and because* it is re-presentative of an identifiable category or class, an identifiable political subject and interest: the identity, subjectivity, and interest of black, native, lesbian, white, or working women, for example.

Organizing under and identifying with the category that articulates our inclusions and exclusions in and from the *polis* (with the category of woman, lesbian, black, native, and so on) may be necessary for winning for ourselves (as women, lesbians, blacks, native women) more and better space within it. But if this is as far as our political gesture goes—if it stops with the already instituted categories themselves—then it is not really subversive of the politics with which it is engaged nor, and this I think is more important, of the ethics upon which that politics depends and which it in turn reproduces in its praxis.[18]

Our lives exceed the categories that organize our relationship to power and to each other. And it is this experience of excess that is the condition of possibility of resistance and dissent in the first place. Claiming that excess against the category that names and contains us broadens the political scope of the category and thus the political scope of our lives. It is, in this sense, liberating. But it leaves the category and the political system it articulates intact and available for recuperation and control by, for, and within the ruling apparatus even if it includes new personnel—if this is all it does. If it does not at the same time continue to pose the ethical question—the question of ethics, the question which is ethics—the question of our *ethical* relations with others. And this means questioning the politics and practices of (political) *re-presentation* itself: the organization of experience and affect into discrete and exclusive categories of being (of identity) through which our encounter with the world and others is mediated as always already predicative and pre-scriptive and, thus, un-response-able to the otherness of others and the possibilities of difference and change.

If politics is only politics—getting the best deal possible, seeking, keeping, and exercising power, that is if politics fails to acknowledge or inhabit or nurture the *space-between* of our ethical relations with others/with otherness, then no matter how radical or subversive its claims and self-conscious ends, it will always end up reproducing the instrumentalities and ends of its point of departure, of the régime it purports to oppose. It is disturbing to see contemporary politics of identity in some of its most accessible and increasingly institutionalized manifestations doing just that: taking familiar political representations of reality at face value (the representations of liberal individualism: the categories of rights and freedoms, self and other, identity and difference) and rejecting or reforming them as the case may be. Speaking not from the *space-between* reality and representation, between context and text, which permits the political critique in the first place, but *from the places prescribed by the ruling representations themselves*: the spaces of the modernist (liberal-democratic) text—of the abstract, disembodied subject of freedom and rights. The politics of identity risks binding us thereby all the more securely and narrowly to and within the politics it is actually struggling against: to and within the re-presentations and categories, the identities and values, of the political status quo; the sedimented meanings, instrumentalities, and ends of liberalism; and the increasingly atomized, volatilized, fragmented, divided, divisive, and impoverished categories of subjective/subjected being upon which the contemporary version of its project depends.

A specifically *ethical* political praxis would consist in resisting this movement of institutionalization: this inherent tendency of contemporary politics to obfuscate and abandon its ethical conditions of possibility in the experience of the *space-between*, in the interest of making claims and consolidating political gains. A specifically ethical political praxis would consist, that is, in honoring and nurturing, acknowledging, inhabiting, and *speaking from* the *space-between* representation and reality, language and life, category and experience: the space of the ethical encounter with others as other and not more of the same—a space and an encounter which puts *me* into question, which challenges and changes me, as well as the other (the otherness of the other) and the socius/the system that contains and sustains us. It is a praxis that will cost me something if it is effective. A praxis of the absolutely particular[19] for which there can be no rules, no codes, no principles, and no guarantees. A praxis of risk and response-ability in which, I believe, lies our only hope for real political change.

NOTES

1. Brian Fawcett, *Cambodia. A Book for People Who Find Television too Slow* (Vancouver: Talonbooks, 1986).
2. Jean-Paul Sartre, *Search for a Method*, trans. Hazel Barnes (New York: Vintage Books, 1963); Jean-François Lyotard, *The Postmodern Condition. A Report on Knowledge* (Minneapolis: University of Minnesota Press, 1984).
3. Jean-Paul Sartre, *Search for a Method*, 48.
4. For *différance*, see note 14 below.
5. Emmanuel Levinas, *Collected Philosophical Papers*, trans. Alphonso Lingis (The Hague: Martinus Nijhoff, 1987), 43.
6. Ibid., 55.
7. Ibid., 56.
8. Ibid., 55.
9. *Who is the 'We'? Absence of Community*, Eleanor Godway and Geraldine Finn (eds.) (Montreal: Black Rose Books, 1994) 101–105.
10. As in the following, for example, Carol Gilligan, *In a Different Voice* (Cambridge: Harvard University Press, 1982); Nel Noddings, *Caring* (Berkeley: University of California Press, 1984); Sara Ruddick, *Maternal Thinking. Toward*

a Politics of Peace (Boston: Beacon Press, 1989); Lorraine Code, Sheila Mullett, and Christine Overall, eds., *Feminist Perspectives: Philosophical Essays on Method and Morals* (Toronto: Toronto University Press, 1988); Marwenna Griffiths and Margaret Whitford, eds., *Feminist Perspectives in Philosophy* (Bloomington: Indiana University Press, 1988).

11. *Sens* in French means both direction (or way) and meaning; *signifiance* (from the verb *signifier*: to signify, mean) refers to signifying as an *activity* (to be distinguished from *signification*: significance, meaning, which refers to the object of activity, or to an already accomplished or given meaning).
12. See chapter 11 in this volume.
13. See, for example, Emmanuel Levinas, *Collected Philosophical Papers.*
14. Chapter 11 describes how the discourse(s) of spirituality and religion, for example, manage/suture this space-between of the ethical encounter with others.
15. "Differance is what makes the movement of signification possible only if each element that is said to be 'present,' appearing on the stage of presence, is related to something other than itself but retains the mark of a past element and already lets itself be hollowed out by the mark of its relation to a future element. This trace relates no less to what is called the future than to what is called the past, and it constitutes what is called the present by this very relation to what it is not, to what it absolutely is not" (Jacques Derrida, "Differance," in *Speech and Phenomena And Other Essays on Husserl's Theory of Signs*, trans. David Allison [Evanston: Northwestern University Press, 1973], 142–43). Derrida's neologism *différance* refers to the activity of differing/deferring which is constitutive of sense/*sens*: to the movement of (the production of) differences without origin or end which makes meaning both possible and ultimately and always undecidable. It designates the incommensurability of language and life—in my terms—the *space-between* category and experience.
16. I am no longer sure that "subordination" is the best description here, or whether the subordination of ethics to politics is as indispensable and inevitable for political practice as I claim. As indicated in the foreword to this chapter, the ideas presented here mark the beginning of a study of the relationship between ethics and politics which is ongoing and which will be elaborated in more detail in a future publication.
17. As, for example, in the discourses and practices of sociology, psychology, psychiatry, criminology, sexology, pedagogy, etc.
18. It is an ethics of freedom and rights that is founded on liberal notions of the self—as discrete, identifiable, proprietorial, and singular with discrete, identifiable, proprietoral, and singular interests, origins, and ends. An ethics which thereby denies the reality of the *space-between* and, thus, the reality of the ethical encounter with others it makes possible; and correspondingly, therefore, the possibility of a different political ethic—an ethic of différance such as the one proposed here.
19. Particularity is not the same as individuality: it does not imply the exclusivity of an I-dentity for which others are Other as individuality does; nor, correspondingly, the inclusivity of a self who is sufficient ("present" in Derrida's sense—see note 14 above) to itself. Particularity, contingency, and the flesh are key terms in my efforts to elaborate a specifically *ethical* political practice. They are the focus of my present work and will be explicated in greater detail in a future publication.

Chapter 13
Thirteen
THE FUTURE OF POSTMODERNISM

The difference between poetry and rhetoric
is being
ready to kill
yourself
instead of your children

I am trapped on a desert of raw gunshot wounds
and a dead child dragging his shattered black
face off the edge of my sleep
blood from his punctured cheeks and shoulders
is the only liquid for miles and my stomach
churns at the imagined taste while
my mouth splits into dry lips
without loyalty or reason
thirsting for the wetness of his blood
as it sinks into the whiteness
of the desert where I am lost
without imagery or magic
trying to make power out of hatred and destruction
trying to heal my dying son with kisses
only the sun will bleach his bones quicker

The policeman who shot down a 10-year-old in Queens
stood over the boy with cop shoes in childish blood
and a voice said "Die you little motherfucker" and
there are tapes to prove that. At his trial
this policeman said in his own defense
"I didn't notice the size or nothing else
only the color" and
there are tapes to prove that, too.

Today that 37-year-old white man with 13 years of police forcing
has been set free
by 11 white men who said they were satisfied
justice had been done
and one black woman who said
"They convinced me" meaning
they had dragged her 4' 10" black woman's frame
over the hot coals of four centuries of white male approval

until she let go the first real power she ever had
and lined her own womb with cement
to make a graveyard for our children.

I have not been able to touch the destruction within me.
But unless I learn to use
the difference between poetry and rhetoric
my power too will run corrupt as poisonous mold
or lie limp and useless as an unconnected wire
and one day I will take my teenaged plug
and connect it to the nearest socket
raping an 85-year-old white woman
who is somebody's mother
and as I beat her senseless and set a torch to her bed
a greek chorus will be singing in 3/4 time
"Poor thing. She never hurt a soul. What beasts they are."

—"Power" by Audre Lorde, *Black Unicorn*

IT SEEMS APPROPRIATE TO close this book with a poem from Audre Lorde and what will probably be my last word on postmodernism. Last because postmodernism is no longer the political or intellectual provocation it once was—as I argue below. But also because the focus of my own work has shifted from the critique of dominant discourse(s) /the discourse(s) of dominance to the articulation of alternatives to them from the standpoint of the space between the categories which organize their rationality and their ends: alternatives that will not (re)produce the politics (of final solutions) of the past, nor therefore a future that is more of the same.

This chapter was originally written for the Royal Society of Canada Conference on "The Future of Post-Modernism" held as part of the Learned Societies' Meetings at the University of Prince Edward Island in Charlottetown, Prince Edward Island, in May 1992. I was asked to speak specifically to the political implications of postmodernism as well as to comment on the other papers presented at the conference, some of which I had received ahead of time. What I decided to do was take the organizing question of the conference seriously—the question of The Future of Postmodernism—and explore the temporal imagination(s) informing postmodernism and the future(s) at stake in its various contestations, and thereby develop a framework for considering the political implications of postmodernism in general and the arguments of the conference papers in particular. I began by reading my prepared text on The Future of Postmodernism, and then signaled briefly and schematically some of the ways the papers we heard in the morning exemplified its arguments.

But first I read the poem by Audre Lorde that appears at the beginning of this chapter, the opening lines of which kept interrupting my concentration as I tried to read Peter McCormick's paper on poetry and postmodernism for the first time:[1]

The difference between poetry and rhetoric
is being
ready to kill
yourself
instead of your children

I first encountered the poem in a collection published in 1978 and decided to read it as the point of departure of my commentary on the politics and future of postmodernism well before the Los Angeles judgment acquitting the white police officers who beat Rodney King forced "race relations" back into the streets and onto the central stage of North American politics—shortly before this conference took place.

I wanted to read *Power* to this Royal Society of Canada Conference on The Future of Postmodernism as an example of a living poetry of the present—of the truly *post* modern, from my point of view—whose relationship to morality, meaning, politics, and life is not in doubt. A poetry which completely dis-places the problematic explored by McCormick through the figure of the modernist Italian poet Eugenio Montale of the relationship between art and reality (the problematic of mimesis or self-referentiality, actual universals or fictional particulars, in his terms), because it speaks from and to an other place and in an other voice: the place and voice of modernism's Other. I offered it, that is, as indicative of a political reality that I argue is ultimately responsible for putting the question of *post* modernism on the intellectual agenda.

Interestingly enough the name, person, and politics of Audre Lorde was invoked earlier in the day by Herta Nagl-Docekal in her presentation on the relationship between feminism and postmodernism. Nagl-Docekal re-cited Lorde's description of herself as "a forty-nine-year-old Black lesbian feminist socialist mother of two, including one boy, and a member of an interracial couple" as a "paradigm case" of "the postmodern concept of fractured identities."[2] What concerned me was that Audre Lorde was the only writer cited in this presentation on Feminism and Postmodernism to be so particularized. And I invite you, the reader, as I did the conference participants, to consider why this might be so and what its political implications are. Especially in the light of the fact that Audre Lorde's contribution to postmodernist and/or feminist theory was not considered by Nagl-Docekal in her presentation, nor were the original context and intentionality of Lorde's self-description provided—nor even supplied as a reference for the citation merely re-cited its prior citation by another.[3] What is at stake in these differential sightings/citings/sitings of the place and voice, and the theory and practice, of the postmodern is made more explicit in the comments which follow.

THE FUTURE OF POSTMODERNISM[4]

"Time is not a line but a network of intentionalities."[5]

Postmodernism designates not so much a reality or a set of beliefs about reality, as the taking up of a position toward it: a position of distance, differentiation, and discontinuity from the ancestors in general and from the more immediate ancestors of modernism and modernity in particular.[6] The invocation of the *post* in postmodernism is performative rather than descriptive, therefore, referring to a praxis that *creates* the distance and defines the differences between the modern and the postmodern rather than to a simple taxonomy or chronology that merely registers them as one thing after another.

In a recent article in *Critical Inquiry*, Kwame Anthony Appiah described the praxis of the *post* of postmodernism as a "space-clearing gesture,"[7] and its project as the transcending of modernism: "Which is to say, some relatively self-conscious, self-privileging project of a privileged modernity."[8] Thus postmodernism intends a future that does not repeat the modernist past nor reproduce the temporal imagination that animated it, that supplied it with its condition of possibility, and its ends, and with the necessities of its logic. The future of postmodernism is, therefore, very much dependent upon the past of modernism, upon how that past is assumed by and within the space-clearing ancestor-distancing gestures that constitute it as a *post.*

"A past and a future spring forth when I reach out towards them."[9]

Gestures are not just actions done for effect. They are also and perhaps primarily, expressive actions, movements that express meaning, emotion, feeling. The space-clearing ancestor-distancing gestures of postmodernism are not univocal. They express different feelings about the modernist past and attribute different meanings to it, according to how that past has been experienced, received, and lived through by those who invoke the *post* of postmodernism as the context of their praxis. The space-clearing gestures of postmodernism embody different intentionalities, that is, different attitudes toward the past, and therefore different futures, according to the positions the originators of those gestures have assumed or been assigned in the project of modernity. The future of postmodernism is thus a contested future. Not accidentally but constitutively. For it is the contestation with and against the ancestors and the ancestral project of modernity that defines postmodernism: directing its gestures, organizing its praxis, and determining its future. A future which cannot be anticipated, nor even posed as a question as it is in this symposium, without at the same time engaging in its contestation and creation.

"He who speaks (and that which he understands tacitly) always co-determines the meaning of what he says, the philosopher is always implicated in the problems he poses."[10]

Those heavily invested in or served by the terms and practices of the culture and institutions of modernism, who believe or once believed in its various rhetorics and reasons and in the values and ends of the Enlightenment and the projects of European Imperialism that coincide with it, have clearly found themselves in a panic at the prospect of its end. Faced as they are with what appears to them to be the collapse of *all* reason, meaning, and ends, and the impossibility of *all* value. The space-clearing, ancestor-distancing gesture of this version of postmodernism, the postmodernism of those who once believed in the modernist project, does not so much transcend or even contest the modernist past as assume it as an absolute loss, and the future, therefore, as the project of its repetition or recovery.

Those not so heavily invested in or served by the values and ends of modernism have found much to celebrate and affirm in the collapse of its authority and control. For it has opened up spaces in culture and consciousness where we can speak, hear, and recognize each other and the heretofore subordinated histories, realities, reasons, subjectivities, knowledges, and values of those who have been silenced and suppressed and/or excluded from the project of modernity. The space-clearing, ancestor-distancing gesture of this version of postmodernism *does* contest the modernist past and transcend to one degree or another the limitations of its horizons. This version of postmodernism does not assume the past as a loss to be recuperated or mourned but as a personal, political, and ethical responsibility to be taken up and translated into a future that will be different.

It is of some concern to me, therefore, that the increasingly hegemonic voice of the postmodern, the voice that is claiming and controlling the category and thereby the rites/rights of inclusion and exclusion in and from the theories, practices, places, and futures it organizes, is not the plural, multivocal, situated, and ex-static voice of those for whom there *is* life after modernism, for whom modernism has never been *all* life is or can be. But the singular, univocal, unsituated, and in-sistently modernist voice of those for whom there is no future if it is not a reproduction or repetition—a re-citation—of the Same: the voice of those who continue to speak as and on behalf of *the* subject of (post)modernism as if there were only one subject and one *post* of modernity and in the name of us all: *our* culture, *our* past, *our* civilization, *our* relationship to language and the Other, as if we, too, were also only One. It is a totalizing voice, the still totalizing voice of Enlightenment Reason, which by universalizing the particularities of its own experience of the distance between modernism and postmodernity as a *loss* or *dead* end, erases the traces of the experience of others whose continuing *contestation* of modernism constitutes postmodernism as a praxis of *affirmation* and *generation*: of a future that is not more of the Same, nor a dead end, nor a re-citation or continuation of the past. I have spoken elsewhere of this erasure of the *contestation* that constitutes postmodernism, as a *hijack*:[11] a seizure by force of the ill-gotten gains, the illicit goods so to speak, of those who would displace or transcend the privileges and exclusivities of modernism on behalf of its dispossessed margins, by and for the sake of its traditional benefactors, beneficiaries, and authorities: white, middle-class, Western Man. The question of this symposium offers a good example of how this hijack can work.

> "We shall miss that relationship—which we shall call here the openness upon the world (ouverture au monde)—the moment that the reflective effort tries to capture it."[12]

The question seems innocent enough at face value. It invites us to consider the future of postmodernism: whether or not postmodernism has a future, and what kind of future that might be. But it is *not* an innocent question. It is a trick question that offers with one hand what it takes away with the other: a future for postmodernism, a postmodernism with a future. Because it does not explicitly problematize the postmodernism of which it speaks, does not that is acknowledge that postmodernism is a *contested* category, that is, a category of contestation which designates a praxis constituted in, by, as, and through its contestation of the taken-for-granted past and future of modernity, the question we are asked to consider, the question of postmodernism's future, begs the necessary prior question of postmodernism's *present and past*—the central question of the meaning, "sens," directionality, and intentionality of postmodernism itself and the corresponding question of its temporality, of the temporal imagination specific to it as a gesture of a *post*.

The question does not throw postmodernism into question, but its future. As if the contestation that defines postmodernism were already a thing of the past. As if postmodernism itself were already a thing of the past. As if the category of the postmodern designated not a continuing praxis of contestation but a coherent, uncontested, recognizable reality or set of beliefs which has already had its day in the sun, and whose future is now in question. Like Marxism in Eastern Europe, and the fishing industry in Newfoundland.

This question, which does not throw postmodernism into question but its future, pre-empts the question and more importantly the *challenge of (post)modernism's present*: the very concrete, particular, and localized challenge the various space-clearing, ancestor-distancing gestures postmodernism presents to and against the established authorities of the modern; authorities like the Royal Society of Canada and the various disciplines of the Learned Societies; challenges to their canons, creeds, and curricula and to their own quite specific and insistent political correctness. This question, which does not throw the present of (post)modernism into question but its future, obfuscates the contestation that defines postmodernism and at the same time and by the same gesture *resolves it* in favor of one of its contestants: in favor of the conservative neo-modernist version of postmodernism described above, which continues to speak as and on behalf of the ancestral One of modernity: one past, one future, one experience of Western culture, one *post* of postmodernity. The question thus secures the future of postmodernism (of a particular version of postmodernism) by consigning it to the past (of a continuing modernist project), while at the same time withholding the future from postmodernism by refusing to acknowledge the possibility of a postmodernism that makes a difference.

The hijack I spoke of earlier has been accomplished. The space-clearing, ancestor-distancing gesture of postmodernism has been recuperated and reclaimed by and for the old authorities: by and for the modernist past and the continuing dialectic of Enlightenment Reason and European Imperialism that coincides with it. The local, particular, contingent, and concrete contestations of modernism, which have put the question of the future of a *post*modernism on the agenda, have been successfully disappeared by and into the question itself, by and into the familiar totalizing gesture(s) of Western Man. And the possibility of imagining, and thus creating, a future that will be different from the past, has likewise and once again been disappeared and disavowed by, in the name of, and on behalf of, more of the Same.

* * *

It seems to me that neither Nagl-Docekal nor McCormick can imagine a future—an ethics or an aesthetics, respectively—which is not more of the Same: the same old values of Reason and Universality, the regulating categories and ends of what Habermas calls Modernity, which both feminism and postmodernism alike have systematically disavowed and displaced from philosophical and political centrality. Though disappointed by their conclusions I was not, however, surprised, for they were anticipated in their respective points of departure which positioned each speaker as a temperamental if not a philosophical modernist engaging with or against postmodernism as his or her Other, rather than as a postmodernist engaging with the modern. McCormick's focus on Eugenio Montale's poetry, for example, and Nagl-Docekal's characterization of postmodernism as both dead and meaningless,[13] signaled to me what I call above a conservative neo-modernist tendency directing their engagements with the postmodern. McCormick's subsequent concern with problems of referentiality and mimesis confirmed this perception, as did Nagl-Docekal's focus on North American feminists like Gilligan and Noddings,[14] whose work has *not* grown out of nor engaged with the principal developments in twentieth-century European thought (structuralism, psychoanalysis, deconstruction, French feminism) that have recently forced postmodernism onto the otherwise resisting North American intellectual agenda.

By comparison it seems to me that Suzanne Foisy[15] does not return us to more of the Same but, on the contrary, challenges us to "resouvenir autrement": to articulate an aesthetics that neither re-cites the values and ends of the modernist past nor lapses into the nihilism of "anything goes." Her opening paragraph, which establishes postmodernism as a political critique of the principles and practices of modernity—"une réaction contre la raison en tant que domination," prepares us for this conclusion, and likewise the choice of artists and texts with which she makes her argument. Unlike McCormick and Nagl-Docekal, Foisy positions herself as a postmodernist engaged in its praxis of confrontation, critique, innovation, etc., in what I describe above as its "local, particular, contingent and concrete contestations of modernism." Not surprisingly therefore she can and does imagine a future which is different, which does not repeat the past, which is perhaps indeed the future of postmodernism.

NOTES

1. Peter McCormick, "Post-Modernism and Literature" in *Transactions of The Royal Society of Canada*, 1992/sixth series/vol. 3 (Ottawa: The Royal Society of Canada, 1993), 107–26.
2. Herta Nagl-Docekal, "Feminism and the Post-Modern" in *Transactions of the Royal Society of Canada*, 1992/sixth series/vol. 3 (Ottawa: The Royal Society of Canada, 1993), 152.
3. Ibid., 160. The citation is from Regenia Gagnier, "Feminist Postmodernism: The End of Feminism or the Ends of Theory," in *Theoretical Perspectives on Sexual Difference*, ed. D. L. Rhode (New Haven/London: Yale University Press, 1990), 23. The original quotation is from Audre Lorde, *Sister Outsider* (New York: The Crossing Press, 1984), 114.
4. First published in *Transactions of the Royal Society of Canada*, 1992, series 6, vol. 3 (Ottawa: Royal Society of Canada, 1993), 185–92.
5. Maurice Merleau-Ponty, *Phenomenology of Perception*, trans. Colin Smith (London: Routledge and Kegan Paul, 1962), 417.
6. I owe this characterization of the *post* of postmodernism as a distancing of the ancestors to Kwame Anthony Appiah. See his "Is the Post- in Postmodernism the Post- in Post-Colonial," *Critical Inquiry* 17 (Winter 1991): 336–57.
7. Ibid., 348.
8. Ibid., 343.
9. Merleau-Ponty, *Phenomenology of Perception*, 421.
10. Maurice Merleau-Ponty, *The Visible and the Invisible*, trans. Alphonso Lingis (Evanston: Northwestern University Press, 1968), 90.
11. See chapter 8, this volume.
12. Merleau-Ponty, *Phenomenology of Perception*, 35.
13. Nagl-Docekal, "Feminism and the Post-Modern," 147.

14. Carol Gilligan, *In a Different Voice* (Cambridge: Harvard University Press, 1982), Nel Noddings, *Caring* (Berkeley: University of California, 1984).
15. Suzanne Foisy, "Amnésie, esthésie et anesthésie (les arts de l'ère postérieure à la moderne)," in *Transactions of the Royal Society of Canada*, 1992/sixth series/vol. 3 (Ottawa: The Royal Society of Canada, 1993), 127–46.

BIBLIOGRAPHY

Althusser, Louis, and Etienne Balibar. *Reading Capital.* Translated by Ben Brewster. London: N.L.B., 1970.

———. *Lenin and Philosophy and Other Essays.* Translated by Ben Brewster. New York and London: Monthly Press Review, 1971.

———. *L'Avenir dure longtemps.* Suivi de les Faits. Edited by Oliver Corpet and Yann Moulier Boutang. Paris: Stock/IMEC, 1992.

Appiah, Kwame, Anthony. "Is the Post- in Postmodernism the Post- in Post-Colonial." *Critical Inquiry* 17 (Winter 1991): 336–57.

Barthes, Roland. *Mythologies.* Translated by Annette Lavers. London: Paladin Press, 1973.

Baudrillard, Jean. *De la Seduction.* Paris: Editions Galilee, 1979.

———. *For a Critique of the Political Economy of the Sign.* Translated by Charles Levin. St. Louis: Telos Press, 1981.

Beers, William. *Women and Sacrifice: Male Narcissism and the Psychology of Religion.* Detroit: Wayne State University Press, 1992.

Berger, John. *Ways of Seeing.* London: BBC and Pelican Original, 1971.

Benjamin, Walter. *Reflections, Essays, Aphorisms, Autobiographical Writings.* New York and London: Harcourt Brace Jovanovich, 1978.

Benston, Margaret. "Feminism and the Critique of Scientific Method." In *Feminism in Canada: From Pressure to Politics*, edited by Angela Miles and Geraldine Finn, 47–66. Montreal: Black Rose Books, 1982.

Braidotti, Rose. "Envy: Or with My Brains and Your Looks." In *Men in Feminism*, edited by Alice Jardine, 233–41. New York: Methuen, 1987.

Burstyn, Varda. "Censorship: Problems and Alternatives." *Parallelogramme*, 9, no. 3 (February/March 1984): 44–47.

———, ed. *Women Against Censorship.* Vancouver and Toronto: Douglas and McIntyre, 1985.

Cavell, Stanley. *The World Viewed. Reflections on the Ontology of Film.* Enlarged edition. Cambridge: Harvard University Press, 1979.

Chion, Michel. *La Voix au Cinema.* Paris: Editions de L'Etoile, 1982.

Code, Lorraine; Sheila Mullett; and Christine Overall, eds. *Feminist Perspectives: Philosophical Essays on Method and Morals.* Toronto: University of Toronto Press, 1988.

Coetzee, J. M. *Waiting for the Barbarians.* London: King Penguin, 1982.

Cohen, G. *Karl Marx's Theory of History: A Defence.* Princeton, N.J.: Princeton University Press, 1978.

Cooper, Barry. *Merleau-Ponty and Marxism: From Terror to Reform.* Toronto: University of Toronto Press, 1979.

———. "Hegelian Imperialism." In *Sojourns in The New World*, edited by Tom Darby, 25–67. Ottawa: Carleton University Press, 1986.

Darby, Tom, ed. *Sojourns in the New World* Ottawa: Carleton University Press, 1986.

de Beauvoir, Simone. *The Second Sex*. Translated by H. M. Parshley. New York: Bantam Books, 1961.

Debord, Guy. *Society of the Spectacle*. Detroit: Black and Red, 1977.

Delphy, Christine. *Close to Home. A Materialist Analysis of Women's Oppression*. London: Hutchinson, 1984.

Deleuze, Gilles, and Felix Guatarri. *The Anti-Oedipus: Capitalism and Schizophrenia*. Translated by Robert Hurley, Mark Seem, and Helen Lane, New York: Viking Press, 1977.

Derrida, Jacques. "Differance." In *Speech and Phenomena And Other Essays on Husserl's Theory of Signs*. Translated by David Allison, 129–60. Evanston: Northwestern University Press, 1973.

Doane, Mary Ann. "Women's Stake: Filming and the Female Body," *October* 17 (Summer 1981): 22–36.

Dover, K. J. *Greek Homosexuality*. Boston: Harvard University Press, 1978.

Edgley, Roy. "Reason and Violence: A Fragment of the Ideology of Liberal Intellectuals." In *Practical Reason*, edited by S. Korner, 113–35. Oxford: Blackwell, 1974.

Farrington, Benjamin. *Greek Science: Its Meaning for Us*. Melbourne: Penguin Books, 1953.

Fawcett, Brian. *Cambodia. A Book for People Who Find Television too Slow*. Vancouver: Talon Books, 1986.

Fee, Elizabeth, "Is Feminism a Threat to Scientific Objectivity." Paper presented at the annual meeting of the American Association for the Advancement of Science, Toronto, Canada, January 1981.

Finn, Geraldine. "Feminism and Socialism: Towards a New Synthesis." Unpublished, 1980.

———. "Understanding Social Reality: Marx, Sartre and Levi-Strauss." Ph.D diss., University of Ottawa, 1981.

———. "Why Althusser Killed His Wife." *Canadian Forum* (September–October 1981): 28–29.

———. "Women and the Ideology of Science." *Our Generation*, 15, no. 1 (Spring 1982): 40–50.

———. "Reason and Violence: More Than a False Antithesis: A Mechanism of Patriarchal Power." *Canadian Journal of Political and Social Theory* 6, no. 3 (Fall 1982): 162–68.

———. "Patriarchy and Pleasure: The Pornographic Eye/I." *Canadian Journal of Political and Social Theory* 9, nos. 1–2 (1985): 81–95.

———. "Against Sexual Imagery. Alternative or Otherwise." *Parallelogramme* 12, no. 1 (Autumn 1986): n.p.

———. "Managing the Difference." *Canadian Journal of Political and Social Theory* X, no. 3 (1986): 176–84.

———. "*Women Against Censorship*: A Response." *Canadian Dimension* 30, no. 4 (July/August 1986): 34–36.

———. "Sexual Representation and Social Control." *Perception* 9, no. 4 (March/April 1986): 24–26.

———. "Nobodies Speaking: Subjectivity, Sex, and the Pornography Effect." *Philosophy Today* 33, no. 2 (1989): 174–81.

———. "Taking Gender into Account in the 'Theatre of Terror': Violence, Media and the Maintenance of Male Dominance." *Canadian Journal of Women and the Law* 3 (1989–90): 375–94.

———. "The Politics of Spirituality. The Spirituality of Politics." In *Shadow of Spirit. Postmodernism and Religion*, edited by Philippa Berry and Andrew Wernick, 111–22. London: Routledge, 1992. Also in *Listening. Journal of Religion and Culture* 27, no. 2 (Spring 1992): 119–32.

———. "The Politics of Contingency. The Contingency of Politics." In *Merleau-Ponty, Hermeneutics and Postmodernism*, edited by Thomas Busch and Shawn Gallagher, 171–87. Albany, N.Y.: SUNY Press, 1992.

———. "Why Are There No Great Women Postmodernists?" In *Relocating Cultural Studies. Developments in Theory and Research*, edited by Valda Blundell, John Shepherd, and Ian Taylor, 123–52. London: Routledge, 1993.

———. "Introduction." In *Limited Edition. Voices of Women, Voices of Feminism*, edited by Geraldine Finn, 1–11. Halifax: Fernwood Publishing, 1993.

———. "The Future of Postmodernism." In *Transactions of the Royal Society of Canada 1992*, series 6, vol. 3, 185–92. Ottawa: Royal Society of Canada, 1993.

———. "The Space-Between Ethics and Politics. Or, More of the Same?" In *Who Is This 'We'? Absence of Community*, edited by Eleanor Godway and Geraldine Finn. Montreal: Black Rose Books, 1994.

Foisy, Suzanne. "Amnesie, esthesie (les arts de l'ere posterieure a la moderne)." In *Transactions of the Royal Society of Canada 1992*, series 6, vol. 3, 127–46. Ottawa: The Royal Society of Canada, 1993.

Foucault, Michel. *The Order of Things. An Archeology of the Human Sciences*. New York: Vintage Press, 1973.

———. *Language, Counter-Memory, Practice*. Edited by Donald Bouchard. Cornell: Cornell University Press, 1977.

———. *The History of Sexuality*. Vol. 1. Translated by Robert Hurley. New York: Vintage Books, 1980.

———. *Power/Knowledge*. Edited by Colin Gordon. New York: Pantheon Books, 1980.

———. *The Use of Pleasure*. Vol. 2, *The History of Sexuality*. Translated by Robert Hurley. New York: Pantheon Books, 1985.

Gallagher, Bob. "The Importance of Sexual Images." *Parallelogramme* 12, no. 1 (Autumn 1986): n.p.

Gidal, Peter. "Against Sexual Representation in Film." *Screen* 25, no. 6 (November/December 1984): 24–29.

Gilligan, Carol. *In a Different Voice*. Cambridge: Harvard University Press, 1982.

Godway, Eleanor. "Towards a Phenomenology of Politics: Expression and Praxis." In *Merleau-Ponty, Hermeneutics and Postmodernism*, edited by Thomas Busch and Shaun Gallagher, 161–70. New York: SUNY Press, 1992.

Goldenberg, Naomi. *Returning Words to Flesh: Feminism, Psychoanalysis, and the Resurrection of the Body*. Boston: Beacon Press, 1990.

Gordimer, Nadine. *The Essential Gesture. Writing, Politics, Places*. Edited by Stephen Clingman. New York: Alfred Knopf, 1988.

Grant, George. *Time as History*. Toronto: Canadian Broadcasting Corporation, 1969.

Griffin, Susan. *Pornography and Silence. Culture's Revenge Against Nature*. New York: Harper Colophon, 1981.

Griffiths, Marwenna, and Margaret Whitford, eds. *Feminist Perspectives in Philosophy*. Bloomington: Indiana University Press, 1988.

Guirand, Felix, ed. *The New Larousse Encyclopedia of Mythology*. London and New York: Hamlyn Publishing Group, 1982.

Habermas, Jurgen. "Modernity—An Incomplete Project." In *The Anti-Aesthetic: Essays on Postmodern Culture*, edited by Hal Foster, translated by Sela Benhabib, 3–15. Port Townsend, Wash.: Bay Press, 1983.

———. *The Philosophical Discourses of Modernity: Twelve Lectures.* Translated by Frederick G. Lawrence. Cambridge, Mass.: MIT Press, 1987.

———. *The Theory of Communicative Action.* 2 vols. Translated by Thomas A. McCarthy. Boston: Beacon Press, 1984.

Havel, Vaclav. "Letter to Dr. Gustav Husak." In *Living in Truth*, edited by Jan Vladislav, translated by A. G. Brain. London: Faber and Faber, 1987.

Heath, Stephen. *The Sexual Fix.* London: MacMillan Press, 1982.

Hein, Hilde. "Women and Science: Fitting Men to Think about Nature." Paper presented at the Annual Meeting of the American Association for the Advancement of Science, Toronto, Canada, January 1981.

Hollway, Wendy. "'I just wanted to kill a woman!' Why? The Ripper and Male Sexuality." *Feminist Review* 9 (October 1981): 33–40.

Hutcheons, Linda. *The Canadian Postmodern: A Study of Contemporary English-Canadian Fiction.* Oxford: Oxford University Press, 1988.

Jardine, Alice, ed. *Men in Feminism.* New York: Methuen, 1987.

Jay, Nancy. "Sacrifice as a Remedy for Having Been Born a Woman." In *Immaculate and Powerful*, edited by Clarissa Atkinson, Constance Buchanan, and Margaret Miles, 283–309. Boston: Beacon Press, 1985.

———. *Throughout Your Generations Forever: Sacrifice, Religion and Paternity.* Chicago: University of Chicago Press, 1992.

Kaite, Berkeley. "The Pornographer's Body Double: Transgression Is the Law." In *Body Invaders. Panic Sex in America*, edited by Arthur and Marilouise Kroker, 150–68. Montreal: New World Perspectives, 1986.

Kaplan, E. A. *Women in Films. Both Sides of the Camera.* London and New York: Methuen, 1983.

Karol, K. S. "The Tragedy of the Althussers." *New Left Review* 24 (1980): 93–95.

Kellner, Douglas, ed. *Postmodernism. Jameson. Critique.* Washington: Maissoneuve Press, 1989.

Kroker, Arthur, and David Cook. *The Postmodern Scene: Excremental Culture and Hyper-Aesthetics.* Montreal: New World Perspectives, 1986.

Kroker, Arthur, and Marilouise Kroker, eds. *Body Invaders. Panic Sex in America.* Montreal: New World Perspectives, 1987.

Kruks, Sonia. *The Political Philosophy of Merleau-Ponty.* Sussex: Harvester Press, 1981.

Kuhn, Thomas. *The Structure of Scientific Revolutions.* Chicago, University of Chicago Press, 1970.

Kundera, Milan. *The Unbearable Lightness of Being.* New York: Harper Colophon, 1985).

Langer, Monika. "Merleau-Ponty: The Ontological Limitation of Politics." In *Domination*, edited by Alkis Kontos, 102–14. Toronto: University of Toronto Press, 1975.

Leiss, W. *The Domination of Nature.* New York: Doubleday, 1972.

Levin, Charles. "Introduction." In *For a Critique of the Political Economy of the Sign*, edited by Jean Baudrillard, translated by Charles Levin, 5–28. St. Louis: Telos Press, 1981.

Levinas, Emmanuel. *Collected Philosophical Papers.* Translated by Alphonso Lingis. The Hague: Martinus Nijhoff, 1987.

Levi-Strauss, Claude. *Conversations with Claude Levi-Strauss*. Edited by G. Charbonnier. London: Johnathan Cape, 1969.

———. *The Elementary Structures of Kinship*. Edited by James H. Bell, John Richard von Sturmer, and Rodney Needham. Boston: Beacon Press, 1969.

———. "Answers to Some Investigations." In *Structural Anthropology II*. New York: Basic Books, 1976.

Lloyd, Genevieve. *The Man of Reason*. Minneapolis: University of Minnesota Press, 1984.

Lorde, Audre. "Power." In *Black Unicorn*, 108–9. New York: Norton, 1978.

Lyotard, Jean-François. *The Postmodern Condition. A Report on Knowledge*. Minneapolis: University of Minnesota Press, 1984.

Marcil-Lacoste, Louise. "Reason and Violence: Three Figures of Their Relationship." *Canadian Journal of Social and Political Theory* 6, no. 3 (Fall 1982): 170–81.

Marx, Karl. "The Economic and Philosophical Manuscripts." In *Early Writings*, edited by T. B. Bottomore. New York: McGraw-Hill Paperbacks, 1963.

McCormick, Peter. "Post-Modernism and Literature." In *Transactions of the Royal Society of Canada 1992*, series 6, vol. 3, 107–26. Ottawa: The Royal Society of Canada, 1993.

Merchant, Caroline. *The Death of Nature. Women, Ecology and the Scientific Revolution*. New York: Harper and Row, 1980.

Merleau-Ponty, Maurice. *Phenomenologie de la Perception*. Paris: Editions Gallimard, 1945. English translation by Colin Smith, *Phenomenology of Perception*. London: Routledge and Kegan Paul, 1962.

———. *The Primacy of Perception and Other Essays*. Edited by James Edie. Evanston: Northwestern University Press, 1964.

———. *Sense and Non-Sense*. Translated by H. L. Dreyfus and P. A. Dreyfus. Evanston: Northwestern University Press, 1964.

———. *The Visible and the Invisible*. Edited by Claud Lefort. Translated by Alphonso Lingis. Evanston: Northwestern University Press, 1968.

———. *Humanism and Terror*. Translated by John O'Neill. Boston: Beacon Press, 1969.

Michaelis, Loralea, and Dieter Misgeld. "Critical Theory, Feminist Theory and Modernity." Paper presented at a conference on Feminism, Critical Theory and the Canadian Legal System, at the University of Windsor, Ontario, June 1988.

Morris, Meaghan. *The Pirate's Fiancee: Feminism. Reading. Postmodernism*. London: Verso, 1988.

Morrison, Toni. *Beloved*. New York: Plume Books, New American Library, 1988.

Mort, Frank. "Sex, Signification and Pleasure." In *Formations of Pleasure*, 36–43. London: Routledge and Kegan Paul, 1983.

Mulvey, Laura. "Visual Pleasure and Narrative Cinema." *Screen* 16, no. 3 (Autumn 1975): 6–18.

Murdoch, Iris. *The Sovereignty of Good*. London: Routledge and Kegan Paul, 1970.

Nagl-Docekal, Herta. "Feminism and the Post-Modern." In *Transactions of the Royal Society of Canada 1992*, series 6, vol. 3, 147–62. Ottawa: The Royal Society of Canada, 1993.

Nelson, Joyce. *The Perfect Machine: Television in the Nuclear Age*. Toronto: Between the Lines, 1987.

Noddings, Nell. *Caring*. Berkeley: University of California Press, 1984.

O'Brien, Mary. "Reproducing Marxist Man." In *The Sexism of Social and Political Theory*, edited by Lorenne Clark and Lynda Lange, 99–116. Toronto: University of Toronto Press, 1979.

———. *The Politics of Reproduction*. London: Routledge and Kegan Paul, 1981.

O'Neill, John. *Five Bodies. The Human Shape of Modern Society*. Cornell: Cornell University Press, 1985.

Rajchman, John. "Postmodernism in a Nominalist Frame." *Flash Art* 137 (November/December) 1987, 49–51.

Penguin English Dictionary. (1965)

Person, Ethel. "Sexuality as the Mainstay of Identity: Psychoanalytic Perspectives." *Signs. Journal of Women in Culture and Society* 5, no. 4 (Summer 1980): 605–30.

Pinch, Trevor. *The Social Production of Scientific Knowledge*. Edited by E. Mendelsohn. Boston: D. Reidel Publishing Co., 1977.

Popper, Karl. "Utopia and Violence." In *Conjectures and Refutations; The Growth of Scientific Knowledge*, 355–63. New York: Harper and Torchbooks, 1968.

———. "Reason and Revolution." *Archives Europeenes de Sociologie*, XI (1970): 252–62.

Reynaud, Emmanuel. *Holy Virility. The Social Construction of Masculinity*. Translated by Ros Schwartz. London: Pluto Press, 1981.

Rubin, Gayle. "The Traffic in Women: Notes on the 'Political Economy' of Sex." In *Towards an Anthropology of Women*, edited by Rayna Reiter, 157–210. New York: Monthly Review Press, 1975.

Ruddick, Sara. *Maternal Thinking: Towards a Politics of Peace*. Boston: Beacon Press, 1989.

Sagan, Eli. *At the Dawn of Tyranny: The Origins of Individuality, Politics, Oppression and State*. New York: Alfred Knopf, 1985.

Sartre, Jean-Paul. *Search for a Method*. Translated by Hazel Barnes. New York: Vintage Books, 1963.

———. *Situations*. New York: Fawcett World Library, 1969.

———. "A Plea for Intellectuals." In *Jean-Paul Sartre. Between Existentialism and Marxism*, translated by John Matthews, 228–85. London: New Left Books, 1974.

———. *Critique of Dialectical Reason*. Translated by Alan Sheridan-Smith. London: New Left Books, 1976.

Saxe-Fernandez, Eduardo. "Marxism, Revisionism and Technological Determinism." Master's thesis, Ottawa University, 1981.

Schor, Naomi. "Dreaming Dissymetry: Barthes, Foucault and Sexual Difference." In *Men in Feminism*, edited by Alice Jardine, 98–110. New York: Methuen, 1987.

Silverman, Kaja. *The Acoustic Mirror. The Female Voice in Psychoanalysis and Cinema*. Indianapolis: Indiana University Press, 1988.

Skeat, Rev. Walter. *A Concise Etymological Dictionary of the English Language*. Reprint, New York: Perigree Books, 1980.

Small, Christopher. *Music—Society—Education*. New York: Schirmer Books, John Calder, 1977.

Smith, Dorothy. "A Sociology for Women." In *Prism of Sex: Essays in the Sociology of Knowledge*, edited by J. Sherman and E. T. Beck, 135–87. Madison: University of Wisconsin Press, 1979.

———. *The Everyday World as Problematic*. Toronto: University of Toronto Press, 1987.

Snitow, Ann, Christine Stansell, and Sharon Thompson, et al., eds. *Powers of Desire. The Politics of Sexuality*. New York: Monthly Review Press, 1983.

Sontag, Susan. *Against Interpretation and Other Essays*. New York: Delta Books, 1966.

———. *On Photography*. New York: Delta Books, 1973.

Turner, Bryan. *Descent into Discourse. The Reification of Language and the Writing of Social History*. Philadelphia: Temple University Press, 1990.

Vigier, Rachel. "Philosophy in the Key of Life." Paper presented at SWIP, Toronto, October 1981.

Wallsgrove, Ruth. "The Masculine Face of Science." In *Alice Through the Microscope. The Power of Science Over Women's Lives* (Brighton Women and Science Group), 228–40. London: Virago Press, 1980.

Warnock, G. J. "Reason." In *The Encyclopedia of Philosophy*, vol. 7–8, edited by Paul Edwards, 83–85. New York: Macmillan, 1972.

Weldon, Fay. *Praxis*. New York: Pocketbooks, 1978.

Wolff, Robert Paul. "On Violence." *The Journal of Philosophy* 66 (1969): 601–16.

Woolf, Virginia. *Three Guineas*. London: Hogarth Press, 1938.

Whiteside, Kerry. *Merleau-Ponty and the Foundation of an Existential Politics*. Princeton, N.J.: Princeton University Press, 1988.

Yawney, Carole. "To Grow a Daughter: Cultural Liberation and the Dynamics of Oppression in Jamaica." In *Feminism. From Pressure to Politics*, edited by Angela Miles and Geraldine Finn, 177–202. Montreal: Black Rose Books, 1989.

INDEX